Building a Eucharistic Pedagogy for the Presbyterian Church of Korea

Building a Eucharistic Pedagogy for the Presbyterian Church of Korea

Hyoung Seop Shin

WIPF & STOCK · Eugene, Oregon

BUILDING A EUCHARISTIC PEDAGOGY
FOR THE PRESBYTERIAN CHURCH OF KOREA

Copyright © 2013 Hyoung Seop Shin. All rights reserved. Except for brief quotations in critical publications or reviews, no part of this book may be reproduced in any manner without prior written permission from the publisher. Write: Permissions, Wipf and Stock Publishers, 199 W. 8th Ave., Suite 3, Eugene, OR 97401.

Wipf & Stock
An Imprint of Wipf and Stock Publishers
199 W. 8th Ave., Suite 3
Eugene, OR 97401
www.wipfandstock.com

ISBN 13: 978-1-62032-393-9
Manufactured in the U.S.A.

All scripture quotations, unless otherwise indicated, are taken from the Holy Bible, New International Version®, NIV®. Copyright ©1973, 1978, 1984 by Biblica, Inc.™ Used by permission of Zondervan. All rights reserved worldwide.

Contents

List of Illustrations / vii
Foreword / ix
Preface / xiii

1 **INTRODUCTION / 1**
   Thesis Statement
   Research Method and Resources
   Outline

2 **CRITICAL ANALYSIS OF FORMATIVE ROOTS OF KOREAN PRESBYTERIAN EUCHARISTIC PRACTICES / 12**
   Confucianism as a Sociocultural Formative Root
   Frontier Worship as a Theological, Liturgical Formative Root
   Nevius Methods as a Pastoral, Liturgical Formative Root
   American Presbyterian Liturgy as a Historical, Liturgical Formative Root
   Need for a New Contextual Approach for Eucharistic Pedagogy

3 **LITURGICAL FOUNDATIONS FOR AN ALTERNATIVE EUCHARISTIC PEDAGOGY / 33**
   Peter Phan's Liturgical Inculturation Focusing on Sociocultural Life Experiences
   Jung Young Lee's Liturgical Inculturation Focusing on a Contextual Epistemology
   Critical Analysis of Korean Presbyterians' Eucharistic Practices in View of Phan's and Lee's Liturgical Contextualization
   Liturgical Implications

Contents

4 EDUCATIONAL FOUNDATIONS FOR AN ALTERNATIVE EUCHARISTIC PEDAGOGY / 68

Roberta Berns' Ecological Socialization Pedagogy
Pedagogical Implications

5 BUILDING A NEW EUCHARISTIC PEDAGOGY FOR THE PRESBYTERIAN CHURCH OF KOREA / 98

Defining a Contextualized Eucharistic Pedagogy
Reconceptualization of Eucharistic Pedagogy
Reformation of Eucharistic Pedagogy
Three Generative Educational Principles from the New Eucharistic Pedagogy
Conclusion

Appendix A / 135
Appendix B / 156
Appendix C / 160
Bibliography / 179

List of Illustrations

Figure 1: Diagram of Individual Ecological Socialization / 73

Figure 2: The Five-Step Cycle of the Contextualized Eucharistic Pedagogy / 110

Figure 3: Contextualized Diagram of Korean Students' Ecological Socialization / 112

Figure 4: The Five-Step Cycle of Eucharistic Learning / 123

Foreword

How can people from different cultures, times, and places celebrate the Eucharist in a way that connects with their own culture, history, and daily lives? This is the central question that lies beneath Hyoung-Seop Shin's remarkable investigation of the history of Eucharistic practice in the Korean Presbyterian Church. In this book, the author uncovers the story of colonial mission work that insisted that the Eucharist in the Korean church must look exactly like it did in the U.S. From its earliest days, missionaries who brought the gift of Christian faith to Korea also demanded that the celebration of the Lord's Supper look, taste, smell, sound, and feel like it did back in their home congregations. These first missionaries carefully guarded this tradition by building strict regulations about who was allowed to lead communion and how it should be done correctly. Shin peels back the layers of communion practice in the Korean church to demonstrate how these rules reinforced the missionaries' own authority and power while unwittingly linking the Gospel with the hierarchical, patriarchal, sacrosanct values of the Confucian society at large. In adopting this parallel structure, churches in Korea maintained the central ritual act of the Eucharist in a way that removed it from the radical claims of table practice in the Gospels and the life of the early church as well as disconnected it from the daily lives of Korean people.

What is deeply ironic about this approach is that Eucharistic practice in the U.S. has changed dramatically during the last hundred years. Many protestant churches in the U.S., have changed the elements (from wine to grape juice and included different kinds and amounts of bread and wafer), the presider's wardrobe (running a gamut from Genevan gowns to academic robes to albs to business suits), the rules about who may participate (adult believers to baptized children to open table practices), the liturgical texts that are used, and a host of other changes. Yet, in Korea, the Presbyterian Church has remained virtually frozen in time as they continue to observe the ways that 19th Century missionaries taught them to approach the table.

Foreword

Nowhere is this clearer than in the pedagogical materials that support this practice. Shin uncovers the single lesson that a young person who grows up in the church will receive during his/her formative years. A Sunday School teacher holds up a picture of Leonardo da Vinci's painting of the Last Supper before a classroom of young Korean boys and girls. Here the effects of colonialism are dramatically on display. Not only does this pedagogical approach ignore the major developments of educational theory and liturgical theology, it fundamentally fails to provide a way for students to place themselves imaginatively into a constructive conversation about the church's history, theology, and practice of celebrating communion.

Recent work on the Eucharist has uncovered a wide diversity of practices within the life of the early church that can be traced from descriptions within the biblical material through the early centuries of the church. It is becoming abundantly clear, in almost every imaginable way, that Christian in different parts of the ancient world found their own unique ways to celebrate this meal. Similarly, in a parallel way, Shin shows how recent work in educational theory requires curriculum and teachers who welcome students to bring their social locations, imaginations, and experiences to the classroom in order that together the group can discover ways to make this ancient meal practice come alive again.

What is remarkable about this work is that Shin lays out this new approach without reproach or blame about the past, but with a sense of gratitude for the hard work and sacrifice of 19th Century Protestant missionaries who brought the Gospel to Korea in hopes to show them a new way of life. Instead of attacking them for their shortcomings and cultural biases, Shin simply declares that it is time for a reassessment of cultural assumptions and practices. Here, Shin opens the door for the hard work of inculturation to begin. There is no prescriptive formula, but Shin provides an analysis of the ways that historical perspectives have prematurely dismissed central aspects of the Korean culture. Here is an invitation to start an open dialogue about the places where Korean culture and experience can serve as a fertile ground for the proclamation of the Gospel as well as an analysis of the ways that historical perspectives have prematurely dismissed central insights of the Korean people. Readers will find the appendices particularly suggestive both in providing an English translation of the current curricular material as well as providing a couple of suggestive new liturgical texts to use in Korean congregations.

Foreword

This work offers a much needed corrective course for bringing new life into the celebration of the Eucharist in the Korean Presbyterian Church. It provides a sorely needed diagnosis of the inadequacies of the current pedagogical model and points to ways that new curriculum can finally free the Eucharistic celebration from the tyranny of the past in order to invite participants to encounter the richness and diversity of the Gospel's message as Christians gather around the table. Shin shows how building on new educational models can open the path to a renewed Eucharistic practice which in turn will breathe new life into congregations.

In the final analysis, though, this work is not simply a descriptive analysis that is limited to the Korean Presbyterian Church. This is an exemplary model of the kind of careful work of inculturation that is so desperately needed by churches around the world. This work anticipates the day when Christians once again celebrate the Eucharist with a vast array of distinctive voices, postures, gestures, attire, elements, and theological nuances. The hard work of liturgical renewal invites us all to reconceptualize our curriculums and open up our tables in order that we no longer simply repeat rituals based on what we were told we should do in this celebration. Instead, Eucharistic renewal invites us to study the biblical, historical, theological, and cultural influences which have shaped these distinctive Christian table practices precisely so that we may once again engage in celebrations where our own lives are transformed by the Spirit's work among us.

It is with deep appreciation for its theological insights and great hope for its pedagogical perspectives that I commend this work to you as a model from which we can all learn as we go about the process of linking Christian faith to our own unique cultures, histories, and daily lives.

Paul Galbreath
Professor of Worship and Preaching
Union Presbyterian Seminary, Richmond, Virginia

Preface

WITHIN THE LAST TWO decades, some Christian educators have investigated the relationship between liturgical practices and Christian education with attention to students' congregational life, culture, and faith transformation. Contextualization issues of eucharistic practices rooted in Asian contexts, however, have not been given adequate attention in the field of Christian education.

This book presents a eucharistic pedagogy for the Presbyterian Church of Korea. Current eucharistic practices of the Presbyterian Church of Korea are analyzed in view of the liturgical contextualization works of two major Asian theologians, Peter Phan and Yung Young Lee. In light of this analysis, Roberta Berns' ecological socialization pedagogy reflecting students' contexts provides educational foundations to present a new model of eucharistic pedagogy through the critical conversations between current Korean Presbyterian students' eucharistic experiences in a class and at the table of the Eucharist and in their daily lives in the world. Since Berns emphasizes the critical examination of students' multilayered sociocultural environments rooted in students' specific local contexts, two Asian theorists—Phan and Lee—who deal with eucharistic experiences in view of Korean Presbyterians' own life experiences and Asian way of thinking are invited as main conversation partners along with Berns.

Based on the critical conversations between Berns, Phan, and Lee, this book suggests an alternative eucharistic pedagogy for the Presbyterian Church of Korea by reforming eucharistic and curricular practices with attention to students' specific local contexts. This process includes the formulation of the definition of the new eucharistic pedagogy, the reconceptualization of concepts regarding the eucharistic pedagogy, and five steps as pedagogical strategies for a new eucharistic pedagogy for the Presbyterian Church of Korea, including pedagogical guidelines for teachers and students.

This book is a fruit of seven and a half years of my studying at Union Presbyterian Seminary in the United States. Since my first year of studying in the United States in 2004, Union Presbyterian Seminary has been my academic and spiritual home where I have explored my theological and educational issues regarding the relationship between Christian education and worship. In this school, I studied under the continuous support and Spirit-filled guidance of my dissertation committee members: Professors Dr. Paul Galbreath, Dr. Jane Vann, Dr. Pamela Mitchell-Legg, and Dr. Syngman Rhee.

Without Professor Paul Galbreath's constructive criticism on my study of theological and liturgical perspectives, this book would never have been undertaken. Professor Jane Vann's prominent perspective on the role of Christian education in the context of worship contributed to the building of this study from the beginning to its conclusion. Professor Pamela Mitchell-Legg showed me who a teacher is as an encourager and facilitator by her support and passion. Professor Syngman Rhee unselfishly contributed a large portion of his time and energy not only by sharing his life-based knowledge regarding Asian theology but also through the study of Asian philosophy, Korean mission history, and religious sociology.

I also want to express my appreciation to outstanding professors in my study at Union Presbyterian Seminary such as Karen-Marie Yust, Henry Simmons, Gwen Hawley, and Cindy Kissel-Ito. Professor Karen-Marie Yust helped me shape and sharpen my thoughts critically on the study of education and worship through her knowledgeable teaching and comments. Professor Henry Simmons' inductive teaching on curriculum enabled me to draw a big picture for this book rooted in my local contexts. Professor Gwen Hawley's teaching helped me to find a blind spot in terms of my life journey within patriarchal, hierarchical, and Confucian society. Cindy Kissel-Ito's student-centered pedagogy demonstrated how the relationship between a teacher and students as collaborative partners can be actualized in a concrete classroom by a teacher's efforts.

For writing this book, I also owe much to my family members, friends, mentors, church members, and school colleagues. Finally, I should give my greatest gratitude to wife, Yun Young Kim, and my two children, Colleen Haein Shin and a blessed baby to be born in this next year, who have always been a powerful and priceless presence through their own self-giving and commitments to me in all my journey both in Korea and in the United States. Through unchanging love and care, they have taught me how to love and how to be loved as a Christian in my daily life.

Preface

After completing my doctoral degree regarding interdisciplinary study between Christian education and liturgy at Union Presbyterian Seminary (Richmond, VA), I came back to Korea and started to serve a local church in Seoul, Choongshin Presbyterian, as the director of Christian education. I also serve Presbyterian College and Theological Seminary as an instructor of Christian education. Both a Christian educator in a local church and an instructor in a seminary, my context in Korea strongly keep calling me to continue an interdisciplinary work between Christian education and worship, between gospel and culture, and between church and the world. As a Korean pastor, I sincerely anticipate that this study will open the door for ongoing educational, liturgical discussions of work of contextualization in churches and help Korean Presbyterians participate in learning the context of the Eucharist actively with a new lens for Korean culture as the soil of Christian faith, and a new hope for education and liturgy to be Christian authentically and appropriate culturally. However, this task will not be finished overnight. Instead, this work invites others to ongoing discussions of liturgical contextualization between teachers, students, and liturgical presiders in the Presbyterian Church of Korea in order to build Christian education and liturgy not only *in* Korea but also *of* Korea.

Chapter 1

Introduction

Since the early church, the Eucharist has been celebrated as the heart of Christian worship. At the table of the Eucharist, Christians gathered to worship God and experienced God's grace as the central liturgy of Christian worship from the outset.[1] With regard to the centrality of the Eucharist in Christian worship, John Calvin asserts that worship in the New Testament (Acts 2:42 and 1 Corinthians 11:20) and the early church included both the Word and the Eucharist as the central order which cannot be reduced.[2] Moreover, the Eucharist has provided participants with the norm of Christian life in terms of thanksgiving, self-giving, and serving. As people participate in the Eucharist, their faith and lives are formed and shaped through their participation in eucharistic practices, which are constitutive and normative for what they believe and how they live in the world.[3] Kevin W. Irwin states that the Eucharist is integrative of participants' Christian lives.[4] The way church members live their lives is formed, challenged, and shaped through participating in the eucharistic practices within the reciprocal relationship between *lex ordandi* (the law of prayer), *lex credendi* (the law of belief), and *lex vivendi* (the law of living).[5] However, throughout the history of the Presbyterian Church

---

1. Bower, *Companion to the Book of Common Worship*, 7; Galbreath, *Leading from the Table*, xiii.

2. Calvin, *Institutes of the Christian Religion*, 4.17.44.

3. Carvalhaes, "Globalization and the Borders," 182; Anderson, *Worship and Christian Identity*, 193.

4. Irwin, *Models of the Eucharist*, 294.

5. Ibid., 30. Irwin mentions that the essential enactment of the Eucharist is not only about what they say (*lex ordandi*) and what they believe (*lex credendi*) in the table of the Eucharist but also about how they live (*lex vivendi*) in their daily lives.

of Korea,[6] the Eucharist has rarely been recognized and practiced as the heart of worship and the norm of Christian life. In most local churches in Korea, the Eucharist has not been celebrated weekly, but as a supplementary liturgy for special occasions such as baptism, Easter, and Christmas. Furthermore, it has been practiced as one of the most Western culture-centered liturgies in the Presbyterian Church of Korea. It is not easy for Korean participants to find ways to connect and reflect on their daily lives given the eucharistic texts, foods (bread and wine), table, chalice, music, clothes, and even plates used in this celebration.

When I was a seminary student in Korea, I had a chance to guide a travel seminar from Union-PSCE (now called Union Presbyterian Seminary) in 2000. After attending a Sunday worship service in a local church in Seoul that included the Eucharist, one group member shared his reflections with me. "Pastor Shin, it is very interesting to me that, in terms of space, music, and worship elements, there are no differences between today's worship service in Korea and the worship service in my hometown in the U.S." His comment interested me because one of the purposes for the group in attending a local Sunday service was not only to experience the service but also to discuss the uniqueness and differences of Sunday worship services in Korea in view of differences in culture, history, and theology. As both a Christian educator and pastor, I was challenged to reconsider: What is lacking in current Korean Presbyterian worship? Unless worship experiences reflect Korean congregations' culture, is it possible for their faith and daily life to be formed and transformed through the worship experiences? If congregations' faith and lives are nurtured by participating in Sunday worship service, what does the Sunday school curriculum of the Presbyterian Church of Korea say about their worship experiences? How can I as a Christian educator help students' faith and lives grow through their worship experiences?

These questions raised serious concerns for me about the way that many within the Korean church focus on a separation between worship and Korean culture, between worship experiences and life experiences, and between Christian education and liturgy. I believe that this existing separation might cause Korean students to understand the relationship between faith and culture exclusively and to identify Christian worship with a fixed-form liturgy based on historically inherited traditions. Moreover, I believe that

---

6. The name "Presbyterian Church of Korea" refers to the Presbyterian Church in South Korea ([Korean font>]대한 예수교 장로회 통합) throughout this document.

it might lead worship and churches to be built *in* Korea but not ultimately *of* Korea. Even though some Western Christian educators who considered worship experiences seriously from an educational perspective—such as John Westerhoff III, C. Ellis Nelson, Maria Harris, and Charles Foster—had been introduced and discussed in the seminary classroom in Korea, the studies and discussions were mostly focused on theoretical discussions of these scholars and their theories rather than contextual analysis and reflections of a Korean context. In the research for my MDiv thesis, "Directions of Christian Education in the Period of Postmodernism," in 2002, I recognized that in the U.S., academic studies of the reciprocal relationship between Christian education and worship were being discussed and developed, theoretically and practically, within an interdisciplinary framework. Given these concerns, interests, and expectations, I resolved to study Christian education in the U.S.

Throughout my studies for my MACE, ThM, and PhD from Union Presbyterian Seminary (Richmond, VA), I learned theories related to academic concerns from the fields of critical pedagogy, curriculum theory, Asian theology, liturgy, ritual, and sociology. As I researched, studied, and struggled with these theories focusing on a Korean context, I found that the Eucharist in the Presbyterian Church of Korea is a matter of primary importance, as well as one of the most problematic, in view of theology, liturgy, and pedagogy. This dissertation is an outcome of my research and a response to the educational context of the Eucharist in the Presbyterian Church of Korea.

Thesis Statement

This dissertation presents an alternative eucharistic pedagogy for the Presbyterian Church of Korea. It starts with a critical analysis of the historic eucharistic practices of the Presbyterian Church of Korea and examines current eucharistic texts of the Presbyterian Church of Korea with attention to the work of selected scholars on liturgical contextualization.[7] In light of

---

7. Jo, *Korean Protestant Church*, 188; Francis, *Shape a Circle Ever Wider*, 59. Francis understands liturgical contextualization as the critical sociocultural dialogues between faith and culture focusing on the mutual enrichment of both the church and the culture in which the faith is proclaimed. With attention to the reciprocal relationship between Christian liturgy and culture, Jo asserts that liturgical contextualization is a liturgical imperative work in the context of the Korean church.

this analysis, Roberta Berns' pedagogy reflecting students'[8] contexts will provide educational foundations to present a new model of eucharistic pedagogy through critical conversations between current Korean Presbyterian students' eucharistic experiences in a class[9] and at the table of the Eucharist and in their daily lives in the world.

Historically, the Eucharist in the Presbyterian Church of Korea was formed under a strong Western influence, which has prescribed and imposed liturgical practices since the nineteenth century. Because of this Western influence, Korean scholars in the field of liturgy and education have requested a new eucharistic pedagogy with appropriate contextual practices in the Presbyterian Church of Korea.[10] This dissertation envisions that a new eucharistic pedagogy for the Presbyterian Church of Korea will help Korean Presbyterian students participate actively in the Eucharist as a formative liturgy to reflect, reinterpret, and reshape their life experiences critically and creatively through contextualized eucharistic practices rooted in ways specific to Korean students' local culture.

Research Method and Resources

This dissertation is a critical conversation about Korean Presbyterians' eucharistic practices in order to identify new ways to teach about the Eucharist. In order to complete this project, I will use a method of cultural analysis focusing on (1) current eucharistic texts and curriculum for the Eucharist of the Presbyterian Church of Korea and (2) the understanding

---

8. Throughout this proposal, the word "students" refers to participants in both worship and children's, youth, and/or adult Christian education.

9. The phrase "students' eucharistic experiences in a class" means their learning experiences about the Eucharist in a class. It includes not only learning the biblical, theological, historical, and liturgical knowledge regarding the Eucharist but also preparation and reflection for students' participation in the Eucharist.

10. S. W. Kim, "Cultural Application," 145; Jung, "Examining the Lima Liturgy, 346; K. J. Kim, *Formation of Presbyterian Worship*, 111; Koh, *Contemporary Christian Education Thought*, 261. In the field of liturgy, Korean scholars such as S. W. Kim, Jung, and K. J. Kim mention that Korean Presbyterians' eucharistic practices have been influenced and shaped based on the Western church's practices without reflecting Korean congregation members' life experiences in terms of historical and sociocultural contexts since the beginning of the Presbyterian Church of Korea. In the field of Christian education, Koh asserts that Korean Presbyterian eucharistic practices which are disconnected from participants' current life and culture cannot be experienced as authentic educational practices that help them live their Christian lives according to God's calling.

by scholars of liturgy and education regarding the relationship between students' eucharistic practices and their faith formation.

First, my cultural analysis will focus on current "eucharistic texts"[11] and curriculum materials[12] in the Presbyterian Church of Korea. The "Nairobi Statement on Worship and Culture" states that the contextualization of worship rooted in diverse local cultures is an indispensable task of the evangelizing church, to incarnate the gospel into a particular culture, since the gospel transcends all cultures and cannot be identified with any culture.[13] The core issues of eucharistic practices raised by scholars of liturgical contextualization include the relationship between contextual theology and liturgical practices, the relationship between gospel and culture, the continuity between liturgical experience and liturgical life, and justice and equality in eucharistic practices. In view of these issues, I will analyze *The Book of Common Worship for the Presbyterian Church of Korea* (BCW [PCK]) and *God's Kingdom: Call and Responding* with attention to liturgical contextualization.

Second, my analysis will focus on how scholars of liturgy and education understand the relationship between Korean Presbyterian students' eucharistic experiences[14] and their life experiences in the world. A cultural analysis regards that the particular context is one of the most significant resources in terms of the formulation and development of the theory.[15] In this respect, such an analysis of Korean eucharistic experiences from liturgical, educational perspectives demands comparative and critical conversations between each theorist's context and Korean students' contexts. This cultural analysis will provide significant pedagogical implications and a foundation for the construction of a new creative eucharistic pedagogy that pays careful attention to the contexts of the Presbyterian Church of Korea.

11. Reforming Committee, *Book of Common Worship* [PCK]. This book includes the up-to-date version of eucharistic texts of the Korean Presbyterian Church. Throughout this project, the phrase "eucharistic texts" refers to the texts and rubrics of the Eucharist that are written in *Book of Common Worship* [PCK].

12. Curriculum Committee, *God's Kingdom*. This is the latest official curriculum series book for the Presbyterian Church of Korea.

13. Scherer and Bevans, "Lutheran World Federation's Nairobi Statement," 182, quoted in Phan, *In Our Own Tongues*, 73.

14. In the view of reciprocal relationship between eucharistic experiences in the Eucharist and learning experiences in the class of the Eucharist, the phrase "eucharistic experiences" refers to both students' experiences at the table of the Eucharist and their learning experiences in the classroom of the Eucharist throughout this proposal.

15. Bal, *Double Exposures*, 16.

Liturgical Contextualization as Resources for Analysis of Eucharistic Practices.

I will use the resources of liturgical contextualization to provide an analysis of Korean Presbyterian students' eucharistic practices in order to prepare the way for the creation of a new eucharistic pedagogy with attention to their specific life contexts. This critical reflection on students' liturgical experiences focuses on the inseparable relationship between participants' liturgical practices and their life contexts, such as economic, political, class, ethnic, cultural, and gender situations. Liturgical contextualization demands that critical analysis of liturgical experiences be conducted not only through intentional processes but also through unintentional processes[16] and not only through formal processes but also through informal processes.[17] The critical analysis not only reflects the students' direct socialization agents such as a family and a faith community but also their indirect socialization agents such as political ideology and socioeconomic change.[18]

The work of liturgical scholars in the area of contextualization offers a significant critique of the eucharistic practices of the Presbyterian Church of Korea, especially through an analysis of the relationship between eucharistic practices and individuals' life experiences in their specific contexts. By giving serious attention to the inseparable, reciprocal relationship between faith and culture, Asian liturgical scholars who have focused on issues of contextualization, such as Peter C. Phan, Anscar J. Chupungco, Soon Whan Kim, Jang Bok Jung, Ki Yeon Jo, and Jung Young Lee, have contributed to the revitalization and development of the essential relationship between a congregation's liturgical practices and their life contexts.[19] The study of liturgical contextualization has developed around the basic theological presupposition that contextual theology is an imperative. Just as contextual theology understands not only "traditional loci of scripture and tradition" but also local culture and social change as essential sources of "the theological enterprise,"[20] liturgical contextualization focuses on the

---

16. Lee and Phan, *Journeys at the Margin*, 113.

17. Phan, *In Our Own Tongues*, 89.

18. Chupungco, *Liturgical Inculturation*, 38.

19. Chupungco, *Liturgical Inculturation*; Phan, *In Our Own Tongues*; idem, *Christianity with an Asian Face*; S. W. Kim, "Cultural Application"; Jung, "Examining the Lima Liturgy"; Jo, *Korean Protestant Church*; Lee, *Marginality*; and Lee and Phan, *Journeys at the Margin*.

20. Bevans, *Models of Contextual Theology*, 11.

contextual, dialectical conversations between a congregation's life experiences and its liturgical practices.[21]

In order to analyze Korean Presbyterians' eucharistic practices with a view toward contextualized eucharistic pedagogy, I have chosen two Asian liturgical scholars, Peter Phan[22] and Jung Young Lee,[23] as conversation partners and their recent books and articles[24] as main resources. This project calls for the critical examination of eucharistic practices with special attention to two areas of Korean sociocultural context: (1) Korean Presbyterians' own life experiences and (2) Asian ways of thinking. First, Phan's liturgical contextualization works, which focus on the interdynamics between congregations' liturgical practices and their life experiences in the world, offer the Presbyterian Church of Korea significant analytic criteria to critically examine eucharistic practices. His works focus on issues of contextualization by nurturing faith without rejecting or destroying local culture. Phan asserts that a congregation's own life experiences are an effective source for the eucharistic liturgy—that church liturgy can be effective and meaningful as long as a congregation's life experiences are linked to it.[25] With three methods drawn from liberation theologians, socioanalytic mediation, hermeneutical mediation, and practical mediation,[26] Phan asserts that

---

21. Schreiter, *Constructing Local Theologies*; Bevans, *Models of Contextual Theology*; K. Y. Jo, "Asian Understanding of the Baptism." In Schreiter, *Constructing Local Theologies*; Bevans, *Models of Contextual Theology*; and Jo, "Asian Understanding of the Baptism," the authors emphasize sociocultural interpretation of theology and liturgical practices with attention to a congregation's local culture.

22. Phan is one of the most active and recent Asian-American liturgists who reform liturgical practices with attention to Asian congregations' sociocultural contexts.

23. Jung Young Lee is a Korean-American theologian who deals with the inculturation process of liturgical practices from an Asian epistemological perspective. There are several Korean/Korean-American liturgical theologians who address this issue, such as Se Kwang Kim, Soon Whan Kim, and Jang Bok Jung. Jung Young Lee is a frontier theologian who first attempted to reinterpret Christian liturgical practices from an Asian epistemological perspective.

24. Phan, *In Our Own Tongues*; *Christianity with an Asian Face*; *Being Religious Interreligiously*; "Culture and Liturgy"; Lee, *Marginality*; *Trinity in Asian Perspective*; *Korean Preaching*; Lee and Phan, *Journeys at the Margin*.

25. Phan, *Being Religious Interreligiously*, 272.

26. Phan, *Christianity with an Asian Face*, 18–21. Socioanalytic mediation is to analyze the ground of the people' lives critically by using social sciences such as sociology, anthropology, history, literature, and politics as critical conversation partners. Hermeneutical mediation is to provide sociohistorical data with theological interpretations by using proper biblical stories and symbols. Practical mediation is to have a circular

liturgical practices need to be based on the congregation's cultural, religious, economic, and political life experiences rather than on Western culture.[27]

Second, Lee's contextual theological works, which focus on the relationship between liturgical practices and contextual epistemology, help the Presbyterian Church of Korea to examine critically Korean Presbyterian students' eucharistic practices in view of Asian ways of thinking.[28] In *The Trinity in Asian Perspective*, Lee emphasizes that Asian ways of thinking are fundamentally different from Western ways of thinking, and so he argues that Western theologies that are communicated through Western thought forms and philosophies cannot deal with the totality of Christian faith and human existence for Asian congregations.[29] Lee understands the yin-yang symbolic thinking as an epistemological paradigm for Korean people for over a thousand years.[30] He describes three distinctive epistemological characteristics of Asian ways of thinking based on the yin-yang symbolic thinking: a both/and way of thinking, a relational way of thinking, and a threefold way of thinking.[31] In this respect, Lee proposes that Asian con-

---

movement between praxis and theory. Praxis examines theory critically, and then theory modifies praxis.

27. Chupungco, *Liturgical Inculturation*, 30. As Chupungco defines liturgical contextualization as "the process of inserting the texts and rites of the liturgy into the framework of the local culture," he illustrates it by using the formula A+B=C as compared to the formula A+B=AB.

28. Lee, *Trinity in Asian Perspective*, 12. Lee insists that a way of thinking is one of the most fundamental elements in Christian theology because God cannot be restricted or limited in an absolute theology based on a certain context or way of knowing because God "transcends human beings' thinking."

29. Ibid., 13. According to Lee, whereas a Western epistemology understands the human being as the center of the cosmos (an anthropocentric cosmology) focusing on a twofold dynamic between God and human beings, an Asian epistemology understands the human being as belonging to the cosmos and as a microcosm of the cosmos (a cosmocentric anthropology) focusing on a threefold dynamic between the heaven, the earth, and human beings. For more on Lee's understanding of the difference between Western and Asian epistemologies, see chapter 3.

30. Ibid., 18–19. Based on an Asian cosmocentric anthropology, Lee explains yin-yang symbolic thinking through the diagram of the Great Ultimate in terms of the waxing and waning of the moon. The yin-yang symbolic thinking has "touched almost all areas of life in the past," and "remained relevant to the way of thinking" for Korean people to the present day in important areas of Asian philosophy, Confucian morality, Asian medicine, Oriental arts, Korean architecture, religions, and even on the Korean national flag. I will deal with yin-yang symbolic thinking in detail in chapter 3.

31. Since there is a diversity of epistemologies in both Western and Asian epistemologies, the characterization of a Western epistemology (as an either/or way of thinking

Introduction

gregations reinterpret their liturgical experiences critically and creatively with attention to the distinctive characteristics of Asian ways of thinking.

Ecological Socialization Pedagogy as a Foundational Framework

This dissertation uses Roberta Berns' ecological socialization pedagogy as an educational framework for a new eucharistic pedagogy for the Presbyterian Church of Korea with attention to its pedagogical strategy. It provides educational foundations and implications for the dynamic relationship between the transformation of students' learning experiences and their eucharistic experiences within a faith community. Berns understands that the process of individuals' socialization takes place ecologically and their sociocultural interactions, experiences, and abilities are built and affected by complicated sociocultural, political processes between individuals and their environments.[32] Based on this understanding of the ecological socialization process, Berns develops an ecological socialization pedagogy that focuses on building effective teaching and learning practices. Berns asserts that the processes of students' socialization in the context of education are intrinsically connected to the contents and methods of teaching in the class. In this respect, such socialization processes need to be ecologically connected and reflected to the complex structural dynamics between students' life experiences in their multilayered socialization environments[33] and course teaching contents and pedagogical methods.

However, even though Berns' theory provides several significant reconceptualizations of pedagogical concepts in terms of students' life-reflected pedagogy, it is not adequate for analyzing Korean Presbyterian contexts of eucharistic pedagogy in light of Korean Presbyterian students'

---

and an anthropocentric way of thinking) and an Asian epistemology (as a both/and way of thinking and a cosmocentric way of thinking) cannot be generalized from two monolithic, dichotomous views. In this respect, even though this book understands that the characteristics of distinctive Asian epistemologies are a both/and way of thinking, a relational way of thinking, and a threefold way of thinking, this view does not mean that I ignore other diverse epistemologies in both the West and the East or scholarly given, but that it belongs to a particular Asian theologians who deals with liturgical contextualization from an Asian perspective such as Phan and Lee.

32. Berns, *Child, Family, School, Community*, 20.

33. Ibid., 21–26. Berns describes the process of socialization as the ecological inter-dynamics between four basic structures: (1) microsystem, (2) mesosystem, (3) exosystem, and (4) macrosystem. For more on these structures of ecological socialization, see chapter 4.

cultural contexts. Because it is grounded in Western thinking, Berns' theory has a limited capacity to reflect Korean students' life experiences from their particular contexts from a postcolonial perspective.[34] Thus, on the one hand, Berns' theory provides this project with an alternative educational strategy to understand the ecological dynamics between students' learning experiences and their specific local context and to reflect on them in classroom settings. On the other hand, her theory has a limited capacity to reflect Korean students' life experiences critically from their own specific contexts from a postcolonial perspective. Since Phan's and Lee's works on liturgical contextualization provide a critical view on Korean Presbyterian students' particular local contexts in terms of a postcolonial perspective, they can help this project build a new eucharistic pedagogy that reflects Korean Presbyterian students' own life experiences.

Therefore, as far as Berns' pedagogical theory has a critical conversation with Phan's and Lee's contextualization works regarding Korean Presbyterian students' eucharistic experiences, it is appropriate for Berns' theory to be used in this project. That is, it will help Korean Presbyterian teachers seriously consider multilayered dynamics of students' contextual socialization experiences and encourage students to critically examine their own life experiences such as Confucianism and Western-culture-oriented eucharistic practices.

Outline

The dissertation is composed of five chapters. The second chapter investigates the historical, sociocultural roots of current Korean Presbyterian eucharistic practices through the critical examination of liturgical books.[35] After describing the historical, sociocultural, and religious formative roots

---

34. Giroux, "Paulo Freire," 182–83. Throughout this book, "postcolonialism" refers to an intellectual discourse concerning reactions to, and analysis of, the cultural legacy of colonialism—specifically Confucianism and Western imperialism—through various forms of patriarchalism, ageism, hierarchalism, and Western culture chauvinism.

35. Presbyterian Church [in citations, "Presbyterian Church" refers to the Presbyterian Church of Korea (Chosen); references to other Presbyterian churches will include the full name], *Constitution*; Clark, *ChonChiMunDap JoYe*; *MokSaJiBop*; idem, *Korean Church and the Nevius Methods*; Underwood, *Chanyangga*; Moffett, *Wi Wonip Koin Kyujo*; Reforming Committee, *Book of Common Worship* [PCK].

of the Eucharist in the early period of the Presbyterian Church of Korea,[36] I will provide my own critical analysis.

The third chapter analyzes the current eucharistic texts from the Presbyterian Church of Korea in light of the liturgical contextualization works of two major Asian theologians (Phan and Lee). The liturgical analysis will help this dissertation prepare the way to build a new eucharistic pedagogy with attention to students' specific contexts by identifying current Korean students' eucharistic experiences both at the table of the Eucharist and in the classroom and their specific contexts.

The fourth chapter provides educational foundations for educational reform for the Presbyterian Church of Korea by having critical conversations about Korean Presbyterian students' eucharistic experiences through the examination of current eucharistic texts and curriculum of the Eucharist from the perspective of Berns' ecological socialization pedagogy. Since Berns' theory emphasizes the critical examination of students' multilayered sociocultural environments rooted in students' specific local contexts as its pedagogical strategy, two Asian theorists—Phan and Lee—whose works concern eucharistic practices in the view of Korean Presbyterians' own life experiences and Asian way of thinking are invited into the process of the critical analysis of Korean Presbyterian students' eucharistic experiences both in a class on the Eucharist and at the table of the Eucharist.

The fifth chapter suggests an alternative eucharistic pedagogy for the Presbyterian Church of Korea by reforming the curriculum of the Eucharist in light of critical conversations between Berns, Phan, and Lee in an effort to create a life-reflected eucharistic pedagogy. This process will include the formulation of the definition of the a new eucharistic pedagogy and reconceptualization regarding the eucharistic pedagogy such as teaching content, learning objectives, the role of the teacher, and the role of students. Based on the newly formulated definition of the eucharistic pedagogy for the Presbyterian Church of Korea and the reconceptualization of eucharistic pedagogy, I will suggest five steps as pedagogical strategies for a new eucharistic pedagogy for the Presbyterian Church of Korea including pedagogical guidelines for teachers and students. Furthermore, I will describe three generative educational principles for the Presbyterian Church of Korea from the new eucharistic pedagogy.

---

36. Throughout this book, the early period of the Presbyterian Church of Korea refers to the years from 1874 (when the first Korean Christians started to have worship services) to 1925 (when Japanese forced Koreans to practice Japanese Shintoism).

CHAPTER 2

Critical Analysis of Formative Roots of Korean Presbyterian Eucharistic Practices

WITHIN THE LAST TWO decades, Christian educators such as John Westerhoff III, Brett Webb-Mitchell, E. Byron Anderson, Robert L. Browning, Roy A. Reed, J. Frank Henderson, Debra Dean Murphy, and Robert K. Martin have investigated the relationship between liturgical practices and Christian education with attention to students' congregational life, culture, and faith transformation.[1] However, contextualization issues of eucharistic practices rooted in Asian contexts have not been given adequate attention in the field of Christian education. In order to build a new eucharistic pedagogy, this book will give special attention to ecological socialization pedagogy as it provides educational foundations by focusing on students' socialization process between their learning experiences and their socialization agents as well as the inseparable relationship between students' learning practices and their real-life experiences based on specific contexts in their daily lives.

In order to build an alternative eucharistic pedagogy with attention to the ecological socialization process of Korean Presbyterian students and their experiences at the table of the Eucharist, this book first explores the historical, sociocultural roots of current Korean Presbyterian eucharistic

---

1. Westerhoff, *Will Our Children Have Faith?*; Webb-Mitchell, *School of the Pilgrim*; *Christly Gestures*; Anderson, *Worship and Christian Identity*; Browning and Reed, *Sacraments in Religious Education*; Henderson, Larson, and Quinn, *Liturgy, Justice*; Murphy, *Teaching That Transforms*; and Martin, "Education and the Liturgical Life." Christian educators who deal with the relationship between liturgy and education focus on the transformation of students' faith and life through the experience of liturgical practices. Thus, in terms of the building of teaching strategies in the context of the Eucharist and in a class of reflection and preparation for students' eucharistic practices in the view of liturgical inculturation theory and ecological socialization pedagogy, these scholars' works on liturgical enculturation pedagogy are connected to what I propose in this book.

practices through the critical examination of liturgical books. The critical analysis of Korean Presbyterian eucharistic practices shows that there have been four historical, sociocultural, and religious formative roots in its development since the early period of the Presbyterian Church of Korea: (1) Confucianism as a dominant socio-cultural environment, (2) frontier worship introduced by missionaries, (3) Nevius Methods as basic mission strategies, and (4) the liturgy of the American Presbyterian church as the model for the formation and practices of Korean liturgy.

Confucianism as a Sociocultural Formative Root

In the 4th century, Confucianism was introduced to Korea from China, and it came to have an enormous influence on Korean views of politics and culture. Confucianism was imported during the three kingdoms of ancient Korea: *Kokuryu, Paikjae,* and *Shilla*.[2] The three kingdoms all accepted Confucianism as the nation's ruling ideology for building government structures, social norms, and training of the government elite.[3] In the beginning of the tenth century, Confucianism was used to lay the groundwork for the nation in the beginning of the *Koryo* dynasty.[4] By the end of the *Koryo* dynasty, when Buddhism came to be seen as depraved because of the close and corrupt relationships between political and religious authorities, Confucianism arose to combat Buddhism and to reestablish the ideas of Confucianism as the foundation of society.[5] "It was this school of thought, particularly as set forth by the Chinese philosopher *Chu Hsi*, which became the official ideology of the state under the *Chosun* Dynasty for over 500 years."[6] In the beginning of the *Chosun* dynasty in the fifteenth century, King *TeJo* adopted Confucianism, which regarded *Chung* (loyalty; 忠) and *Hyo* (filial piety; 孝) as the basis of political ideology. That is because he had ascended to the throne by force and then realized that he could not rule over the nation only by force.[7] Gradually, Confucian ethics became the basis of political principles in Korea.[8] As the *Chosun* dynasty founded a

2. Ministry of Culture, *Religious Culture in Korea*, 60.
3. K. J. Kim, *Christianity and the Encounter*, 87.
4. D. H. Kim, *Ethical Researching*, 25.
5. S. Son, "Historical Relationship," 67.
6. Adams, *Christ and Culture*, 65.
7. N. O. Kim, *Study of Ancestor Worship*, 13.
8. Adams, *Christ and Culture*, 70–71.

nation, Confucianism started to influence the history, culture, politics, and education of the *Chosun* dynasty over the next five hundred years.

When Christianity was introduced into Korea, Confucianism had dominated Korean religion, society, and culture since the sixteenth century.[9] In the early period of the Presbyterian Church of Korea, Korean society was deeply linked to Confucian culture and thought. Paul Crane observes that even contemporary Korean Christians are Confucians who attend a church.[10] He points out that Confucian ways of thinking even influence the ways that Korean Christians believe in God. Julia Ching also points out:

> Whether they like it or not, Korean Christians . . . cannot but assert themselves as Christians of Confucian background and values. This implies . . . that Korean Christians, as long as they are Koreans as well as Christians, cannot avoid the religio-cultural legacy of Confucianism, which has been the sole cumulative tradition during the past five centuries in Korea.[11]

Because the primary goal of most missionaries in the early period of the Presbyterian Church of Korea was to propagate Christianity to Korean people, they sought to distance Christianity from the older religious-cultural traditions of Korean society.[12] Not all missionaries approached Korean sociocultural traditions with the purpose of excluding them, but most missionaries did not fully understand them. Even though there were a few missionaries who tried to understand Korean cultural traditions, many missionaries regarded Korean cultural elements as anti-Christian or evil, with a strong sense of the superiority of Western culture.[13] In this context, most missionaries insisted that Korean religious cultural traditions be discarded and replaced with Christianity based on Western culture.[14] However, the roots of Confucianism were so deep that liturgy in Korean worship was nevertheless formed under the strong influences of Confucianism in terms of its values and patterns such as conservatism, authoritarianism, and hierarchicalism.[15]

---

9. Adams, *Christ and Culture*, 65.
10. Park, *Influence of Confucianism*, 24.
11. Ching and Kung, *Christianity and Chinese Religions*, 85.
12. Jo, *Korean Protestant Church*, 33.
13. S. W. Kim, *Worship in the Twenty-First Century*, 185.
14. K. J. Kim, *Early Korean Presbyterian Worship*, 175–76.
15. C. H. Kim, *Study of Worship Renewal*, 50–51; H. Y. Kim, *Wang Yang-Min and Karl Barth*, 3–4. C. Kim and H. Kim mention that the cultural and religious legacy of

From the very beginning, Confucianism was built on a strong basic confidence by Confucius in the *Han* dynasty. He believed that the ultimate solution might come from the restoration of *In* (benevolence rooted in love; 仁). According to Confucius, *In*, as the highest, ideal value, is a moral nature that is immanent in every single human being from heaven.[16] As Confucius interpreted the character *In* by its components—person (人) and two (二)—the meaning of *In* is to love; to live with other people and to love them. That is, love is the foundation of *In* and human beings can become genuine human beings as long as they love others and live with others.[17]

What is distinctive about the character of Confucian *In*, as love, is that *In* should keep the position at the center of oneself, and then it should extend outward to family, society, and the world. Confucian *In* is self-centered but it is not egoistic selfishness because it is supposed to flow outward. Since Confucius thought that equality for everyone was impossible in a society, he claimed that to love all people equally is to deceive oneself. The concept of equality in Confucianism does not mean that everyone should be treated equally in society, but that everyone needs to fulfill their own *In* according to their own social position for the sake of social harmony and order. For this reason, Confucianism places compulsory responsibility on everyone for the order of a society. *Tu Yu Myung* calls this "Inclusive Humanism."[18] From this perspective, *Hyo* (filial piety; 孝) and *Jesa* (ancestor worship; 祭祀) are understood as follows: *Hyo* means to respect, serve, and love one's own parents; *Jesa* as ancestor worship is understood to be filial affection as the most representative expression for *Hyo*.[19] When people practice *In* in their daily lives, *Ye* (禮) can be the concrete form and explicit expression of *In*.

Confucianism has had an effect on not only Korean society but also Korean Presbyterian worship. H. Kim asserts that the need for a Confucian-Christian dialogue is particularly imperative in the Korean Church for the following three reasons: "(1) Korea is the only country in East Asia where Christianity is no longer a small minority religion, but takes a leading role in society; (2) In the history of east Asia, Korea was most strongly influenced by Confucianism, and still is; and (3) Korean Christianity is basically a Confucian Christianity."

16. Lee, *Confucian Asceticism*, 10.
17. Baek, *Is Confucianism Unfair Thought?*, 37.
18. Ibid., 51.
19. M. H. Kim, *Ancestor Worship*, 236.

Based on this understanding of *In*, Confucianism has two central characteristics: ritual formalism and patriarchal conservatism.[20] Confucius believed that human society needed a certain social system in order to solve the problems of social disorder. His ideal model for a real society was the *Chu* dynasty, and so Confucius put together, carried over, and synthesized ancient *Chu* traditions and culture, such as the concepts of "mandate from heaven" (天命), "ancestor worship" (祭祀), and the "institution of *Ye*" (禮).[21] He emphasized that ancient traditions and their rituals from the *Chu* dynasty, performed mainly by the eldest man in a group, should be accepted as essential and unchangeable resources for "an ideal model for a real society."[22] These characteristics are evident in the central rituals of Confucianism, such as *Je-Rye* (ancestral worship; 祭禮), *Kwal-Rye* (celebration of coming of age; 冠禮), *Sang-Rye* (funeral rite; 喪禮), and *Hol-Rye* (marriage rite; 婚禮). In most Confucian rituals, the eldest man presides over ritual practices, following traditional Confucian customs, orders, and conventions.[23] This presupposition of Confucian ritual based on sacrosanct, male-oriented, and male-led ritual practices influenced Korean Presbyterians' understanding of liturgical practices as unchangeable, hierarchical, and patriarchal.

The Directory of Worship of the Presbyterian Church of Korea[24] shows a strong tendency to reinforce sacrosanct eucharistic practices. In chapter 11 (The Lord's Supper), there is only a single form of celebration of the Eucharist in terms of eucharistic prayer, the Words of Institution, prayer after communion, gesture, and movement.[25] In the chapter of "Ordinances in the Particular Church" in *ChonChiMunDap JoYe* (*What Is the Presbyterian Law?*), the patriarchal conservatism in the liturgy of the Presbyterian Church of Korea is clearly observed. "The minister should himself offer the prayers in the Sunday morning worship and Sunday evening prayer meeting. . . . At the prayer meetings, the male communicants are to take part under the general supervision of the pastor. Female communicants also can

20. Park, *Influence of Confucianism*, 33.
21. Baek, *Is Confucianism Unfair Thought?*, 37.
22. D. H. Kim, *Ethical Research*, 8.
23. Korean National Commission, *Korean Anthropology*, 176.
24. Presbyterian Church, *Constitution*, 78–80, quoted in K. J. Kim, *Early Korean Presbyterian Worship*, 239–41.
25. In an appendix, I will provide the English translation of chapter 11 (the Lord's Supper) of *The Directory of Worship of the Presbyterian Church of Korea*.

Critical Analysis of Formative Roots of Korean Presbyterian Eucharistic Practices

lead the prayer but it is subject to the discretion of the pastor and elders of the churches."[26] Furthermore, these tendencies were reinforced by missionaries, who conveyed to the Korean Presbyterians the celebration of the Eucharist from their own restricted Western culture–centered understanding and with their own patriarchal and formal practices.[27] In this context, there was an unusual parallel between the Confucian values underlying the Korean culture and Western colonial values brought by the missionaries in terms of ritual formalism, patriarchal conservatism, and the sense of the superiority of Western culture.

The Eucharist, however, is not sacrosanct; nor is it a ritual of injustice theologically and liturgically. First, since the era of the New Testament and early church, there was "no single authoritative origin"[28] for the Eucharist. In their book *Many Tables*, Dennis E. Smith and Hal E. Taussig explain that there were various eucharistic practices and interpretations in the first-century church by examining biblical, historical texts, and recent studies and articles regarding the Eucharist. As their book title indicates, Smith and Taussig emphasize that these diversities of eucharistic practices can provide significant foundations for liturgical renewal today to have "more creative directions"[29] beyond the formal repetition of eucharistic practices. In *Eucharistic Origins*, Paul Bradshaw points out that there were variations in the eucharistic practices of the early church, such as cup-bread or bread-cup thanksgiving pattern, celebration with only bread or only wine, celebration by using water instead of wine or wine mixed with water, celebration with a bread ritual or a whole meal, and celebration in the morning or evening.[30] According to Bradshaw, the Eucharist in early Christian worship kept evolving according to "new surroundings" in terms of the development of the church and the society.[31] Through the comparative study of early Christian traditions such as the *Acts of John*, the *Anaphora of Addai and Mari*, the Strasbourg Papyrus, the *Sacramentary*

---

26. Clark, *ChonChiMunDap JoYe* (*What is the Presbyterian Law?*), ch. 7, quoted in K. J. Kim, *Early Korean Presbyterian Worship*, 227.

27. B. J. Kim, "Study of Korean Presbyterian Liturgy," 36.

28. Smith and Taussig, *Many Tables*, 37.

29. Ibid., 16.

30. Bradshaw, *Eucharistic Origins*, 59–61. Bradshaw explores various eucharistic practices in early Christian worship by examining eucharistic materials of early Christian ritual meals such as the symposium, 1 Corinthian texts, the apostolic tradition, and papias.

31. Ibid., 137.

of *Serapion*, and *The Apostolic Tradition*, Bradshaw asserts that the early church's eucharistic prayers evolved and developed variously in different geographical regions.[32] In his recent book, *Reconstructing Early Christian Worship*, Bradshaw attempts to disclose the diverse patterns of eucharistic practices and prayers in early church. For example, with regard to the structure of eucharistic celebrations, he points out that the *Didache*, as a very early Christian text, includes two different parallel variants of eucharistic prayers in chapters 9 and 10.[33] While the prayer in chapter 9 describes the practices of eating the bread and drinking the cup as clearly separated from each other, the prayer in chapter 10 illustrates them as a continuous whole. In view of the contents of eucharistic prayer, Bradshaw explores the ways that the elements of eucharistic prayers, such as creation, the saving acts of Christ, a narrative of institution, prayer for communicants, epiclesis, and general intercession, have been developed diversely according to participants' political, economic, geographical, and sociocultural contexts from different historical periods.[34] In this respect, Smith, Taussig, and Bradshaw understand that the Eucharist was not formed as a ritual of sacrosanctity grounded on one authoritative single tradition or one single eucharistic prayer but developed in various traditions and eucharistic prayers in the relationship to new sociocultural contexts throughout the period of the New Testament and the early church.[35]

Second, the Eucharist is a place of hospitality, equality, and justice. In *What Happens in Holy Communion*, Michael Welker emphasizes that the first Eucharist was a meal table of equality and hospitality. Through the examination of the biblical texts regarding the Eucharist, he highlights that all participants were accepted in the first Eucharist unconditionally and equally.[36] Welker observes that Jesus invited all his disciples equally and allowed them to participate in the Last Supper with hospitality in spite of Judas' betrayal and Peter's denial. He underlines that Jesus' hospitable and equal acceptance of the marginalized and suffering as "characteristic of the

---

32. Ibid., 116.

33. Bradshaw, *Reconstructing Early Christian Worship*, 41.

34. Ibid., 52.

35. White, *Introduction to Christian Worship*, 230. Even though it is true that the various eucharistic traditions and prayers were developed with the mutual dynamics of people's sociocultural contexts in the early church, it became more static during the fourth century in the West. White explains that, in the post-Nicene era, the variety and rich diversity in eucharistic rites were simplified in form and practice.

36. Welker, *What Happens in Holy Communion?*, 69.

pre-Easter Jesus practice of table fellowship" attains to "an exemplary apex" in Jesus' Last Supper.[37] Welker also points out that the "unworthy eating and drinking" in Corinth came from the misuse of the eucharistic meals in terms of inequality and injustice between the rich and the poor.[38] In the eucharistic table of the Corinthian church, the rich consumed their own food, which they brought in the name of the celebration of the Eucharist and which they ate before the poor arrived. "In light of the callously oblivious behavior of the rich, the poor are once again reminded of their oppressive situation."[39] Welker understands that, in the context of Corinthian eucharistic practices, there was not a meal of mutual acceptance and justice but "the perverted meal" of inequality and injustice.[40] In his book *Leading from the Table*, Galbreath also points out justice issues in the context of the Eucharist. He insists that all participants need to identify justice issues and theological presuppositions of current eucharistic practices through a critical perspective.[41] Since participants are guided to have Christian virtues and practices through their participation in the Eucharist, critical reflection on current eucharistic practices with attention to "giving up power," "caring for all God's creations," and "practicing hospitality" is demanded by all participants in the Eucharist.[42] In this sense, the misunderstanding of the Eucharist as an unchangeable, hierarchical, and patriarchal rite in the early Korean Presbyterian Church under the strong sociocultural influence of Confucianism needs to be reconceptualized theologically and ritually to be a meal of variety, equality, justice, and hospitality.

Frontier Worship as a Theological, Liturgical Formative Root

Missionaries in the early Korean Protestant church introduced and practiced forms of frontier worship as the basic worship form for Korean Protestant Christians. Even though the missionaries came from various nations (such as the U.S., Canada, and Scotland) and various denominations (such as Presbyterian, Methodist, and Baptist), frontier worship spread across the early Korean Protestant church commonly as the most traditional worship

37. Ibid., 72.
38. Ibid., 74.
39. Hofius, *Paulusstudien*, 220, quoted in Welker, *What Happens in Holy Communion?*, 78.
40. Welker, *What Happens in Holy Communion?*, 78.
41. Galbreath, *Leading from the Table*, 125.
42. Ibid., 129.

form. Because frontier worship was a very popular worship pattern in the U.S. in the eighteenth and nineteenth centuries through the Great Awakening and revival movements, most missionaries were familiar with frontier worship and introduced it to Korean Protestant Christians in order to spread the gospel to them effectively.[43] Frontier worship, focusing on evangelism, emphasized individual salvation and conversion with attention to people's repentance depending on God's forgiveness through Jesus' suffering and death.[44] According to *MockSaJiBub* (*The Works of the Pastors*), published by Clark in 1919, the goal of Sunday morning worship is to save people from judgment and their sins.[45]

Early Korean Presbyterian worship that was based on frontier worship emphasized individual salvation through the repentance of sin. In this context, the Eucharist was understood as a supplementary solemnized liturgical occasion. The liturgical tracts of the early Korean Presbyterian Church such as *Kurisudo Mundap* (*Christian Catechism*) and *Songgyong Mundap* (*Bible Catechism*) assert that the meaning of the Eucharist is to memorialize Jesus' suffering and death for the forgiveness of people's sins.[46] K. J. Kim points out that "there was no mention of remembering the resurrection of Jesus Christ in those books," and he mentions that the Eucharist was understood and practiced as a gloomy liturgy focusing on remembering the death of Jesus Christ.[47] Jin Hwan Han describes the early Korean Presbyterian Church's Eucharist as "a mere symbolic rite to help people commemorate the death of Christ, or most critically speaking, . . . as an audio-visual aid to commemorate vividly the passion of Christ."[48] An interesting note on the Lord's Supper is seen in Clark's book *MokSa ChiBop* (*The Works of Pastors*; 牧師之法 [1919]). He proposed that "two white tablecloths ought to be prepared, one for covering the table and the other for covering the

---

43. Jo, *Korean Protestant Church*, 34.

44. K. Kim, *Early Korean Presbyterian Worship*, 28; White, *Protestant Worship*, 177. White explains that the worship pattern of frontier worship style was made of three parts: (1) passionate praising for a long time, (2) a strong evangelical sermon emphasizing salvation through the dichotomy between God's grace and human beings' depravity, and (3) an invitation to accept the gospel and conversion.

45. Jo, *Korean Protestant Church*, 41, quoted in C. H. Kim, *Study of the Revival*, 153.

46. Nevius, *Kurisudo Mundap*, 30; Underwood, *Songgyong Mundap*, 9, quoted in K. J. Kim, *Formation of Presbyterian Worship*, 101.

47. K. J. Kim, *Early Korean Presbyterian Worship*, 207.

48. Han, *Historical and Theological Analysis*, 207.

Critical Analysis of Formative Roots of Korean Presbyterian Eucharistic Practices

vessels, which contained the elements."[49] It is customary to cover the dead with a white cloth in Korea; therefore, these tablecloths show that the Lord's Supper of the Presbyterian Church in Korea focused on the passion and death of Christ by creating a deep penitential mood.[50] According to *MokSa ChiBop*, elders need to prepare two white tablecloths for covering eucharistic elements in the practice of the Lord's Supper: (1) before the worship service, elders (or deacons) not only need to prepare the communion vessel and the elements but also cover them with the white tablecloth; (2) at the beginning of the Lord's Supper, elders come to the table, lift the tablecloth, fold it, and put it away in a safe place; (3) and at the end of the Lord's Supper, elders come to the table and "cover the elements with this tablecloth.[51]

Even though *The Directory of Worship of the Presbyterian Church of Korea*[52] encourages liturgists to say a thanksgiving prayer and a post-Communion prayer focusing on thanksgiving and glorification, it does not provide any specific texts for the prayer. K. J. Kim points out that "in *HongSang YesikSoe* (Forms of Marriage and Burial) this post-communion prayer of thanksgiving was omitted along with other exclusions, such as exhortations for the communicants and for the spectators, which had been included in *The Directory of Worship of the Presbyterian Church of Korea* in the order of service."[53] Under this influence many ordained pastors in the Korean Presbyterian Church continue to have a tendency to: (1) strictly adhere to the Words of Institution focusing on the passion of Christ, and (2) skip the preface (including Sanctus and Benedictus), the epiclesis of thanksgiving prayer (including intercession prayer, Trinitarian doxology, and Great Amen), or a post-Communion prayer focusing on thanksgiving and glorification.[54]

However, the Eucharist is not a gloomy ritual focused solely on remembering Jesus' passion and death, but a joyful ritual focused on participating in the presence of the risen Christ. According to John Calvin, the Protestant reformer, the Eucharist does not illustrate only the body of

---

49. Presbyterian Church, *HongSang YesikSoe*, 26.

50. K. J. Kim, *Formation of Presbyterian Worship*, 207.

51. Ibid.

52. Presbyterian Church, *Constitution*, 68–88. The Constitution consisted of five parts: (1) the Confession of Faith, (2) the Westminster Shorter Catechism, (3) a Form of Government, (4) a Book of Discipline, and (5) the Directory of Worship.

53. K. J. Kim, *Formation of Presbyterian Worship*, 208.

54. Ibid.

Christ but a genuine feast and holy banquet.[55] In the Eucharist, people do not merely recall what Christ has done for us, or merely partake of the benefits he has won, but also communicate with the living savior himself in the fullness of his glorified person, not only with his Spirit or divine nature, but with his flesh and blood.[56] For Calvin, sign and reality are inseparable in the Eucharist. The Eucharist is given with the signs that are not merely empty signs but joined with the reality of the risen Christ. Even though the body of Christ is subject to the common limits of a human body and cannot be in more than one place at the same time, after Christ's ascension to heaven, the Spirit truly unites things separated in space.[57] The Holy Spirit is the bond of our union with Christ in the Eucharist. Calvin contends that we do not drag Christ down from heaven; rather, he pulls us up to himself, and that is how we enjoy his presence.[58] God gives us grace through sign and reality and human beings acknowledge God's grace as a gift and respond to God with gratitude in the Eucharist. In this respect, Calvin understands that the Eucharist is a joyful feast as the sacramental real presence and a sign of the guarantee of a present reality. The meal is a gift of God, but it is also an invitation to give thanks. Calvin writes:

> We call it either "the Lord's Supper" or "the Eucharist" because in it we both are spiritually fed by the liberality of the Lord and also give him thanks for his kindness. In this sacrament (the Eucharist) . . . the Lord recalls the great bounty of his goodness to our memory and stirs us up to acknowledge it; and at the same time he admonishes us not to be ungrateful for such lavish liberality, but rather to proclaim it with fitting praises and celebrate it by giving thanks. . . . We see that this sacred bread of the Lord's Supper is spiritual food, sweet and delicious to those to whom it shows that Christ is their life. . . . All the delights of the gospel are laid before us.[59]

B. A. Gerrish mentions that the Eucharist is the liturgical enactment of the theme of God's grace and human beings' gratitude that lies at the heart of Calvin's entire theology. He summarizes Calvin's eucharistic theology in

---

55. Calvin, *Institutes*, 4.17.1.

56. Ibid., 4.17.5; John Williamson Nevin, *The Mystical Presence: A Vindication of the Reformed or Calvinistic Doctrine of the Holy Eucharist* (Philadelphia: S.R. Fisher & Co, 1846), 57-58.

57. Calvin, *Institutes*, 4.17.26, 27, 33.

58. Gerrish, *Grace and Gratitude*, 175.

59. Ibid., 19–20.

the form of five propositions: (1) the Eucharist does not merely remind us of a gift but is a gift; (2) the gift is Jesus Christ himself, (3) "the gift is given with the signs"; (4) "the gift is given by the Holy Spirit"; and (5) "the gift is to be received by faith."[60] In this sense, Gerrish confirms that Calvin understands the Eucharist as God's grace in Christ through the Holy Spirit and human beings' thanksgiving.

Moreover, the Eucharist is a communal participatory ritual rather than a private spiritual one. Laurence Hull Stookey asserts that the Eucharist is a corporate, communal serving rite rather than an individualistic and self-serving rite. As Stookey mentions that the Eucharist involves God's story, including creation, covenant, Christ, church, and coming kingdom, he points out that the term *anamnesis* is not about solitary experience involving mental recall but about a corporate act in which the event remembered is experienced anew through ritual repetition.[61] In his book *Leading from the Table*, Paul Galbreath points out the misguided interpretation of 1 Corinthians 11:27–28 regarding the Eucharist. Galbreath asserts that the Apostle Paul's attention is focused not on a private spiritual condition but on the external communal eating practices in a meal community.[62] Galbreath also emphasizes the importance of the basic physical actions (such as breaking, pouring, passing, eating, and drinking), which have been overshadowed in some eucharistic traditions.[63]

In this sense, it is an urgent theological, liturgical imperative that the Eucharist as focused on the private recalling of Jesus' death rooted in frontier worship needs to be reformed critically. It cannot be used as a means of effective propagation of the gospel and individuals' conversion but should be a joyful, communal heavenly banquet where people participate in the presence of God with attention to God's grace and human beings' gratitude.

Nevius Methods as a Pastoral, Liturgical Formative Root

The Nevius Methods as a pastoral, liturgical formative root had an effect on the understanding of the Eucharist in the early Presbyterian Church of Korea not as the main part of worship but as a marginalized part of it. The methods were originally established by John L. Nevius, a missionary with

60. Ibid., 135–38.
61. Stookey, *Eucharist*, 28.
62. Galbreath, *Leading from the Table*, 22.
63. Ibid., 26.

the Presbyterian Church of United States of America in Shan-Tung province (China) in order to propagate the gospel in a non-Christian society.[64] Most missionaries, such as H. G. Underwood in Korea, accepted these methods as the basic principle for the Korean mission in 1891 since they heard that the methods were already studied and practiced in the mission field of China.[65] After the Presbyterian Church in the USA Mission adopted the Nevius Methods as official mission policies for Korea in 1895, they became "the backbone of the Korean mission policies" in both name and practice.[66] The Nevius Methods were built and practiced on the ground of the Three-Self principles: (1) self-propagation, (2) self-government, and (3) self-support.[67] For the effective propagation of the gospel in Korea, Nevius insisted that the gospel should be spread by native lay people and that worship should be conducted in the local language in simple worship patterns. This is because he thought that the lay people in a mission field were not trained to conduct a formal, long worship service or the sacraments.[68] Nevius' suggestion for a simple worship pattern was: (1) praise, (2) prayer, (3) reading the Bible, (4) congregational prayer, (5) praise, (6) teaching/interpretation the Bible, (7) prayer, (8) offering, and (9) praise. This simplified worship style encouraged by Nevius provided the basic form of Korean Presbyterian Sunday worship as appearing in official liturgical books such as *Chosen Yesugyo Changnohoe Honsang Yesikso* (*Forms of Marriage and Burial of the Presbyterian Church of Korea*), *MoksaChibop* (*The Works of Pastors*), and *Yebae Chopkyong* (*Aids for Public Worship*). All three books do not describe the Eucharist as part of regular Sunday worship service but only as part of occasional Sunday worship service such as a baptismal service.[69] Even though

---

64. K. J. Kim, *Formation of Presbyterian Worship*, 66.

65. Park, *Influence of Confucianism*, 28.

66. K. J. Kim, *Formation of Presbyterian Worship*, 67.

67. Clark, *Korean Church and the Nevius Methods*, 33–34. Clark described the methods as follows: I. Self-propagation: every believer is a teacher for someone and a learner from someone else; every individual and group seeks by the "layering methods" to extend the work of the church. II. Self-government: each group is governed under its chosen unpaid Leaders; circuits under their own paid Helpers, who will later yield to Pastors; circuit meeting training for district, provincial and national leaders. III. Self-supporting: all chapels are built and funded by local believers; each group, as soon as founded, begins to pay towards the circuit Helper's salary; no pastor of a single church should be provided by foreign funds.

68. K. J. Kim, *Formation of Presbyterian Worship*, 69. In the early Korean Presbyterian Church, most native lay leaders were farmers, artisans, and merchants.

69. Presbyterian Church, *Yesugyo Changnohoe Honsang Yesikso*, 1; Clark, *MokSaJiBop*,

The Directory of Worship (1922) mentions that "The Lord's Supper is to be celebrated frequently," it set the limit of celebration: "the exact number of its frequency may be determined by the Session accordingly for its edification."[70] In this respect, native people never really developed authentic Korean liturgies under the influences of the Nevius Methods. Even though the Nevius Methods emphasized the use of native language and the liturgical practices of native people, the building of authentic liturgy cannot be completed simply by changing languages or liturgists from the foreign to the native. I think that this failure of building authentic liturgy in the early period of the Korean Protestant church is also related to the Confucian conservatism that is reluctant to allow ritual change. For Korean people who lived under a strong ritual authoritarianism and hierarchicalism, the simplified worship style without the Eucharist that was suggested, decided, and taught deductively by foreign missionaries was easily understood as the most traditional form of the Korean Sunday worship service, which could not be changed or altered.[71] Therefore, because of the virtual lack of native ordained ministers to preside over the Eucharist and the overall lack of education about the Eucharist, the Eucharist was marginalized from regular Sunday worship service in the early years of the Korean Protestant church.[72]

In contrast, John Calvin emphasizes the centrality of the Word and the Eucharist as the normative pattern for the Sunday worship service.[73] As Calvin mentions that worship in the New Testament (Acts 2:42 and 1 Cor 11:20) and early church included both the Word and the Eucharist as the central order, which cannot be reduced,[74] Calvin criticizes the limited observance of the Eucharist in the Protestant church in Geneva (four times a year).[75] According to Calvin, the Eucharist is the means of grace in association with the Word. It is a "testimony of divine grace toward us,

---

195–97; Soltau, *Yebae ChopKyoung*, 1–2.

70. Presbyterian Church, *Constitution*, 214.

71. Jo, *Korean Protestant Church*, 164.

72. K. J. Kim, *Formation of Presbyterian Worship*, 206. Kim mentions that "there are no specific records to indicate exactly on what dates the Korean Church observed the Lord's Supper, however, it is likely that the Lord's Supper was celebrated on Easter, Thanksgiving, Christmas, and at the end of the week of prayer of the Korean New Year season (lunar calendar)."

73. Bower, *Companion*, 7.

74. Calvin, *Institutes*, 4.17.44.

75. Bower, *Companion*, 7–8; Calvin, *Institutes*, 4.17.46. Calvin calls the Roman Catholic custom an "invention of the devil" and the Geneva custom "a defect."

confirmed by an outward sign, with mutual attestation of our piety toward him [God]."[76] In his *Institutes of the Christian Religion,* Calvin suggests the proper structure of the celebration of the Eucharist for the Sunday worship service on the basis of two liturgical poles: the Word and the Eucharist.[77] It shows that Calvin understood the Eucharist as a central liturgical part of Sunday worship. *The Book of Common Worship* clearly reflects and articulates Calvin's understanding of Word and Sacrament as the normative weekly service. It affirms that Christian worship was shaped distinctively on the basis of the "reading and proclamation of the Scripture" and the "celebration of the Eucharist" as its central norm from the period of the New Testament.[78] The Eucharist, making the Word of God visible and concrete, is not an additional liturgy but an integral liturgy for each Sunday worship service.[79] *The Companion to the Book of Common Worship* also states the reciprocal relationship between the Word and the Eucharist.

> Word and Sacrament are interdependent. The Word amplifies the Sacrament, and the Sacrament magnifies the Word. Word and Sacrament become more fully themselves when each stands next to the other.... Word and Sacrament each contribute to the integrity of the other. The Word reduces the possibility that the Sacrament will turn into superstition or an empty observance; and the Sacrament reduces the possibility that the Word will mutate into moralizing or unenacted words.[80]

In this sense, it is unfortunate that the Eucharist had been understood and practiced not as the central liturgy of worship but as a marginalized liturgy in the Presbyterian Church of Korea.

American Presbyterian Liturgy as a Historical, Liturgical Formative Root

In the early stages of the Presbyterian Church of Korea, liturgies were established and dictated mainly by missionaries.[81] After the first independent

---

76. Calvin, *Institutes,* 4.14.1.
77. Ibid., 4.17.43.
78. Presbyterian Church (USA), *Book of Common Worship,* 41.
79. Ibid.
80. Bower, *Companion,* 7–8.
81. K. J. Kim, *Formation of Presbyterian Worship,* 111.

Critical Analysis of Formative Roots of Korean Presbyterian Eucharistic Practices

presbytery in the Korean church was established in 1907, the Presbyterian Church of Korea formed official liturgies concerning the roles of ordained pastors, such as exercising jurisdiction and discipline, performing baptism, and presiding over the Eucharist.[82] In the process of liturgical formation, Korean people were not permitted to prepare liturgical texts. Instead, foreign missionaries such as S. A. Moffett,[83] H. G. Underwood,[84] and Charles Allen Clark[85] played a vital, decisive role in the preparation, translation, writing, and publishing of official liturgical materials such as *The Confession of Faith, ChonChiMunDap JoYe (What Is the Presbyterian Law?*; 政治問答), *The Directory of Worship, MockSaJiBub (The Works of Pastors*; 牧師之法), *Chanyangga (Hymns of Praise)* and *Wi Wonip Koin Kyujo (Manual for Catechumens)*.[86] Korean cultural contexts were not seriously considered in the establishment of liturgies in the Presbyterian Church of Korea. For example, *The Confession of Faith* originally made for the Presbyterian Church of India was adopted officially in 1907 by the Presbyterian Church of Korea.[87] *ChonChiMunDap JoYe (What Is the Presbyterian Law?)* was adopted

82. Ibid., 117.

83. Clark, *Digest*, 64; K. J. Kim, *Formation of Presbyterian Worship*, 254. S. A. Moffett was the first moderator of the Presbyterian Church of Korea, and he was the chair of the committee preparing, reporting, and adopting "rules, by-laws, and forms for the ordination of officers and administration of the Sacraments" for the establishment of constitution of the Presbyterian Church of Chosen to the General Assembly. He also wrote and published the *Wi Wonip Koin Kyujo (Manual for Catechumens)*, which includes basic instructions of liturgies and church politics with prayers and hymns.

84. K. J. Kim, *Formation of Presbyterian Worship*, 108, 254. H. G. Underwood, who was the second moderator of the Presbyterian Church of Korea as well as one of the early missionaries in Korean Protestant Christianity, published several significant liturgical materials such as *Songkong Mundap (Bible Catechism)*, *Yeosukyo Mundap (Presbyterian Catechism)*, and *Chanyangga (Hymns of Praise)*, which was the first Presbyterian hymn book written in Korean.

85. Clark, *Mokhoehak*, 1–2. Clark was the professor of worship and preaching in Presbyterian Theological Seminary at Pyeongyang from 1908 to 1944. He wrote and published many liturgical books and materials for the Presbyterian Church of Korea such as *ChonChiMunDap JoYe (What Is the Presbyterian Law?)*, *MokSaJiBop (The Works of the Pastors)*, and *Kangdohak (Homiletics)*.

86. Presbyterian Church, *Constitution*; Clark, *ChonChiMunDap JoYe*; idem, *MokSaJiBop*; Underwood, *Chanyangga*; and Moffett, *Wi Wonip Koin Kyujo*.

87. Clark, *Digest*, 114–15. According to the preface of the Confession, "in presenting the following proposed Confession of Faith, we desire to state that the committee has not attempted to formulate a new Confession.... The preamble only being changed, it is the Confession of Faith adopted last year by the recently organized Presbyterian Church of India."

in 1919 by translating the book *What Is the Presbyterian Law as Defined by the Church Courts?* by missionary J. A. Hodge, without any revision in the light of Korean Presbyterian contexts.[88] The *Directory of Worship*, adopted and published in 1922, combined parts of *The Directory for Worship of the American Presbyterian Church* (Southern) and *The Directory for Worship of the American Presbyterian Church* (Northern) with certain modifications.[89] Chapters 1–16 of *The Directory of Worship of the Presbyterian Church of Korea* were exact copies of the same chapters of *The Directory for Worship of the American Presbyterian Church* (Southern).[90] Chapters 17–19 were adopted directly from *The Directory for Worship of the American Presbyterian Church* (Northern).[91]

In the early Korean church, liturgy had been formed and practiced not based on Korean congregations' sociocultural contexts but guided according to what missionaries had done in the Presbyterian Church in the U.S.[92] That is, while the liturgy of the American Presbyterian church (Southern and Northern) became the model for the formation and practices of Korean liturgy, Korean people's culture and daily lives were marginalized from liturgical practice. L. George Paik mentions that "one of the interesting features connected with the organization of the Korean Presbyterian Church was the introduction of American usage and customs."[93] Under the strong influence of missionaries regarding the formation of Korean liturgy, most Korean Presbyterian congregations were taught Western culture–oriented liturgies as the best model for Christian liturgy.[94] Moreover, many missionaries had a conviction that Korean culture was inferior to Western culture or even evil.[95] For the worship practices, including the celebration of the Eucharist, many missionaries guided Korean congregation members

---

88. K. J. Kim, *Formation of Presbyterian Worship*, 119.

89. Presbyterian Church, *Constitution*, 71, quoted in K. J. Kim, *Formation of Presbyterian Worship*, 122. In *The Directory of Worship of the Presbyterian Church in Korea*, one sentence about the posture of prayer was added in Section V: "kneeling in prayer or prostrating oneself is proper."

90. Presbyterian Church in the United States, *Directory for the Worship of God*.

91. Presbyterian Church, *Constitution*; Presbyterian Church in the United States, *Constitution*.

92. K. J. Kim, *Formation of Presbyterian Worship*, 123.

93. Paik, *History of Protestant Missions*, 337–38.

94. Jung, "Examining the Lima Liturgy," 346.

95. Davies, *Missionary Thought*, 3–36, quoted in S. W. Kim, *Study of the Liturgical Reconsideration*, 308.

to use Western instruments, hymnals, clothes, and food without serious consideration of and respect for Korean cultural contexts. For instance, according to *The Directory of Worship of the Korean Presbyterian Church*, there is no option for eucharistic elements except Western bread and grape wine in the early Korean Presbyterian Church.[96] At the eucharistic table, rice as the symbol of life to Korean people was marginalized by the use of Western bread.[97] The songs in the Korean hymnal were not composed by Korean people but translated by foreign missionaries from American hymns. The fact that hymn singing was not accompanied by Korean folk music instruments but by Western instruments did not adequately reflect Korean Presbyterian congregations' sociocultural contexts.[98] Even though there were attempts to incorporate Korean culture by several missionaries in the early Korean Protestant church, their efforts did not succeed because they also did not understand Korean traditions, culture, and religion in depth.[99] For example, according to the *Centennial History of Yongdong Presbyterian Church*, James Gale, a missionary during the early period of the Korean Presbyterian Church, tried to use native Korean tunes, called *Yangsando karak*, for Sunday worship service at Yongdong Presbyterian Church in Seoul. For this, Gale was severely criticized by other missionaries, who thought that only Western music was proper for worship services.[100]

However, eucharistic theology and practices are inherently contextual, not predetermined, because authentic theology cannot be separated from congregation members' real lives within their cultures.[101] Since the early church, the Eucharist has been formed and developed not in a vacuum but

---

96. Presbyterian Church, *Constitution*, 205–9, quoted in K. J. Kim, *Formation of Presbyterian Worship*, 196.

97. S. W. Kim, *Symbol of the Eucharist*, 134–35.

98. Kim, *Task for the Korean Hymnal*, 414. For example, *Chansongga* (1894), the first Korean hymnal book in the early period of the Presbyterian Church of Korea, consisted of mainly the British-American songs of the eighteenth and nineteenth centuries: 110 of the 117 songs were composed by foreigners.

99. Davies, *Missionary Thought*, 3–36, quoted in S. W. Kim, *Study of the Liturgical Reconsideration*, 308. According to Davies, when missionaries in the early Korean Presbyterian Church took a firm attitude about idolatry or shamanistic superstition, they could not discern clearly what was authentic Korean culture or religious idolatry. In this context, most of them taught Western culture–oriented worship style as the best model for Christian liturgy.

100. K. J. Kim, *Formation of Presbyterian Worship*, 118; Kyohoe, *Yongdong Kyohoe Paengyonsa*, 196–98.

101. Ting, "Eucharistic Homily," 62.

through the dynamics within congregations' cultures.[102] In his book *Shape a Circle Ever Wider*, Mark R. Francis, a Catholic liturgical theologian, asserts that "except for the period of 400 years after the Council of Trent," the liturgy of Christian worship has interplayed continuously with new cultural contexts throughout its history:[103] the liturgy of the New Testament (with Jewish and Hellenistic culture); the liturgy of the early church (with the Greco-Roman culture); the liturgy of the Middle Ages (with various local cultures in Western Europe); and the liturgy of the missionary outreach of the sixteenth and seventeenth centuries (with diverse local cultures in mission fields such as Latin America and China). In his book *God Is Rice*, Masao Takenaka, a Japanese theologian, insists that the Eucharist needs to be practiced and expressed according to the local culture because that culture is a means by which people interpret and express their Christian faith in the context of their real lives.[104] In 1996, the Nairobi Statement, an ecumenical consultation on culture and liturgy by the Lutheran World Federation, categorizes four models dealing with the relationship between liturgical traditions and culture: (1) a trans-cultural model focusing on invariable elements given by God beyond cultures, (2) a contextual model focusing on creative "cultural adaptation," (3) a counter-cultural model focusing on criticizing that which is "dehumanizing and contrary to the good news," and (4) a cross-cultural model focusing on a dialogical dynamic of contextualization.[105] Similarly, Stephen Bevans categorizes five models focusing on the relationship between gospel and culture: a translation model, anthropology model, synthetic model, praxis model, and transcendence model.[106] According to Bevans, since each model is distinct but also conjunctive with each other model, there is no one perfect model that can be

---

102. Chupungco, *Worship*, 21.

103. Francis, *Shape a Circle Ever Wider*, 58.

104. Takenaka, *God Is Rice*, 6.

105. Lutheran World Federation, "Nairobi Statement," quoted in Francis, *Shape a Circle Ever Wider*, 68–69.

106. Bevans, *Models of Contextual Theology*, 27. According to Bevans, if the translation model's main concern is "the preservation of Christian identity" rooted in Scripture and tradition rather than other theological resources, the anthropological model's main concern is the "establishment of cultural identity" rooted in the congregation's culture. While the synthetic model attempts to "keep each of the four elements," Scripture, tradition, social change, and local culture "in perfect balance," the praxis model focuses on the active response to current social change. The transcendental model focuses on "the subject who is articulating and expressing one's faith personally in an authentically contextual manner" rather than on "a content to be articulated."

Critical Analysis of Formative Roots of Korean Presbyterian Eucharistic Practices

"applicable to all situations of faith."[107] In a society of "radical plurality and ambiguity," the best answer to the question of which model is the most adequate for a certain local congregation and for building concrete liturgical contextualized practices depends on the congregation's context.[108] No matter which model is developed, the congregation's own culture and life context always need to be respected, since authentic theology cannot be separated from a people's context.

In this sense, it is lamentable that the Eucharist based on Western culture was conveyed and applied to the Presbyterian Church of Korea according to American Presbyterian liturgical practices with no critical reflection by missionaries on Korean congregations' culture and contexts. There was little or no space for the Eucharist in the early stages of the Presbyterian Church of Korea to be formed and developed with serious attention to the relationship between eucharistic practices and Korean culture.

Need for a New Contextual Approach for Eucharistic Pedagogy

Most contemporary Korean scholars of liturgy, such as Jang Bok Jung, Kyeong Jin Kim, Ki Yeon Jo, and Soon Whan Kim, agree that these formative roots of the early period of the Presbyterian Church of Korea—the formation of official liturgy modeled after the liturgy of the American Presbyterian church (Southern and Northern), frontier worship style introduced by missionaries, the Nevius Methods as basic mission strategies, and Confucianism as a dominant sociocultural environment—still dominate the understanding and practices of the Eucharist in the Presbyterian Church of Korea.[109] On the basis of these historical, sociocultural formative roots, I can describe eucharistic practices in the Presbyterian Church of Korea as sacrosanct, hierarchical, male liturgist–oriented, solemnized, marginalized, and Western culture–centered. These characteristics show two levels of the lack of dynamics in the view of liturgy and education. One is the lack of mutual dynamics between liturgists and congregation members in the context of eucharistic practices. The other is the lack of

---

107. Ibid.

108. Ibid., 112.

109. Jo, *Korean Protestant Church*, 189; S. W. Kim, *Study of the Liturgical Reconsideration*, 28; K. Y. Kim, "Early Korean Presbyterian Worship"; Jung, *Theology of Worship*, 38–41, 365–66.

interactive dynamics between eucharistic practices and the congregation's sociocultural life experience. In this respect, there is a contextual pedagogical need for the Presbyterian Church of Korea to build a new model of eucharistic pedagogy that pays attention to students' transformative socialization process in the multilayered structural dynamics within their sociocultural environments. This pedagogical process needs to be based on collaboration between teachers and students regarding critical reflections and actions on their learning experiences.

In the next chapter, in order to prepare the way for the creation of a new eucharistic pedagogy focusing on Korean Presbyterian students' local contexts, I will seek liturgical implications as I critically examine the current eucharistic texts of the Presbyterian Church of Korea in light of Phan and Lee's works on liturgical contextualization.

3

Liturgical Foundations for an Alternative Eucharistic Pedagogy

CHRISTIAN THEOLOGY NEEDS TO be contextual because it cannot be separated from people's own culture.[1] In and through culture people interpret and express their faith.[2] According to Anscar J. Chupungco,[3] Christ's incarnation explains the reason for local churches to contextualize their liturgies in accordance with local culture in terms of the pattern of encounter between the church and culture.[4] Chupungco sees Christ's incarnation and life as the primary analogue of liturgical contextualization,[5] and he asserts that liturgical contextualization needs to take place in all local churches. God showed God's love and salvation within a particular culture and society through Christ's incarnation as a Jew. Local churches need to help people see the mystery of God's love and salvation through the contextualization of their liturgies based on people's specific local, social, and cultural circumstances.[6] Chupungco states that this occurs most effectively when liturgical texts and rites are united with the local cultural patterns through mutual interactions with local traditions and cultures. Chupungco understands that the process of liturgical contextualization is

---

1. Bevans, *Models of Contextual Theology*, 112; Chupungco, *Liturgical Inculturation*, 29; Francis, *Shape a Circle Ever Wider*, 10.

2. Takenaka, *God Is Rice*, 6.

3. Anscar J. Chupungco is a Filipino Catholic theologian and professor at the Pontifical Liturgical Institute in Rome.

4. Chupungco, *Liturgical Inculturation*, 19.

5. E. Kilmartin, "Culture and the Praying Church," quoted in Chupungco, *Liturgical Inculturation*, 18.

6. Chupungco, *Liturgical Inculturation*, 17.

a reciprocal assimilation between liturgy and local culture and results in the dynamic of transculturation.[7]

In terms of the inseparable and mutual relationship between Christian faith and congregation members' local contexts, the term "contextualization" appeared first in the theological literature of Shoki Coe and Aharon Sapsezian, theological educational directors of the World Council of Churches, in 1972.[8] It refers to the process of contextualizing the Christian faith into local cultures and contexts. In the field of Christian liturgy and missiology, the concept of contextualization has been used and developed with the accompanying neologism "inculturation." This term is a response to an ecclesiastical need to connect the relevance of the gospel to contemporary contexts of local community, such as economic, political, cultural, and social contexts. In the 1960s, the French Catholic theologian J. Masson used the term inculturation for the first time.[9] In 1973, G. L. Barney, a Protestant missionary, used it to argue that the essential nature of both gospel and a new culture should neither be lost nor distorted in the context of frontier missions.[10] In 1979, Pope John Paul II employed the term inculturation officially as a newly coined word to explain the reciprocal relationship between Christian faith and culture through the analogy of Christ's incarnation in his "Address to the Pontifical Biblical Commission."[11]

After Pope John Paul II's official use of the term, it has become one of the most significant concepts in Christian liturgy and missiology. In his book *Toward a Theology of Inculturation*, Aylward Shorter defines inculturation as a creative ongoing process in the context of mission through the dynamic relationship between the Christian message and the surrounding culture.[12] In his book *Shape a Circle Ever Wider*, Mark R. Francis defines inculturation as a transformative conversation between faith and culture that

---

7. Ibid. 30.

8. TEF Staff, *Ministry in Context*, 20; Coe, "Contextualization as the Way toward Reform," 48.

9. J. Masson, "Catholicism That Is Incultured," 1038; quoted in Francis, *Shape a Circle Ever Wider*, 58.

10. Barney, "Supracultural and the Cultural," quoted in Chupungco, *Liturgical Inculturation*, 25. Barney writes, "The essential nature of these supracultural components should neither be lost nor distorted but rather secured and interpreted clearly through the guidance of the Holy Spirit in inculturating them into this new culture."

11. John Paul II, "Address to the Pontifical Biblical Commission," 5, quoted in Chupungco, *Liturgical Inculturation*, 26.

12. Shorter, *Toward a Theology of Inculturation*, 11.

enriches both.¹³ Francis insists that liturgical inculturation is an essential aspect of Catholic heritage and an indispensable process for effective evangelization.¹⁴ According to Francis, liturgical inculturation is a creative effort to help local congregations experience the gospel understandably and accessibly within their own liturgical practices. He asserts that through liturgical inculturation, local congregations can express their faith in the context of the liturgy through practices reflecting their own specific sociocultural contexts.¹⁵ Other concepts such as liturgical indigenization,¹⁶ liturgical adaptation,¹⁷ and liturgical acculturation¹⁸ have been related to liturgical contextualization, but the term liturgical inculturation is understood as a distinct technical term that pays special attention to the reciprocal relationship between liturgy and culture as well as their enrichment.

In this chapter, I will invite Peter Phan and Jung Young Lee as conversation partners for critical conversations about Korean eucharistic practices and their sociocultural contexts in the light of liturgical contextualization (or liturgical inculturation).¹⁹ Phan is one of the most active and recent Asian-American liturgists who urges the reformation of liturgical practices with attention to Asian congregations' sociocultural contexts. Lee is a Korean-American theologian who deals with the contextualization pro-

13. Francis, *Shape a Circle Ever Wider*, 58.

14. Ibid., 50.

15. Ibid., 42; Schreiter, *Constructing Local Theologies*. Schreiter uses the term "localization" as a synonym of inculturation.

16. Chupungco, *Liturgical Inculturation*, 16–17. Chupungco explains that liturgical indigenization refers to the spontaneous process of conferring on Christian liturgy a native cultural form of the local community by native people. However, he asserts the impossibility of liturgical indigenization because "it [Christian liturgy] does not spring spontaneously from any cultural soil; it has always been transmitted by means of an apostolic dialogue which inevitably becomes part of a certain dialogue of cultures."

17. Ibid., 24–25. According to Chupungco, while adaptation in the field of Christian liturgy refers to "the general program of Church renewal or updating" to "adapt more suitably to the needs of our times those institutions that are subject to change," inculturation is "one of the ways of achieve it."

18. Francis, *Shape a Circle Ever Wider*, 60. Francis defines acculturation as "culture contact when two cultures come together and produce a juxtaposition of elements that remain unrelated to one another, not really influencing each other."

19. With attention to mutual relationship between liturgical practices and congregation members' life experiences, he intentionally calls his own works "liturgical inculturation." Since Phan names his works on contextualization as "inculturation" consistently in all of his books, I will use the term "liturgical inculturation" as a synonym of liturgical contextualization throughout this book.

cess of liturgical practices with attention to Asian ways of thinking. Even though recently several Korean theologians have written about liturgical contextualization, most of their works focus on criticizing the separation between Korean liturgical practices and Korean culture. However, Phan and Lee go further in suggesting alternative ways of liturgical contextualization in Asian churches with serious consideration of congregations' own specific contexts. In their works on liturgical contextualization, there are unique, and important characteristics: autobiographical,[20] experience oriented,[21] and Asian context centered.[22] Furthermore, although Phan and Lee are both Asian-Americans, their works are eventually concentrated and developed with attention to the contexts of Asian churches.[23]

In this sense, I will critically analyze current Korean Presbyterian eucharistic texts in view of Phan and Lee's liturgical contextualization with attention to each scholar's sociocultural context. The critical analysis of Korean Presbyterian eucharistic texts will provide Korean Presbyterians with significant liturgical foundations for an alternative eucharistic pedagogy in the Presbyterian Church of Korea.

Peter Phan's Liturgical Inculturation Focusing on Sociocultural Life Experiences

Peter Phan[24] introduces a contextual theology—he calls it "intercultural theology"[25]—rooted in Asian-Americans' experiences in the U.S. by dealing with Asian-American political, ethical, religious, cultural, and philosophical contexts and in the realities of prejudice, racism, colonialism, and ethnocentrism. Reflecting on his life journey as a Vietnamese refugee in

---

20. Phan's and Lee's works begin from their own personal life histories rather than building on other liturgical scholars' official theoretical works.

21. Phan's and Lee's works of liturgical contextualization are basically oriented to critical reflections on their own life experiences.

22. Phan's and Lee's works focus on Asian contexts by giving priority to Asian situations such as poor people, religious pluralism, and multicultural society.

23. Lee and Phan, *Journeys at the Margin*, 113. Interestingly, Phan mentions that his theory regarding contextual theology and liturgical contextualization is originally based on Lee's understanding of Asian ways of thinking in terms of the both/and way of thinking rooted in yin-yang symbolic thinking.

24. Peter Phan is a professor and chair of Catholic social thought at Georgetown University.

25. Lee and Phan, *Journeys at the Margin*, 114.

1975 to an immigrant Roman Catholic professor teaching theology, Phan describes his life as "betwixt and between" at the boundary of the East and the West in terms of his theological scholarship and his social life.

Understanding Betwixt and Between and Intercultural Theology

Phan describes his experiences in his article, "Betwixt and Between: Doing Theology with Memory and Imagination."[26]

> To be betwixt and between is to be neither here nor there, to be neither this thing nor that. Spatially, it is to dwell at the periphery.... Politically, it means not residing at the centers of power of the two intersecting worlds but occupying the precarious and narrow margins where the two dominant groups meet and clash. ... Socially, to be betwixt and between is to be part of a minority, a member of a marginalized group. Culturally, it means not being fully integrated into and accepted by either cultural system.... Linguistically, the betwixt-and-between person is bilingual but may not achieve a mastery of both languages.... Psychologically and spiritually, the person does not possess a well-defined and secure self-identity.[27]

According to Phan, most Asian American people share this situation of a marginalized life, so the betwixt-and-between life is the hallmark of marginalized migrants' lives. However, being betwixt-and-between is not just a predicament of suffering of total disadvantage and negativity, but also a resource for creative reinterpreting of both cultural traditions by fusing both worlds and cultures, by finding respective resources from them, and by reforming tradition anew. Since marginalized people are betwixt-and-between, both insiders and outsiders, dwelling in both worlds and cultures, they can see the weaknesses and strengths of both cultures more objectively,[28] and can live not only "in-between" but also "in-both" and "in-beyond."[29]

With this understanding of betwixt-and-between, Phan explains an intercultural theology as his contextual theology. His theology has two

26. Ibid., 113–33.
27. Ibid, 113.
28. Phan, *Christianity with an Asian Face*, 9.
29. Jung Young Lee's three models of marginality. See the subsection "Theology of Marginality" below in this chapter.

basic affirmations.³⁰ One is that God transcends all cultures and cannot be contained to a certain philosophical, ethical, and political tradition. The other is that theology is not only contemplated by humans located in history and shaped by tradition but also reformed by human imagination with a perspective to fashioning a possible future. In the view of God's transcendence of human culture, Western theology, which has been considered as a canonical theology, cannot be the absolute theology for all ethnic Christians, especially for Asian Christians. Thus, Phan's intercultural theology emphasizes critical theological reflections on sociocultural realities such as prejudice, racism, colonialism, and ethnocentrism. In the view of an intercultural theology, memory and imagination interact mutually in the betwixt-and-between situation of Asian Americans. Through the mutual process of memory and imagination, intercultural theology helps people have a chance to creatively build their own theology. Such a theology is not limited by the past but employs the past in order to critically contemplate it for the future.

On the basis of his two theological assumptions, Phan suggests a three-step hermeneutical approach to creating an intercultural theology: suspicion, retrieval, and reconstruction.³¹ First, the step of suspicion is to unveil the hierarchical relationship between the dominant culture and the minority one in terms of the forces of power by interpreting it with suspicion. Second, the step of retrieval is to recover the underside of history, which has been often overlooked, such as immigrants' stories found betwixt-and-between in terms of ethnic, racial, sociopolitical, and economic differences. Third, the step of reconstruction is to form a new culture out of the resources of both cultures, that is, the immigrant culture and the dominant one.

For the method of intercultural theology, drawing from liberation theologians such as Clodovis Boff, Juan Luis Segundo, and Robert Barr, Phan introduces liberation theology's method: socioanalytic mediation, hermeneutical mediation, and practical mediation.³² First, socioanalytic mediation analyzes the ground of the immigrants' lives critically by using social sciences such as economics, sociology, history, and politics as critical conversation partners. Because this step values the immigrants' real lives, their folk songs, dance, drama, rituals, arts, and folk tales are not only

---

30. Lee and Phan, *Journeys at the Margin*, 114–15.
31. Phan, *Christianity with an Asian Face*, 16–18.
32. Ibid., 19–22.

very important resources for reflecting on their common stories but also become privileged resources for intercultural theology. Second, hermeneutical mediation provides sociohistorical data with theological interpretations by using appropriate biblical stories and symbols such as the story of the exodus and the story of crossing the Jordan. This method enables theologians to overcome the limitations of past interpretations. It also demands multifaceted hermeneutical works, which involves conversation with other religions' sacred texts and traditions with mutual respect. Third, practical mediation has a circular, dialectic movement between praxis and theory. Phan asserts that authentic praxis produces sociopolitical transformation with critical questions about the alleged truth of the doctrines. Praxis examines theory critically, and then theory modifies praxis.[33] In the process of practical mediation, the interaction between praxis and theory has an ongoing dialectic tension. In this way, Phan builds an intercultural theology by using socioanalytic mediation, hermeneutical mediation, and practical mediation as his theological methods.

Liturgical Inculturation as the Multiple Dialogues between the Gospel, Cultures, the Poor and Other Religions

Phan deals with liturgical inculturation in view of Christian mission in Asia and Asian theologies by focusing on the relationship between the gospel and culture. Based upon the official documents of inculturation from both the Catholic and the Protestant traditions,[34] he summarizes the main points of agreement on inculturation.

> 1. Inculturation is an integral and constitutive dimension of the church's evangelizing mission.... 2. Inculturation is a double process comprising (a) insertion of the gospel into a particular culture, and (b) introduction of the culture into the gospel.... 3. The result of inculturation is both the transformation of the culture from within by the gospel and the enrichment of the gospel by the culture with its new ways of understanding and living it.... 4.

---

33. Ibid., 22.
34. Federation of Asian Bishops' Conferences, *For All Peoples of Asia*. See also "The World Council of Churches' Jerusalem Statement on Intercultural Hermeneutics" (1995), "The Lutheran World Federation's Nairobi Statement on Worship and Culture," and "The World Council of Churches Commission on World Mission and Evangelism (WCC-WCME) Ecumenical Conference in Salvador, de Bahia, Brazil" (1996), in Scherer and Bevans, *New Directions*, vol. 3., 177–234.

> Gospel is never independent of culture.... 5. Since religion—a system of beliefs, values and practices—is a constitutive dimension of culture, inculturation is of necessity an interreligious dialogue.... 6. Inculturation must also go hand in hand with liberation.... 7. Inculturation as a theological process is governed by the mysteries of the incarnation, death, resurrection of Jesus, and the descent and active presence of the Holy Spirit.... 8. The principal agent of inculturation is the local church, not the experts and the central authorities.... 9. Inculturation must be carried out in all areas of church life.... 10. Inculturation must bring about diversity in unity and unity in diversity.... 11. It must be guided by a robust theology of the local church.[35]

Through this outline of inculturation, Phan understands that the context of Asian churches' liturgical inculturation is the multiple dialogues between the gospel, cultures, the poor, and other religions.

Phan examines two official documents, one Protestant (the Lutheran World Federation's Nairobi Statement on Worship and Culture) and the other Roman Catholic (the Pontifical Council for Culture's *Toward a Pastoral Approach to Culture*).[36] He criticizes the lack of success of churches in dealing with concrete ways to contextualize the Christian faith into cultures with adequate attention to economic, sociocultural contexts.[37] For authentic liturgical inculturation, Phan introduces two guidelines. The first is about the conjunctive relationship between interreligious dialogue and human liberation. That is, liturgical inculturation needs to be a multilayered dialogue that involves not only intercultural dialogue but also interreligious dialogue and the concern for human liberation. In an Asian context, including the metacosmic religions (such as Hinduism, Buddhism, Taoism, Confucianism, Islam, and Shintoism) in this interreligious dialogue is necessary and inevitable in the course of liturgical inculturation because religion and culture cannot be separated. This dialogue cannot be appropriate as long as it forces people to replace one culture with another. When liturgical inculturation proceeds without the serious consideration of human liberation, it also might be the work of elitism and cultural chauvinism. Phan

---

35. Phan, *In Our Own Tongues*, 5–10.

36. Ibid., 72; "The Lutheran World Federation's Nairobi Statement on Worship and Culture," in Scherer and Bevans, *New Directions*; John Paul II, "Toward a Pastoral Approach to Culture," online: http://www.vatican.va/roman_curia/pontifical_councils/cultr/documents/rc_pc_pc-cultr_doc_03061999_pastoral_en.html.

37. Phan, *In Our Own Tongues*, 77.

emphasizes that authentic liturgical inculturation cannot be completed by adapting local language, music, and art perfunctorily and by regarding a certain traditional rite such as the substantial unity of the Roman rite as sacrosanct.[38]

The second guideline is about the relationship of liturgical practices to popular religion. In connecting popular religion with the dialogue with poor people in Asia as well as intercultural dialogue, Phan points out that popular religion is primarily the religion of the poor people in Asia. Phan summarizes seven features of popular religion.[39] He understands that popular religion has a power to liberate people to stand against injustice and inequality. In his view, popular religion is not so much an obstruction to the liberation of people as a crucial and influential force for it. An understanding of the liturgy as the summit of the church's life might result in theological and pastoral deformations such as the separation between spirituality, liturgy, and sociopolitical involvement.[40] In order to avoid such theological and pastoral deformations, Phan proposes to give theological priority to a liturgy of life—which is inevitably tied to popular religion—over an official liturgy of the church. He mentions that the liturgy of life refers to the experiences of "God's self-communication" to all human beings within their daily lives from all concrete contexts that are both sacred and secular and both affirmative and negative.[41] Phan understands the liturgy of life as the source of richness of church liturgy and church liturgy as the real symbol of the liturgy of life. That is, the liturgy of life is symbolized and intensified in the church liturgy through Word, prayer, and the sacraments. In consideration of the inevitable relationship between the liturgy of life and popular religion in Asia, as long as popular religion is not simply adapted without the process of critical theological reflection, it can be a means for people's expression of the liturgy of life, as a source of strength and vigor for church liturgy rather than in opposition to it.

With serious attention to the conjunctive relationship between the gospel, culture, human liberation, and popular religion, Phan strongly rejects the imperialistic, elitist, sociocultural perspectives of the eucharistic

---

38. Ibid., 84.

39. Ibid. As Phan quotes Pieris, "Asian Paradigm," he mentions the seven features of popular religion: "it has a this-worldly spirituality, it is animated by a sense of total dependence on the divine, it longs for justice, it is cosmic, it accords women a key role, it is ecological, and it communicates through story."

40. Ibid., 89.

41. Phan, "Liturgy of Life," 25, quoted in Phan, *In Our Own Tongues*, 89.

liturgy. He emphasizes the reconceptualization of Asian religious-political contexts—that is, religious pluralism and economic injustice—as a significant resource for liturgical contextualization for Asian churches. Phan asserts that the eucharistic liturgy and the liturgy of daily life, especially in terms of popular religion including its texts, rituals, and life experiences, need to be interdependent on each other, to interact with each other, and to enrich each other.[42] In this sense, Phan attempts to propose alternative groundbreaking guidelines for liturgical contextualization based on congregation members' sociopolitical, economic, cultural, and religious contexts. He encourages Asian Christians to have dialogue between the gospel, local cultures and religions, and human liberation. Such a dialogue would be ongoing, multilayered, deep, and wide, and would happen through critical reflection and reconsideration of popular religion, indigenous hidden stories or folk songs, and other religions' texts and traditions.[43]

Critical Reflections on Phan's Liturgical Inculturation

When I examine Phan's liturgical contextualization with critical thinking from a Korean perspective, I find that there are four strengths in his works: (1) revitalizing the value of Asian culture, (2) a commitment to poor people, (3) an openness for interreligious dialogue, and (4) an inductive approach.

First, Phan's liturgical inculturation helps Korean Christians to revitalize the value of Asian culture because his works are based on the dynamic interaction between Christianity and Asian culture, between Christian liturgy and Asian culture, and between the liturgy of church and the liturgy of life. In particular, Phan's work on the relationship between the churches'

42. Phan, *In Our Own Tongues*, 273.

43. Ibid., 126. As a good example of liturgical inculturation, Phan introduces the innovation and practices of the Masses for the celebration of the Lunar New Year, called *Tet*. As the most significant sociocultural, religious feast in Vietnamese society, *Tet* is an occasion for worshiping ancestors from New Year's Eve to the beginning of the new year at least for three days: the first for the cult of ancestors and the current parents, the second for near relatives, and the third for the dead. In 1994, the Vietnamese bishops made an attempt for liturgical inculturation of *Tet* by composing a special series of Masses, which consists of five: the first for giving thanks and asking forgiveness to God, the second for celebrating the passage into the new year, the third for praising God and asking for peace and prosperity, the fourth for praying for ancestors and parents, and the fifth for the sanctification of labor. Each Mass includes a different eucharistic prayer including the mention of congregation members' sociocultural, religious realities such as ancestors, poverty, and political injustice.

liturgies (or official liturgy) and the liturgies of life provides Korean Christians with an alternative perspective on the relationship between liturgy in church and liturgical life in a Korean society. That is, liturgical life—which is not an isolated, separated element but a very important resource for the process of liturgical contextualization—is not an optional element but an essential one.

Second, Phan's work pays attention to the voices and experiences of the poor people of Asia. Considering his hermeneutics (of suspicion) and his method (of socioanalytic mediation), Phan attempts to discover poor people's underside of history in the context of sexism, classism, ethnic discrimination, and political oppression and injustice. Through his commitment to poor people—which is inevitably connected with their culture and religion—Phan's works help Korean Christians to understand that Christian liturgy is not only an individual, confessional ritual practice but also a communal, ethical ritual practice.

Third, Phan's emphasis on interreligious dialogue challenges Korean Christians not to avoid or ignore but to accept the contemporary sociocultural, religious situations of Korean society. It offers them an opportunity to introduce the gospel to other religions and non-Christians not with an imperialistic, superior, and aggressive attitude but with a humble, egalitarian attitude as well as to know other religions and their liturgy and traditions. There has long been a popular aphorism in China: "One more Christian, one less Chinese"[44]; and a similar expression in Korea: "Christianity in Korea is the most exclusive religion of the world."[45] Phan's understanding of popular religion may give Korean people (both Christian and non-Christian) an alternative perspective on Korean popular religion, not as an obstacle for Christian liturgy but as an important resource for Christian liturgy.

Fourth, Phan's work is built and developed not by a deductive approach but by an inductive approach. Because it is built bottom to top rather than top to bottom, it has more space for creativity and openness. Considering various contextual situations such as sociopolitical, economic, political, ethnic, and religious contexts, the inductive approach of Phan's work helps Korean liturgists and pastors develop and create new Korean liturgical forms and practices with freedom and autonomy.

---

44. Levitt, "Review of Chinese Christians in America," 1552.

45. Research Committee of Korean Church History, *Christian Thoughts of Korean Church*, 184.

Jung Young Lee's Liturgical Contextualization Focusing on a Contextual Epistemology

Jung Young Lee is a Korean-American theologian who attempted to break new ground in Asian contextual theology and liturgical contextualization with attention to yin-yang symbolic thinking as an Asian epistemological construct. Through the critical reflection of his life experiences in a minority community in the U.S., Lee proposes his marginality theology as a new model for developing contextual theology. Lee asserts that marginality is not only about the contents of the Christian faith but also is a hermeneutical principle. He suggests a new epistemological understanding of marginality based on an "in-beyond" model rather than an in-between model.[46] Lee proposes the yin-yang symbolic thinking as an Asian contextual epistemology for the Korean church, and he deals with liturgical contextualization by attempting to reinterpret and reform Korean liturgical practices.

Yin-Yang Symbolic Thinking as Contextual Epistemology for the Korean Church

Yin-yang symbolic thinking based on East Asians' understandings of the cosmos is regarded as the foundation of East Asian thinking in China, Korea, and Japan.[47] The cosmology of East Asian people is understood best as the bipolarity of nature, which operates cyclically in terms of the moon's waxing and waning.[48] These opposite poles are known as yin and yang, which represent the basic principle of the universe. In *I Ching* (*Book of Change*), the yin-yang relationship is best illustrated through the diagram of the Great Ultimate.[49]

In the diagram, one circle represents the cosmos. The dark part represents yin and the light part represents yang. In the dark part, there is the light dot (○) signifying the Sun. In the light part, there is the dark dot (●) signifying the moon. The dark and light dots are distinct but share a common shape. They are opposite in character and inseparable. Through the yin-yang dots in both yin and yang, the concept of *in-ness* can be found and

---

46. Lee, *Marginality*, 4.
47. Ibid., 35.
48. Thompson, *Chinese Religion*, 3, quoted in Lee, *Trinity in Asian Perspective*, 24.
49. Thompson, *Chinese Religion*, 4; Fung Yu-lan, *Short History of Chinese Philosophy*, 269–72, quoted in Lee, *Trinity in Asian Perspective*, 26.

expressed. In-ness as the inner connecting principle allows yin and yang to co-exist distinctively and harmoniously in the view of Asian Trinitarian theological thinking.[50] That is, through the concept of in-ness, one can be three and three can be one in the Great Ultimate. One (symbolized by the great circle) is in two (symbolized by yin and yang), and two (symbolized by yin and yang) are in three (symbolized by yin, yang, and yin-yang dots in them), and one is in three: "When yin and yang are manifested in external symbols, the *in* or inner connecting principle manifests itself as an external connecting principle known as *and*."[51] In this respect, yin and yang are existentially opposite but essentially united in the Great Ultimate.

On the basis of Asian cosmology, Lee explains three distinctive epistemological characteristics of the Asian Trinitarian way of thinking based on yin-yang symbolic thinking: (1) an inclusive both/and way of thinking, (2) a complementary relational way of thinking, and (3) a threefold way of thinking.

First, the yin-yang relationship has a characteristically inclusive way of thinking. In the diagram of the Great Ultimate, we can see an inclusive characteristic. Yin (the dark) has a light dot in it and yang (the light) has a dark dot in it. Yin is not only yin but also yang, and yang is not only yang but also yin. Yin and yang cannot be separated. Even though they seem to be opposite, they always co-exist essentially. Thus, the yin-yang symbol represents the inclusive both/and way of thinking: yin is both yin and yang, and yang is also both yang and yin. Through an exclusive either/or way of thinking, the yin-yang symbol cannot be understood.

Second, yin-yang symbolic thinking is not only inclusive but also relational. On account of inclusivity in the yin-yang symbol, yin and yang limit each other. That is, yin cannot exist by itself; it exists only in correlation to yang. When yin is correlated to yang, yang is relative to the whole—which is both yin and yang—as well as yin. For example, light and darkness are not two independent entities. They are not only two distinctively but also one essentially. Thus, the yin-yang relationship emphasizes relationship more than existence. In this situation in terms of relationship, the important thing is the harmony of opposites (yin and yang). In order to harmonize with each other, the yin-yang relationship needs to be understood not as conflict but as complementary. That is, the yin-yang relationship does not

---

50. Lee, *Trinity in Asian Perspective*, 27.
51. Ibid., 59.

express a conflicting dualism (either/or way of thinking) but a complementary dualism (both/and way of thinking), emphasizing harmony.[52]

Third, yin-yang symbolic thinking understands the universe in terms of a threefold cosmology comprising heaven, earth, and human beings. Lee compares two different ways of thinking of the universe rooted in each sociocultural context. From a Western perspective, based on an anthropocentric cosmology, the human being is the center of the cosmos. From an Asian perspective, based on a cosmocentric anthropology, the human being belongs to the cosmos as a microcosm of the cosmos. That is, if the West's cosmology is understood as an anthropocentric cosmology, Asian anthropology can be understood as a cosmocentric anthropology.[53] While the West approaches cosmology in the view of human beings, East Asians do so in the view of cosmology because East Asians conceptualize the human being as a product of the dynamic between heaven (yang) and earth (yin) and also a part of the universe. In this respect, while the West understands the universe as a twofold cosmology (between human being and universe), East Asians understand the universe as a threefold cosmology (between heaven, earth, and human being).

From yin-yang symbolic thinking, Lee finds the basic ideas of a contextual epistemology for Asian Christians in terms of a both/and way of thinking, a relational way of thinking, and a threefold way of thinking. Lee insists that this way of thinking is one of the most fundamental elements in Christian theology because Christian faith is interpreted and expressed by people's own culture and God cannot be restricted to a certain theology rooted in one particular way of knowing. In this sense, Lee understands that yin-yang symbolic thinking can be regarded as a contextual epistemological paradigm for a Korean way of thinking.

Theology of Marginality

In his book *Marginality: The Key to Multicultural Theology*, Lee insists that theology must be autobiographical because a living theology needs to be linked to people's life experiences and to reflect them deeply.[54] As he describes his life in the U.S. as a life of marginality, Lee suggests that marginality can be a hermeneutic key for marginal people to have a biblical

52. Ibid., 31.
53. Ibid., 18.
54. Lee, *Marginality*, 2.

understanding of Christian ways of thinking and living. Based on three different understandings of marginality, Lee delineates three possible models to understand who marginal people are: (1) in-between, (2) in-both, and (3) in-beyond.[55] First, applying the in-between model, marginality is understood as total exclusion (negation) by dominant groups in a society from a centralist perspective. Lee explains that this classical self-negating definition of marginality has been accepted in a society dominated by an Anglo-American culture based on an either/or way of thinking. Marginal people who do not belong to either of two groups fully experience double rejection from both groups. Second, applying an in-both model, marginality is understood as total affirmation based on a conviction affirming one's existence through a positive self-image in both groups to which marginal people are connected.[56] According to Lee, this contemporary self-affirming definition of marginality has been acknowledged in a pluralistic society based on a both/and way of thinking. However, Lee mentions that this total affirmation of both groups is unrealistic and impractical in that the authentic multiethnic society that they imagine does not exist. Third, applying an in-beyond model, marginality is understood as *both* total negation *and* total affirmation through the interpenetration of each other based on a both/and way of thinking. In this view, marginality is a creative core, an inclusive, open-ended, and relational nexus where the total negation and total affirmation harmoniously co-exist not in a confrontational relationship but in a complementary relationship. In such a complementary relationship, negation is not understood as a rejection of affirmation but as the indispensable background of it, and vice versa.[57] An in-beyond model describes a place of reconciliation between marginality and centrality, where the conflict between margin and center disappear into the harmonious coexistence of total negation and total affirmation. Because of this co-existence, the new way of thinking—in-beyond model—can be the most inclusive as well as the most relational form of thinking. Lee asserts that in the third way of thinking, neither/nor (the first way of thinking) and both/and (the second way of thinking) are simultaneously opposite *and* complementary.

In the view of an in-beyond way of thinking, Lee proposes this theology of marginality as an epistemological foundation for Korean contextual theology. He reinterprets Jesus as a new marginal person because he was

55. Ibid., 57–61.
56. Ibid., 66.
57. Ibid., 67.

not Jesus or Christ but Jesus-Christ, as a person who was in-between as well as in-both worlds.[58] In the death of Jesus-Christ, Jesus as a new marginal person who is both in-both and in-between worlds is manifested in that he, as both human and divine, was rejected by dominant groups of his day and God. In the resurrection of Jesus-Christ, whereas his death represents that absolute negation of life (neither/nor), his resurrection represents the absolute affirmation of life (both/and). Jesus' death and resurrection cannot be separated from each other but belong together. In Jesus-Christ as a person who is in-beyond worlds—that is, both in-between and in-both worlds—his death and resurrection as the marginal event of marginality mutually complement each other. Reconciliation occurs at the margin of marginality, which Lee calls the "creative core."[59] In the view of marginal theology, marginal people from an in-between perspective can overcome marginality only when everyone is marginal because "there is no centrality that can marginalize anyone."[60] Lee describes it as marginality overcome through marginality, the way to be a new marginal community based on the In-beyond model.[61] In this way, Lee understands Jesus-Christ as a new marginal person through his death and resurrection, which happens at the margin of marginality. In his death and resurrection, Jesus-Christ who is both human and divine builds reconciliation not only between God and human beings but also among human beings.

Liturgical Contextualization as the Reformation of Liturgy Rooted in Contextual Epistemology

In view of marginality based on the yin-yang symbolic thinking, Lee suggests that the Eucharist needs to be reinterpreted and reformed as (1) the cosmic Trinitarian acts between the Triune God, God's children, and God's creation and (2) an interrelated threefold tense event (past, present, and future). It may seem to be strange for Lee to approach the Eucharist from a cosmic perspective rather than a local perspective because the language of cosmic acts runs in the opposite direction of contextuality. However, as I noted in chapter 1, the uniqueness of Asian ways of thinking comes from a different understanding of the universe as a cosmocentric anthropology

58. Ibid., 98–99.
59. Ibid., 98.
60. Ibid., 151.
61. Ibid.

based on cosmic Trinitarian dynamics between the heaven, the earth, and human beings.[62] In light of an Asian cosmocentric anthropology, a both/and way of thinking was explicated and expressed as one of the distinctive characteristics of Asian ways of thinking through the diagram of the Great Ultimate.[63] Therefore, in view of Lee's both/and way of thinking, cosmic Trinitarian acts cannot be separated or opposed to local contextuality but are the very example of a contextual way for Asians to understand objects in the world. In this respect, Lee's liturgical contextualization of the Eucharist in light of Asian ways of thinking based on cosmic Trinitarian acts may be complementary to the liturgical reformation of the Eucharist. With this understanding of Asian ways of thinking, Lee proposes that eucharistic practices need to be contextualized epistemologically and practically in the context of the Korean church.

First, on the basis of Asian Trinitarian cosmology, Lee proposes that Korean Christians reinterpret and practice the Eucharist as cosmic Trinitarian acts of divine *koinonia* based on the Father God's love, divine commemoration of the Son, and divine service through the power of Holy Spirit between the triune God, God's children, and God's creation. In terms of divine *koinonia*, the Eucharist is a place of open-ended and loving fellowship, in which all people are invited through the Father God's love, which was revealed and expressed in Jesus Christ.[64] In terms of divine commemoration, participants as God's children commemorate the Son's death and resurrection as the basis of our salvation and new life by partaking of bread and wine as God's creatures.[65] In terms of divine service, the Eucharist is connected to serving the world as the people respond to God's love through the power of the Holy Spirit.[66] Just as three are one and one is three in yin-yang symbolic thinking based on Asian Trinitarian cosmology, divine *koinonia* is based on the Father God's love, divine commemoration of the Son, and divine service through the power of Holy Spirit. The three elements are inseparable, complement each other, and co-exist harmoniously in the Eucharist as cosmic Trinitarian acts between the triune God, God's children, and the world.

---

62. Lee, *Trinity in Asian Perspective*, 13.
63. Ibid., 24.
64. Ibid., 184; Bower, *Companion*, 35.
65. Lee, *Trinity in Asian Perspective*, 185.
66. Ibid.

Second, Lee proposes that the Eucharist be an *interrelated threefold-tense* event rather than a *separated time-tense* event. Lee explains the interrelated threefold-tense concept through a both/and way of thinking. In the yin-yang way of thinking, three tenses—past, present, and future—are always correlated. As yin and yang co-exist essentially in the diagram of the Great Ultimate, time also co-exists essentially within different forms, as in the present including the past and the future. From the perspective of yin-yang symbolic thinking, the Eucharist needs to be experienced as an interrelated threefold-tense event where people participate in the presence of God with the remembrance of the past of Jesus' death and resurrection as well as anticipating the future of the kingdom of God in hope. In this sense, Lee maintains that the Asian way of thinking rooted in yin-yang symbolic thinking helps Korean Christians to understand the Eucharist not as a separated time-tense event but as an interrelated threefold tense event.

Critical Review of Lee's Liturgical Contextualization

The concept of in-ness in Lee's liturgical contextualization presents to Korean Christians an opportunity to participate in the Eucharist actively with a more integrative understanding of Jesus' death and resurrection. First, in-ness as the common and essential concept of both yin-yang symbolic thinking and marginality theology provides Korean Christians with an inclusive epistemology to understand Jesus' death and resurrection. From the perspective of in-ness based on yin-yang symbolic thinking, just as yin cannot be meaningful without yang in yin-yang symbolic thinking, Jesus' death cannot be meaningful without resurrection at the eucharistic table and vice versa. In the view of in-ness rooted in the in-beyond model, Jesus' death is understood not only as total negation but also as total affirmation and, by the same token, Jesus' resurrection is regarded as not only total affirmation but also total negation. In this respect, the concept of in-ness helps Korean Christians participate in the Eucharist with gratitude to God from an inclusive epistemology of Jesus' death and resurrection at the Eucharist rather than with sadness from an exclusive epistemology focusing on only Jesus' death.

Second, the concept of in-ness guides Korean Christians to understand the Eucharist as a Trinitarian integrative event in terms of the Father's creation, the Son's redemption, and the Spirit's sustenance harmoniously, reciprocally, and distinctively. In the view of in-ness, the Father's creation co-exists with the Son's redemption as redemption *in* creation, the Son's redemption co-exists with the Spirit's sustenance as redemption *in* sustenance, and the Father's creation exists with the Spirit's sustenance as sustenance *in* creation. Thus, in-ness helps Korean Christians understand the Eucharist as a Trinitarian liturgy where works of the Trinity are not separated but complement each other with harmony and distinctiveness.

Third, the concept of in-ness guides Korean Christians to identify the Eucharist as a threefold liturgy between God, human beings, and nature (sacramental foods) rather than as a twofold anthropocentric liturgy between God and human beings. In the view of an Asian cosmocentric theological approach based on yin-yang symbolic thinking, God represents the heaven, the congregation represents human beings, and sacramental foods represent the earth. When I approach the Eucharist from this perspective (heaven-earth-humanity), the Eucharist can be understood as a liturgy of cosmic union between God, congregation, and nature (sacramental foods). Moreover, in the view of the concept of in-ness as an inner connecting principle, the three are also interconnected at the eucharistic table. Therefore, in this understanding, none of the three may be devalued or isolated.

Critical Analysis of the Current Korean Presbyterian Eucharistic Practices in View of Phan's and Lee's Liturgical Contextualization

The Book of Common Worship of the Presbyterian Church of Korea of 2008 (hereafter, BCW [PCK]) is the latest liturgical book to include eucharistic texts of the Presbyterian Church of Korea. In the preface, managing editor Jang Bok Jung introduces the BCW (PCK) of 2008 as a result of continuous efforts of liturgical contextualization to bring liturgical renewal to the Presbyterian Church of Korea. Historically, the BCW (PCK) originated in the *Directory for Worship of the American Presbyterian Church* (North and South) in 1922 and it was used as the official liturgical material in the Presbyterian Church of Korea under the title *The Directory for Worship of the Presbyterian Church of Korea* until 1960.[67] In 1961, the Presbyterian Church of Korea changed the name to *The Book of Common Worship of the Presbyterian Church of Korea* and began to revise it with attention to the context of Korean Presbyterians' sociocultural lives by giving attention to issues such

---

67. Reforming Committee, *Book of Common Worship* [PCK], 7.

Building a Eucharistic Pedagogy for the Presbyterian Church of Korea

as ancestral worship, funeral rites, marriage rites, and Sunday worship.[68] In 1971, 1987, and 1997, the Presbyterian Church of Korea continuously attempted to revise the BCW (PCK) in light of liturgical contextualization by focusing on the changing contexts of local Korean Presbyterian churches. According to Jung, the liturgical renewal of the BCW (PCK) has been very limited, with minor additions and amendments to traditional liturgical practices.[69] In this respect, the BCW (PCK) of 2008, as the latest version, provides various liturgical models in accordance with various worship contexts and contextual issues. These contexts are categorized into (1) Sunday worship service, (2) weekday worship service, (3) Christian organization worship service, (4) installation worship service, (5) church building dedication worship service, (6) rite of passage worship service, and (7) traditional festival worship service.[70] However, even though diverse versions of worship service formats are introduced according to seven different occasions in the BCW (PCK), only the Sunday worship service part includes the Eucharist.[71]

When I compare the current BCW (PCK) to the 1997 version, I find that there are positive shifts, including an increase in the number of eucharistic prayers from three to eleven and a greater variety in accordance with eucharistic contexts. Each of the eleven eucharistic prayers is made in accordance with a particular Sunday worship context.[72] The first eucharistic prayer (prayer A) is for an ordinary Sunday worship service including the Eucharist. The second and third eucharistic prayers (prayers B and C) are for an ordinary Sunday worship service including both baptism and the Eucharist. The eucharistic prayers D, E, F, G, H, and I are for Sunday worship services including the Eucharist according to the season of the liturgical year. The fourth eucharistic prayer (prayer D) is for Sunday worship services in Advent. The fifth eucharistic prayer (prayer E) is for a Christmas Sunday worship service. The sixth eucharistic prayer (prayer F) is for an Epiphany Sunday worship service. The seventh eucharistic prayer (prayer G) is for a Palm Sunday worship service. The eighth eucharistic prayer (prayer H) is for an Easter vigil service. The ninth eucharisic prayer (prayer

---

68. Ibid.
69. See chapter 2 of this book.
70. Reforming Committee, *Book of Common Worship* [PCK], 12–17.
71. Ibid., 36–38.
72. Since the eleven eucharistic prayers are not named or numbered, I labeled them with alphabet characters from A to K in order.

52

Liturgical Foundations for an Alternative Eucharistic Pedagogy

I) is for a Pentecost Sunday worship service. The eucharistic prayers C, D, E, F, G, H, and I are largely translations from the BCW [PCUSA]'s resources for the liturgical year. The eucharistic prayers C, D, and G are translated almost directly, and the rest are partial translations. This demonstrates how the eucharistic prayers in the Presbyterian Church of Korea still depend on those of the Presbyterian Church (USA). The tenth eucharistic prayer (prayer J) is for intergenerational corporate Sunday worship service. The eleventh eucharistic prayer (prayer K) is for a Sunday worship service that includes a time for prayers of healing and wholeness.

Through the critical lens of Phan's and Lee's liturgical contextualization, it becomes clear that there are several important liturgical and theological characteristics of current eucharistic practices in the Presbyterian Church of Korea: (1) a focus on reaffirming participants' conversion and salvation without reflecting their socio-cultural life experiences; (2) a reflection of Western culture rather than Korean culture in the eucharistic objects and practices; (3) minimal emphasis on unity, hospitality, equality, and justice; and (4) reinforcement of a twofold anthropocentric eucharistic experience rather than a cosmic Trinitarian experience.

Eucharistic Texts Focusing on Reaffirming Participants' Conversion and Salvation

In view of the reciprocal relationship between church liturgy and liturgical life, most eucharistic texts in the BCW [PCK] show a strong tendency to focus on participants' reaffirmation of their own conversion and salvation without critical reflections on their daily life experiences, such as interpersonal relationships, economic transactions, and social responsibilities. For example, the opening dialogue of eucharistic prayer B[73] describes the Eucharist as the memorial rite of Jesus' passion and death with attention to the reaffirmation of participants' conversion and salvation through the recalling and representing of Jesus' flesh and blood.

> The Eucharist is not only for remembrance. It is a place for us to recall, reenact, and meditate on the Lord's broken body and

---

73. In order for the reader to have access to the texts of all eleven eucharistic prayers in BCW [PCK] under examination, I reproduce them in the appendix of this dissertation by translating it into an English version. See the appendix for my translation of these texts into English.

> shedding blood for us. For the Lord's body and blood to be my body and blood, we need to rededicate a new life.[74]

During the distribution of the elements, eucharistic prayer B guides the liturgist to emphasize that the bread and cup is Jesus' wounded flesh and shed blood.

> Now you may ponder on the Lord's flesh, broken for us. And then, you may eat it with your thankful heart.... Now, you may take the cup and ponder on the Lord's shed blood for the forgiveness of our sin. And then, you may drink it with your sincere thankful heart.[75]

In the post-Communion prayer, eucharistic prayer B reminds participants of the Eucharist as the rite of reaffirmation of their conversion and salvation through Jesus' death and resurrection.

> Loving God, thank you for allowing us to participate in the Eucharist by your merciful grace. Thank you for your renewing the grace of forgiveness and salvation. Thank you for helping us reaffirm that we are the Lord's bodies.[76]

The eucharistic prayer B has no space for participants to reflect upon their life experiences such as economic, political, and sociocultural oppression in their family, school, working places and society, but reaffirms their salvation and conversion through the Eucharist.

This lack of emphasis on participants' reflection on their life experiences in favor of a reaffirmation of conversion and salvation comes from the lack of inclusive understanding of the relationship between the Eucharist in church and Christian life in the world. In the BCW [PCK], while only the Sunday worship service part includes the Eucharist in the order of worship, the other six parts, which cover a congregation's general Christian life—marriage service, funeral service, weekday worship service, and traditional festival worship service—do not include the Eucharist in their worship order.[77] When the Eucharist is celebrated only in a Sunday worship service, congregation members may understand that the Eucharist is separated from the rites of passage in their lives.

---

74. Ibid., 68.
75. Ibid.
76. Ibid., 70.
77. Ibid., 12–17.

Moreover, the tendency to concentrate on reaffirming participants' conversion and salvation in the Eucharist is clearly expressed in the eucharistic prayer with a christocentric form. Ronald P. Byars asserts that eucharistic prayer in the Reformed tradition needs to be Trinitarian.[78] In his book *Lift Your Hearts on High*, Byars points out that a Trinitarian form of eucharistic prayer was developed as an important part of its structure in the early church, and reaffirmed during the Reformation era as well as in modern times of Reformed and other Protestant churches, and in the Roman Catholic Church after Vatican Council II.[79] According to Byars, the Trinitarian form of eucharistic prayer guides participants not only to set basic biblical affirmations regarding Christian belief and life but also to give glory to the triune God by giving thanks to the creator Father, by blessing the redeemer Son, and by petitioning the Holy Spirit.[80] However, eight out of eleven eucharistic prayers (excluding prayer C, D, G) in the BCW [PCK] are written not based on a Trinitarian form but on a christocentric form. Seven out of eleven eucharistic prayers—prayers A, B, E, F, H, I, J, and K—do not mention the Holy Father's creation works but rather emphasize Jesus' redemptive works. Furthermore, Jesus' redemptive works are described by focusing mainly on Jesus' suffering and death at the night of Thursday and Friday morning. In the epiclesis, eucharistic prayers B and H focus on restating Jesus' salvation through Jesus' death and resurrection rather than on asking God to pour out God's Holy Spirit upon participants along with the bread and the wine.

> Our Lord who broke your own flesh and shed your own blood, we come to this place with unclean hearts and bodies. Now we are standing in front of the Eucharist reenacting the Lord's flesh and blood. Come to this place and lead us to experience deeply your flesh and blood within our mouths and bodies. May you guide us to encounter you in this place. In the presence of the Holy Spirit, we may participate in the holy Eucharist. In the name of Jesus Christ who broke his own body and shed his own blood for us, Amen.[81]

---

78. Ronald P. Byars is a Presbyterian theologian and emeritus professor of worship and preaching at Union Presbyterian Seminary.

79. Byars, *Lift Your Hearts on High* xix.

80. Ibid., 74.

81. Reforming Committee, *Book of Common Worship* [PCK], 68. This epiclesis comes from eucharistic prayer B.

As the eucharistic prayer with a Christ-centered form highlights Jesus' salvation through his death and resurrection, it guides participants to recall their own conversion experiences and reaffirm their salvation. In this context, there seems to be no space for liturgists and participants to link their sociocultural life experiences to the Eucharist in the light of the hope of God's kingdom, but instead reinforces the participants' own conversion and salvation with attention to Jesus' suffering and death. Eucharistic prayer A, as an example, shows the tendency to concentrate on the affirmation of participants' conversion and salvation.

> Gracious God, thank you for sending your son Jesus Christ as a human being to this world and saving us through Jesus' sacrificial death. The Lord Jesus died as a perfect and holy sacrifice for the forgiveness of our sins. You commanded us to do this remembrance of Jesus until Jesus' second coming. Merciful God, we ask you to bless and make this rice cake and cup holy through the Holy Spirit. By receiving the rice cake of eternal life and the cup of salvation, we want to remember Jesus' suffering, his death by shedding his blood, his resurrection with authority, and his ascension gloriously once again. We ask the Holy Spirit to help us to receive life and grace in this table where Jesus provides. In the name of Jesus, we all pray, Amen.[82]

Eucharistic Objects and Practices Reflecting Western Culture

Eucharistic objects and practices such as eucharistic foods, clothing, and music suggested in the BCW [PCK] reflect Western culture rather than Korean culture. First, the use of bread as eucharistic food echoes that Korean Presbyterian eucharistic practice is not so much Korean culture–centered as Western culture–centered. For the cultural relevance of eucharistic foods, several Korean liturgical theologians such as Jang Bok Jung and Soon Whan Kim criticize the use of Western bread and wine for the celebration of the Eucharist. As Jung mentions that the Presbyterian Church of Korea has a strong tendency to keep "Western culture–oriented worship element as the best" without any critical process of cultural contextualization,[83] he asserts that this phenomenon also happens in the Eucharist. Jung claims that the rejection of Korean indigenous foods as eucharistic foods has implicitly

---

82. Ibid., 58.
83. Jung, "Examining Lima Liturgy," 346.

Liturgical Foundations for an Alternative Eucharistic Pedagogy

reinforced an understanding that Western culture is the most appropriate culture for Christian liturgy. Most Korean Presbyterian churches do not use rice cake and rice wine (which are symbols of life in Korean society) but only Western bread (or Western wafer) and Western wine (or Western grape juice) for the Eucharist.[84] S. Kim also criticizes the use of Western bread and wine at the Eucharist, which has been accepted as a Korean Christian worship tradition in the Presbyterian Church of Korea since the beginning by foreign missionaries.

According to S. H. Kim, rice has been an essential symbol of life, thanksgiving, sharing, peace, and community in agrarian Korean society for thousands of years.[85] Thus, rice cakes and rice wine have been used as indispensible ritual foods at the table of rites of passage such as the first-birthday celebration, coming-of-age ceremony, marriage, and memorial ceremony, and for Korean traditional rituals such as the Lunar New Year's day and the harvest festival of thanksgiving.[86] He insists that because rice is the essential food for Korean Christians, rice cakes and rice wine, rather than Western bread and wine, should be used for the celebration of the Eucharist in the Presbyterian Church of Korea.[87]

With regard to eucharistic foods in the BCW [PCK], I find that there are two separations in Korean Presbyterian eucharistic practices. On the one hand, the use of bread as a eucharistic food indicates the separation between Korean local culture and eucharistic practices in the Presbyterian Church of Korea. Even though the BCW [PCK] names rice cake as the eucharistic food in the texts of eucharistic prayer, it guides liturgists to use bread at the eucharistic table in the practical guidelines. This may have been done as a recommendation that the liturgist use bread as the eucharistic food but call it "rice cake," or it may have been done to allow a liturgist to use either bread or rice cake for the celebration of the Eucharist.[88] These two possibilities indicate that bread is still used officially for the eucharistic table in the Presbyterian Church of Korea. On the other hand, the naming of "rice cake" for bread in eucharistic texts shows the separation between liturgical practices and biblical, historical references regarding eucharistic foods. In all eucharistic texts (from eucharist prayers

---

84. S. W. Kim, *Worship in the Twenty-First Century*, 242.
85. S. W. Kim, *Symbol of the Eucharist*, 145.
86. Ibid., 138.
87. Ibid., 157.
88. BCW (PCK), 56.

A–K), the BCW [PCK] simply substitutes rice cake for bread. For example, when Jesus' Passover meal is treated as a historical reference in the Words of Institution from eucharistic prayer B, a rice cake is placed in the setting.

> The Lord Jesus, on the night he was betrayed, ate the Passover with his loving disciples. At that time, he took *rice cake*, gave thanks, broke it, and gave it to his disciples. Jesus said, "This is my body, which is for you; do this in remembrance of me."[89]

This substitution of rice cake for bread in all eucharistic texts may cause congregation members to confuse and misunderstand Jesus' Passover meal because of the conflicting information in biblical and eucharistic texts. Moreover, the confusion may hinder congregation members in linking biblical texts to their meal experiences in their daily lives in the Eucharist. As I point out in the section on Phan's liturgical contextualization works, authentic liturgical contextualization cannot be completed by simply changing the local language.[90]

Second, Western culture–centered liturgical objects are also observed in Western-styled liturgical garments. The BCW [PCK] identifies a Western-styled liturgical gown, clerical collar, and stole as the official liturgical clothes of the Korean Presbyterian worship service. In the appendix of the BCW [PCK], the history of the liturgical gown is explained in detail as established in Western churches such as the Reformed church in the sixteenth century, the Church of Scotland, and the Presbyterian Church in the U.S.[91] At the end of the historical description of liturgical clothes, the BCW [PCK] recommends Korean Presbyterian liturgists to use a Geneva-styled gown, Reformed-church-styled stole, and Scottish clerical collar as official liturgical clothes.[92] There is no reference to any Korean-styled liturgical gown, stole, and clerical collar.

This tendency to use Western culture–centered liturgical objects and practices occurs along with the use of non-Korean hymns at the eucharistic table. In the appendix, the BCW [PCK] suggests five hymns for the celebration of the Eucharist, all of which are brought from foreign churches: two come from France, one is an African-American spiritual song, another comes from Germany, and one comes from the Philippines.[93] In the view of

89. Ibid., 68.
90. Phan, *In Our Own Tongues*, 84.
91. Reforming Committee, *Book of Common Worship* [PCK], 561–63.
92. Ibid., 565.
93. Ibid., 642–47.

the inseparable relationship between liturgical experiences in a church and liturgical life in a society, Western-styled liturgical clothes and hymns may serve to exclude Korean culture–embedded liturgical clothes and hymns and inhibit the inclusion of socioculturally appropriate liturgical objects and clothes and music in the Presbyterian Church of Korea. In the view of contextual theology, Western culture–centered liturgical objects and practices at the eucharistic table may echo a message that most current Korean Presbyterians already understand, that Western culture is considered the most appropriate for Christian liturgy, and that Korean culture is considered inappropriate or inferior for Christian liturgy. When Western culture–centered liturgical objects and practices are used officially and repeatedly, Korean Presbyterians' cultural prejudice rooted in post-colonialism are reproduced and reinforced. In this sense, eucharistic objects reflecting Western culture rather than Korean culture are stumbling blocks rather than stepping stones for Korean Presbyterians to participate actively in the Eucharist in ways that reflect their own life experiences.

Eucharistic Texts Rarely Expressing Eucharistic Values

The eucharistic texts suggested in the BCW [PCK] rarely manifest eucharistic values such as unity, hospitality, equality, and justice. This can be seen in the multilayered hierarchical separations between a liturgist and congregation members and among congregation members at the eucharistic table in the Presbyterian Church of Korea. The tendency of the hierarchical separation between eucharistic participants is seen clearly through the rubrics in the eucharistic texts. First, in view of the separation between a liturgist and congregation members, in its guidelines for eucharistic practices the BCW [PCK] states that the order of distribution of the elements is to the liturgist first, servers second, and congregation members last.[94] Practically, seven out of eleven eucharistic prayers—prayers A, B, C, H, I, J, and K—plainly restate the order of receiving the eucharistic foods—first the liturgist, second the distribution members, and last the congregation members—in the rubrics of distribution. Moreover, while most rubrics of eucharistic actions focus on a liturgist's postures and movements from opening dialogue to post-Communion prayer in detail as in the BCW [PCK], the only rubric regarding congregation members' actions is shown in just one sentence in each eucharistic prayer from prayers C, H, and J.

94. Ibid., 37.

> [In distribution,] they [congregation members] may have the rice cake by dipping it into the cup or before drinking the cup separately. (Prayer C)[95]
>
> Those who are baptized today receive the rice cake and the cup first, and then serve other congregation members. (Prayer H)[96]
>
> They [congregation members] may have the rice cake with the cup or by dipping it into the cup. (Prayer J)[97]

However, Calvin rejects the division between presiding minister and congregation members at the table of the Eucharist. With the harsh criticism of the medieval Mass that ignores and sometimes excludes the participation of the congregation but heavily depends on the priest's presiding, Calvin emphasizes that congregation members need to participate in the Eucharist actively rather than as bystanders.[98] According to B. A. Gerrish, Calvin understands that congregation members are invited to participate in the Eucharist actively not only by acknowledging it as God's visible grace but also by responding to God with gratitude through reflecting, receiving, praising, and thanksgiving.[99] Similarly, with regards to the importance of the assembly in liturgy, Vatican II calls for congregation members' full, active, and conscious participation in liturgical celebrations.[100] Gilbert Ostdiek mentions that the text of "full, active, and conscious participation of the assembly" refers to congregation members' participation in liturgical practices reflecting their sociocultural specific contexts through external and internal engagements and their full awareness of doing the liturgy as God's people.[101] In view of this criterion of liturgical practices, he raises some critical questions regarding the role of assembly in liturgy: "Was the liturgy truly the assembly's action?" "Were the various liturgical roles distributed and respected?" "Did the ministers serve the assembly?"[102] From this perspective, it is unfortunate that the BCW [PCK] shows an obvious gap of expectation between a liturgist and congregation members. While

95. Ibid., 59.
96. Ibid., 164.
97. Ibid., 206.
98. Calvin, *Institutes*, 4.17.39.
99. Gerrish, *Grace and Gratitude*, 19–20.
100. Vatican Council II, "Constitution on the Sacred Liturgy" (*Sacrosanctum Concilium*), online: http://www.vatican.va/archive/hist_councils/ii_vatican_council/documents/vat-ii_const_19631204_sacrosanctum-concilium_en.html .
101. Ostdiek, *Catechesis for Liturgy*, 38.
102. Ibid., 38–39.

a liturgist is described as an active participant in the Eucharist as well as professional performer of Jesus' Last Supper, congregation members are described as passive participants at best.

Second, the separation between congregation members can be observed through the rubrics of eucharistic texts. According to Lee's understanding of marginality, people who do not belong to either of two groups experience double negations from both groups (the in-between model).[103] Lee asserts that the double negations can be overcome by marginality through marginality. That is, when all people become marginal people by giving up their centrality to control and dominate other people, the conflict between margin and center in the group disappear into the harmonious coexistence of total negation and total affirmation (in-beyond model).[104]

From this perspective, the rubrics for the eucharistic texts in the BCW [PCK] guide congregation members to experience the Eucharist not as a new marginal community of unity, equality, justice, and hospitality but as marginalized persons, depending on age and physical disability. First, with regard to the separation of adults and children, the BCW [PCK] specifies that eucharistic participants are restricted by their age. For example, according to the rubrics in eucharistic prayer J, while adult congregation members can participate in the Eucharist, children may not participate in the Eucharist either by partaking in eating rice cake nor by drinking wine.

> Only baptized congregation members stand in a line before a eucharistic table and receive the rice cake and cup.... Children who are with their parents observe their parents' participation in the Eucharist.[105]

This restriction is directly related to the requirement of baptism in the Presbyterian Church of Korea, because unbaptized congregation members are not allowed to participate in the Eucharist. According to *The Catechism of the Presbyterian Church of Korea*, a congregation member who wants to be baptized should be over fifteen years old.[106] Even congregation members who were baptized as infants cannot participate in the Eucharist because of the age restriction. These restrictions present a serious obstacle for those who are under fifteen to participate in the Eucharist as a place of equality

---

103. Lee, *Marginality*, 57.
104. Ibid., 151.
105. Reforming Committee, *Book of Common Worship* [PCK], 206.
106. Education and Resource Ministry, *Catechism of the Presbyterian Church*, 6.

and hospitality. The rubric in eucharistic prayer J provides a brief guidance for toddlers: "parents may prepare some foods for their babies who cannot understand what the Eucharist is."[107] This may lead parents to guide their toddlers to practice a pseudo-Eucharist without any connection to the eucharistic community. According to the rubrics of the BCW [PCK], it is enough for children to be with adult congregation members and to watch as adults eat and drink eucharistic foods around the eucharistic table.[108] In eucharistic prayer J, there is no further explanation of the rationale for the age restriction in eucharistic participation.

Second, the separation between the handicapped and the unhandicapped also can be observed through the eucharistic texts and rubrics in the BCW [PCK]. Even though there is no explicit restriction or discrimination between the handicapped and the unhandicapped, the separation can be seen tacitly through the rubrics of distribution. Six of eleven eucharistic prayers—prayers A, B, H, I, J, and K—provide rubrics of distribution that allow congregation members to come to the eucharistic table. However, none of the guidelines mention any consideration for those congregants who are unable to walk or to see or to hear.

According to Lee's understanding of the Eucharist as the table of reconciliation through JesusChrist as a new marginal person,[109] the multilayered hierarchical separations observed at the eucharistic table in the Presbyterian Church of Korea do not reflect eucharistic values but rather threaten them by underpinning inhospitality, inequality, and injustice through eucharistic experiences. In this context of separation between the liturgist and congregation members or among participants, Korean Presbyterians are apt to understand themselves, consciously or unconsciously, as the double-negated ones in the view of the in-between model. At the table of the Eucharist, their experiences of separation or restriction cause them to understand themselves as marginalized from the liturgist and other congregation members. In this respect, the multilayered separations hinder participants from being "creative agents of reconciliation"[110] in the context of injustice and inequality around the eucharistic table. On the contrary, the experiences of separation may bring out this double-negated self-identity to participants as passive, oppressed people who experience

107. Reforming Committee, *Book of Common Worship* [PCK], 206.
108. Ibid.
109. Ibid., 95.
110. Ibid., 119.

eucharistic discrimination. Such separation experiences not only weaken eucharistic values such as unity, hospitality, equality, and justice but also mislead participants to understand themselves as double-negated people in the view of the in-between model rather than new marginal community members in the view of the in-beyond model.

Eucharistic Experience as a Twofold Anthropocentric Event

The eucharistic texts in the BCW [PCK] have a strong tendency to describe the Eucharist not as a cosmic Trinitarian event between God, human beings, and God's creation (eucharistic foods) but as a twofold anthropocentric event between God the redeemer and human beings. Most eucharistic prayers in the BCW [PCK] focus on the stories of Jesus' suffering and death with attention to the reaffirmation of participants' salvation and conversion rather than the triune God's works such as God's work in creation and the Holy Spirit's consecration of the eucharistic foods. For example, while only three out of eleven eucharistic prayers—prayers C, D, and G—include the triune God's works upon the eucharistic foods, the rest begin with Jesus' Last Supper with his disciples, focusing on Jesus' suffering and death. Furthermore, four out of eleven euharistic prayers—prayers A, B, I, and J—focus on the story of Jesus' Last Supper without including stories of Jesus' other works such as incarnation, baptism, teaching, preaching, forgiving, healing, resurrection, and ascending. The propensity of overfocusing on Jesus' Last Supper in eucharistic texts may cause Korean Presbyterians to understand the Eucharist as a twofold anthropocentric event between God the redeemer and human beings with attention restricted to the reaffirmation of individual salvation and conversion.

With this understanding of the Eucharist, eucharistic foods as such are regarded not as primary and essential signs that are inseparable and join with the reality of God's presence, but as secondary and supplementary signs that are used for representation of Jesus' Last Supper. However, because the Eucharist is the heavenly banquet where God's people participate in God's presence with, through, and in eucharistic foods, eucharistic foods cannot be secondary and supplementary for the representation of Jesus' Last Supper at the eucharistic table. This understanding of the eucharistic foods agrees with an Asian Trinitarian understanding. In the view of Asian Trinitarian epistemology based on yin-yang symbolic thinking, eucharistic foods become primary signs of God's creation, which join with the reality of God's presence through the concept of in-ness between God as the heaven, God's creation as the earth, and human beings. In this respect, eucharistic foods are not secondary and supplementary signs but essential ones. From an Asian Trinitarian perspective, the Eucharist can be understood not as an anthropocentric event between God and human beings but as a cosmic union between God (the heaven), eucharistic foods (the earth), and human beings. Over-focusing on Jesus' Last Supper in eucharistic texts in the BCW [PCK] reflects the strong tendency of Korean Presbyterians to understand the Eucharist as a twofold anthropocentric event between God the redeemer and human beings. It also causes Korean Presbyterians to understand eucharistic foods not as primary and essential signs but as secondary and supplementary signs at the eucharistic table.

Liturgical Implications

In light of Phan and Lee's liturgical contextualization works, this work on critical analysis of eucharistic texts in the BCW [PCK] identifies that current eucharistic texts have several limits in helping Korean Presbyterians to engage actively in eucharistic practices as critically reflective of participants' sociocultural life experiences. In terms of the reciprocal relationship between liturgical practices and participants' specific local contexts, this critical analysis provides the Presbyterian Church of Korea with significant liturgical implications for the building of an alternative eucharistic pedagogy: (1) valuing congregation members' life experiences as important resources for eucharistic texts, (2) reforming eucharistic objects and practices to better reflect Korean culture, (3) reinterpreting congregation members as active co-celebrants in equality and justice, and (4) revitalizing the value of eucharistic foods as essential signs.

First, Korean Presbyterians' life experiences in their sociocultural contexts need to be valued as important resources of eucharistic texts. In the context of the dichotomous understanding between liturgical experiences and liturgical life, the congregation's life experiences have no space to be considered and reflected in the eucharistic texts. In view of the inseparable relationship between faith and culture,[111] participants' current sociocultural lives need to be linked to their liturgical practices in the Eucharist. However, current eucharistic texts hardly encourage Korean Presbyterians to participate in the Eucharist fully with attention to participants' life ex-

---

111. Lee and Phan, *Journeys at the Margin*, 114.

Liturgical Foundations for an Alternative Eucharistic Pedagogy

periences in their specific local contexts. In order to participate fully in the Eucharist, congregation members must identify their real life issues in their sociocultural contexts at the eucharistic table. In order to bring and reflect participants' life experiences into the Eucharist, their current sociocultural issues and realities need to be echoed and integrated with the eucharistic texts in various creative ways. For example, participants' real life stories, including urgent prayer requests that express both joy for grateful stories and sadness for despairing stories in their sociocultural contexts, can be used for eucharistic prayer texts as well as post-communion prayer texts.[112] Participants' life experiences can become significant vehicles to deliver God's gospel to participants through their own culture at the eucharistic table. Both the Eucharist and local culture are enriched mutually through these practices. An effort to integrate participants' sociocultural life experiences into the eucharistic experience can help Korean Presbyterians have an inclusive view of the relationship between Christianity and Korean culture, between liturgy and local culture, and between liturgy and popular religion, not as opposite and separate but as interactive and reciprocal.

Second, eucharistic objects and practices in the Presbyterian Church of Korea need to reflect Korean culture. When Western culture–centered objects and practices such as Western liturgical clothes, music, and eucharistic foods are used for the celebration of the Eucharist, they do not help Korean Presbyterians participate in the Eucharist with a reflection of their own life experiences. On the contrary, Western culture–centered objects and practices are inclined to impede linkage of their sociocultural life experiences to the eucharistic table. The process of reforming eucharistic objects and practices based on Korean culture cannot be completed simply by switching from Western music to Korean music, from Western-styled clothes to Korean clothes, and from bread to rice cake. There needs to be an ongoing critical conversation between Christian liturgy and Korean culture, both theologically and ritually. Korean culture-oriented eucharistic objects and practices need to be discerned and adopted critically through the contextual and dialectical conversations between the significant sources of the theological enterprise[113]; that is, Scripture, tradition, local culture, and social change. In this conversation, alternative Korean culture-oriented

---

112. For example, congregation members' various life stories and issues in their daily lives, whether sad or joyful—such as a sudden slump in the rice market, an abrupt political crisis in the relationship with North Korea, or a recovery from illness—can be included creatively in the process of the revision of the eucharistic prayer.

113. Bevans, *Models of Contextual Theology*, 11.

liturgical objects and practices in the Eucharist can be examined critically through the collaborative works of memory and imagination.[114] They need to be examined in light of not only memory of the past rooted in Scripture and tradition, but also imagination for the future based on local culture and social change.

Third, the role of congregational members needs to be reinterpreted as active co-celebrants in equality and justice at the eucharistic table. In the eucharistic context of the multilayered separation between a liturgist and congregation members or among participants, the eucharistic table cannot be the table of equality and justice as long as congregation members are double-marginalized from the liturgist and other participants. In order for the eucharistic community to be a new marginal community of equality and justice, all congregation members, including children and disabled people, must be reinterpreted as active co-celebrants who are not marginalized or ignored unequally and unjustly at the eucharistic table. When the liturgist gives up his or her centrality as the only active performer at the eucharistic table, eucharistic marginality can be overcome. When adults and the able-bodied give up their centrality as privileged participants who can access the eucharistic foods without any restrictions at the eucharistic table, eucharistic marginality of the young and disabled can be overcome. The eucharistic community can become a new marginal community, and when that happens, the eucharistic table can be the table of equality and justice.

Fourth, the eucharistic foods need to be revitalized as the essential signs. From an Asian Trinitarian perspective, the Eucharist is understood as a cosmic Trinitarian union between God as the heaven, human beings, and God's creation as the earth. In this union, eucharistic foods cannot be understood as subordinate liturgical elements for the encounter between God and human beings but as essential elements for the cosmic Trinitarian union. However, in the current Korean Presbyterian eucharistic practice, with an over-emphasis on Jesus' Last Supper and a narrow attention on the reaffirmation of participants' individual salvation and conversion, eucharistic foods have been easily understood as subordinate liturgical elements for the representation of Jesus' Last Supper. Eucharistic prayers have been developed not in a Trinitarian form composed of God the Father, God the Son, and God the Spirit but in a christocentric form, only focusing on Jesus' suffering, death, and resurrection. In this sense, the integration of an Asian cosmic Trinitarian perspective can help Korean Presbyterians to revitalize

---

114. Lee and Phan, *Journeys at the Margin*, 115.

the value of eucharistic foods as essential signs at the eucharistic table, and to reform eucharistic texts in a Trinitarian form based on the works of the triune God, including the Father's creation works, the Son's redemptive works, and the Holy Spirit's consecration and helping works.

CHAPTER 4

Educational Foundations for an Alternative Eucharistic Pedagogy

UNDERSTANDING CURRICULUM IS ESSENTIAL and important educational work. The purpose, methods, and environment of education are constructed differently according to how curriculum is understood. Historically, the field of education has been marked by various understandings of the term "curriculum." These differing interpretations have led to a wide variety of educational strategies. For example, traditional curriculum theorists such as Franklin Bobbitt or Ralph Tyler understood curriculum as a tool or system in an effective means-ends model.

THEY BELIEVED THAT EDUCATION needs to prepare students to adjust and match themselves to the existing social order for a successful adult life through teaching and learning experiences. By contrast, reconceptualist curriculum theorists such as Henry Giroux or William F. Pinar, who regard curriculum as a political text, concentrate on empowering students in their daily lives to respond to the political structures with critical thinking and actions.

Reconceptualized curriculum theory has been developed by educators and scholars in an effort to encourage and assist students in forming a critical view of orders and structures in their sociocultural contexts and in responding actively to them.

The contents and pedagogical strategies of reconceptualized curriculum theory are open-ended according to students' real life and learning experiences in the context of education.

This book is an educational work based on reconceptualized curriculum theory in terms of building a new eucharistic pedagogy with attention to Korean Presbyterian students' sociocultural contexts. It understands curriculum as a process of ecological socialization with attention to students' learning experiences closely related to their multilayered sociocultural contexts. In this chapter, I will examine Roberta M. Berns' ecological socialization pedagogy with attention to the relationship between students' ritual experiences and their sociocultural contexts. Berns is a secular scholar in the field of education who developed an ecological socialization pedagogy based on socialization theory from sociology. Her pedagogical work focuses on "a reciprocal dynamic process" between individuals' learning experiences and their multilayered social contexts. As the term "ecological socialization pedagogy" indicates, Berns' theory comes from a broader study of human development based on interdisciplinary works of biology, sociology, anthropology, psychology, economics, politics, ecology, and education. Based on in-depth analysis of students' learning processes from various angles, Berns' ecological socialization pedagogy provides a provocative educational strategy for the teacher to understand students' daily life in their local contexts and to reflect on them, ecologically and effectively, in their teaching practices. In this respect, even though Berns is a Western theorist, her theory provides significant educational resources to the Presbyterian Church of Korea. As I examined in the previous chapter, current eucharistic practices in the Presbyterian Church of Korea have several liturgical, theological, and educational weaknesses, such as the lack of reflecting students' life experiences in the Eucharist; minimal emphasis on unity, hospitality, equality, and justice; and a reliance on Western culture-oriented eucharistic texts, objects, and practices. Moreover, these characteristics are closely related to the current Korean Presbyterian eucharistic pedagogy, which is deductive, hierarchical, and instructive.

Considering how Berns' theory is not only based on an in-depth and broad study of students' learning processes but also takes inductive, life-reflective, and collaborative teaching approaches, I find that her theory can help meet the weaknesses of current Korean Presbyterian eucharistic practices and pedagogy. In her theory, Berns suggests reconceptualizing pedagogical concepts of the teacher's role, the contents of teaching, the building of curriculum, and extended learning environments. The rationale for the use of Berns' theory will be provided later.

Roberta Berns' Ecological Socialization Pedagogy

Roberta Berns, professor emerita of human and community development at the University of California, Irvine, a well-respected researcher and instructor, introduces ecological socialization pedagogy, giving attention to the interactive effects of individuals' sociocultural environments in their learning processes. Based on the understanding of ecological socialization, Berns reconceptualizes the role of a teacher, the role of students, and the functions of socializing agents, and she suggests a six-step model for pedagogical strategies with attention to students' relationship with their multilayered ecological contexts.

Understanding of Ecological Socialization

Berns defines socialization as a reciprocal, dynamic, and human process by which "individuals acquire the knowledge, skills, and character traits that enable them to participate as effective members of groups and society" through interacting with ecological contexts.

Originally, the term "socialization" was developed in the field of sociology during the mid-twentieth century in order to delineate the process of the deliberate shaping of individuals within a society.

In the field of sociology, it is generally understood as the process whereby individuals grow into societal roles and fulfill the expectations of their societal roles within both formal and informal contexts through their social environments.

Regarding the process of socialization between individuals and society, most contemporary sociological theorists reject any exclusive interpretation of the traditional understanding of socialization as either actor-oriented or structure-oriented.

They agree that there is no pure individuality without social interaction and there is no pure sociality without individual response. As contemporary sociologists concentrate on the inclusive societal tensions between individuals and society, they regard the construction of sociocultural knowledge as one of the primary issues in socialization theory.

With attention to the structured interdynamic processes of an individual's socialization within multilayered sociocultural environments, the newly coined term "bioecological socialization" was initially introduced and developed by Urie Bronfenbrenner, a professor of human development at Cornell University, who taught and influenced Berns. In his article "Ecological Systems Theory," Bronfenbrenner insists that developmental science about human beings should involve more than the mere collection of data and explanation of the person and environments. It should also involve the particular processes of the person's development.

With his emphasis on the process of development, Bronfenbrenner's study began to expand and synthesize the level of developmental elements from biology, sociology, anthropology, psychology, economics, politics, and ecology.

In contrast to Piaget's "decontextualized" organism tested in a laboratory setting, Bronfenbrenner suggests a process-person-context-time (PPCT) model for human development, focusing on the reciprocal interactions between an active individual and his or her multilayered ecological contexts as the driving forces of development.

These four interrelated components (process, person, context, and time) are crucial to understanding an individual's development.

Richard M. Lerner, professor and director of the Institute for Applied Research in Youth Development at Tufts University, describes Bronfenbrenner's four components:

> (a) the developmental *process*, involving the fused and dynamic relation of the individual and the context; (b) the *person*, with his or her individual repertoire of biological, cognitive, emotional, and behavioral characteristics; (c) the *context* of human development, conceptualized as the nested levels, or systems, of the ecology of human development he has depicted; and (d) *time*, conceptualized as involving the multiple dimensions of temporality—for example, ontogenetic time, family time, and historical time—constituting the chronosystem that moderates change across the life course.

In his pioneering work *The Ecology of Human Development*, Bronfenbrenner explains that an individual's development is shaped by the interaction, synthesis, and integration of the four components and occurs in the interrelated ecological levels of human development: microsystem, mesosystem, exosystem, and macrosystem.

Bronfenbrenner understands that the development of individuals takes place through a pattern of the developing person's activities, roles, and interpersonal relations in a given face-to-face setting (microsystem) and through the interlinked relationships between two or more settings (mesosystem).

It also occurs through an extension of the mesosystem, which does not involve the individual as an active participant directly but influences his or her behavior and development (exosystem) and through the given culture, subculture, or other broader social contexts that overarch the pattern of micro-, meso-, and exosystem (macrosystem).

Moreover, Bronfenbrenner mentions that individual ecological socialization processes within these four basic structures are influenced by significant historical events of an individual or a society. Bronfenbrenner calls this the *chronosystem*.

Within the conceptual framework of Bronfenbrenner's ecological model of human development, Berns proposes a new pedagogical approach to the understanding of students' learning with attention to their socialization process in an educational setting. In *Child, Family, School, Community: Socialization and Support*, Berns adopts and applies Bronfenbrenner's main concepts—ecology of human development, microsystem, mesosystem, exosystem, macrosystem, and chronosystem—to educational settings.

In view of the ecology of human development, Berns understands that the sociocultural interactions, experiences, and abilities of a student are built and affected ecologically by very complicated sociocultural, political processes between individuals and their life environments.

Like Bronfenbrenner, Berns emphasizes that students' socialization taking place in ecological contexts is a reciprocal dynamic process.

> It [the socialization of individuals] is a reciprocal process in that when one individual interacts with another, a response in one usually elicits a response in the other; it is also a dynamic process in that interactions change over time, with individuals becoming producers of responses as well as products of them.

In this respect, Berns understands that the processes of socialization in the context of education are intrinsically connected not only to the contents and methods of teaching in the classroom but also ecologically, to the complex, structural, reciprocal dynamics between students' sociocultural life experiences and multilayered social agents and teaching contents and pedagogical methods. In the view of the ecological level of human development, Berns suggests the four structures of ecological socialization—microsystem, mesosystem, exosystem, and macrosystem—as the basic framework to understand students' socialization in the educational setting.

Berns asserts that within the four basic structures of ecological socialization, the socialization process of students involves bidirectional interactions and relationships with others. That is, students experience socialization not only in their relationship with significant others in a

Educational Foundations for an Alternative Eucharistic Pedagogy

particular small setting such as family, school, peer group, media, or community (microsystem) but also in the interrelationships between individuals' microsystems, such as having friends at church, friends going to the movies, and guest speakers in a school (mesosystem).

Moreover, students' socialization takes places in a setting that affects individuals indirectly in one of their microsystems, such as parents' work, school boards, community boards, social services, and federal commissions (exosystem). It also occurs in a society or subculture to which individuals belong with specific reference to value systems, belief systems, patterns of social interaction, and lifestyle such as religion, culture, ethnicity, economics, and political ideology (macrosystem).

According to Berns, these four basic structures of ecological socialization are also affected by temporal changes in an ecological system or within individuals (chronosystem). The temporal changes produce new conditions that influence the process of students' socialization over time.

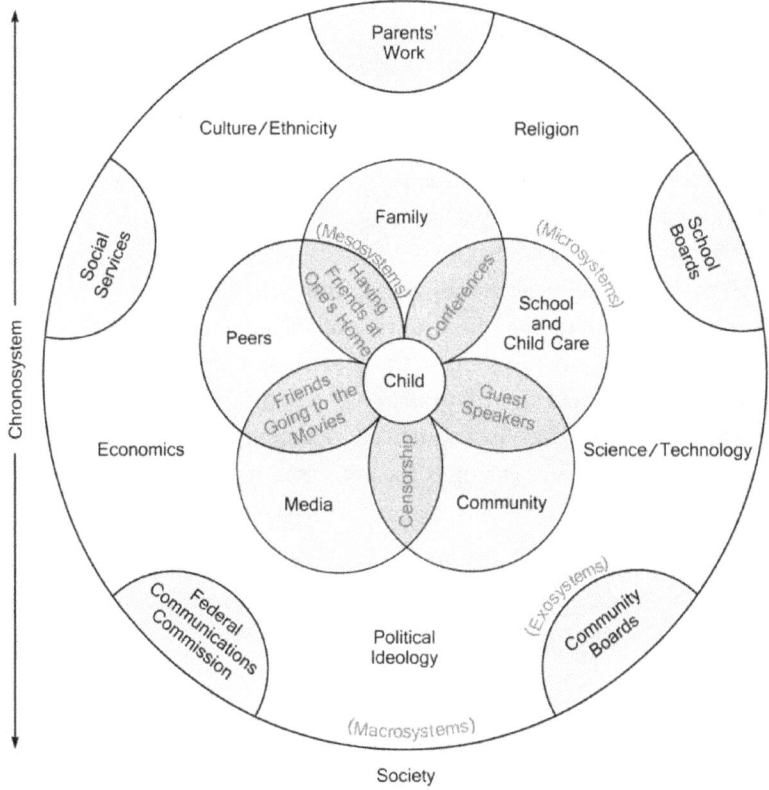

Figure 1: Diagram of Individual Ecological Socialization[1]

1. Ibid., 21.

With a basic understanding of ecological socialization frameworks, Berns identifies five significant socialization agents that exert influence on the process of individual ecological socialization: family, school, peers, mass media, and community. First, the family is the initial reference group bearing major responsibility for socializing the child.[2] Through interactions with family members, individuals begin to learn and practice social values, norms, and behavior patterns toward others.[3] Second, the school is the formal organization that provides individuals with the intellectual and social experiences to develop skills, knowledge, interests, and attitudes for their academic, vocational, social and civic, and personal lives through educational policies, orders, and social relationships in the classroom.[4] Third, peers help individuals satisfy their belonging needs and social interactions within their group activities through socializing mechanisms such as reinforcement (approval and acceptance), modeling (imitation), punishment (rejection and exclusion), and apprenticeship (learning from other expert peers).[5] Fourth, mass media such as books, television, movies, and Internet provide information about the society, ways to respond or interact, role models to follow, and resources to reflect socio-political attitudes.[6] Fifth, a community is a group of people who share fellowship and common interests in places like church, libraries, museums, zoos, and businesses.[7] Within a community, individuals experience emotional security and companionship as well as participate in cooperation with others for practical necessities of life or accomplishment of large and urgent tasks.[8]

Even though Berns examines the functions of the socialization agents belonging to the microsystemic structure of socialization, she emphasizes the influence of the macrosystem on the process of individual socialization. Berns underscores that all socialization agents are closely related to the macrosystem, in that they are influenced by the ongoing changing nature of their macrosystem. For example, the processes of children's socialization

---

2. Ibid., 82.

3. Handel and Elkin, *Child and Society*, 143, quoted in Berns, *Child, Family, School, Community*, 53.

4. Berns, *Child, Family, School, Community*, 215.

5. Ibid., 309.

6. Ibid., 58.

7. Decker and Decker, *Engaging Families and Communities*, quoted in Berns, *Child, Family, School, Community*, 414.

8. Berns, *Child, Family, School, Community*, 403; Warren and Lyon, *New Perspectives on the American Community*, quoted in ibid., 403.

Educational Foundations for an Alternative Eucharistic Pedagogy

within families are affected by the ethnic orientation and religious orientation in which their families are based. The different ethnic and cultural norms and values influence how children are socialized in their families in terms of the basic patterns of thinking and living and expectations for following the behavior patterns of the family. The different religious beliefs and practices affect how family members understand gender roles, parents' responsibility, and children's morality and attitudes in their family lives.[9] Just as the individual socialization processes within the family is affected by the macrosystem, the individual socialization processes within other socialization agents such as school, peer groups, mass media, and community are influenced by the macrosystem. These include such things as ethnic orientation, religious orientation, gender stereotypes, political ideology, and socioeconomic status. In this sense, Berns understands that the process of individual socialization occurs ecologically with bidirectional dynamics among the structures of ecological socialization (microsystem, mesosystem, exosystem, macrosystem, and choronosystem). In particular she emphasizes that the macrosystem as a societal blueprint influences the process of individual socialization within all socialization agents (family, school, peers, mass media, and community) in accordance with their sociocultural contexts.

Pedagogical Reconceptualization: Teacher, Curriculum, Critical Conversation, and Learning Environments

With attention to the individual socialization process based on ecological socialization theory, Berns asserts that the role of the teacher and learning environments in educational contexts needs to be reconceptualized from a classroom-limited perspective to an ecologically expanded perspective. In the view of ecological socialization theory, students' learning experiences take place not only within a microsystemic scale such as in a classroom but also within meso-, exo-, macro-, and chronosystemic scales rooted in their daily life experiences. From this perspective, Berns understands that effective teaching requires the teacher to know students' sociocultural ecological contexts in terms of the microsystem, mesosystem, exosystem, macrosystem, and chronosystem and critically reflect them in their teaching.

---

9. Gollnick andChinn, *Multicultural Education in a Pluralistic Society*, quoted in Berns, *Child, Family, School, Community*, 119.

According to Berns, in order to understand students' ecological sociocultural contexts, the teacher needs to be aware of not only the specific and concrete contexts of students' current microsystem but also its linkages with other ecosystems such as school-family linkages, school-peer group linkages, school-media linkages, and school-community linkages. For instance, many research studies show that students' academic achievement in a school is closely related to the relationship between school and family.[10] Home environments that discourage learning, low parental expectations for student achievement and future careers, and low socioeconomic status tend to result in less effective educational outcomes in the school.[11] In this situation, the teacher can help families become involved in school by creating communication channels such as weekly tutoring sessions, assignment monitoring, and open conferences to help underachieving students.[12] Furthermore, for effective teaching, the teacher needs to recognize not only the contexts of students' exosystem, such as parental employment and income, or the city council's decision to build a highway near the school, but also the contexts of their macrosystem, such as students' ethnicity, cultures, belief systems, socioeconomic status, and sociopolitics.

With serious attention to students' complicated ecological sociocultural situations, Berns suggests that the teacher needs to use various socialization methods: (1) affective method, (2) operant method, (3) observational method, (4) cognitive method, (5) sociocultural method, and (6) apprenticeship method.

First, Berns calls the teacher to develop an affectional attachment to the students, and identifies attachment as the foundation of social interaction and as a basic pedagogical strategy.[13] The affective method is an essential way for students to be socialized because their socialization occurs through person-to-person interactions and human interactions lead to affectional ties. Developing a secure attachment between the teacher and students helps build a sense of trust among them and a feeling of competence and cooperation in the context of education.[14]

---

10. Epstein, *School, Family, and Community Partnerships*; Henderson and Berla, *New Generation of Evidence*, both quoted in Berns, *Child, Family, School, Community*, 241.

11. Haskins and Rouse, "Closing Achievement Gaps," quoted in Berns, *Child, Family, School, Community*, 242.

12. Berns, *Child, Family, School, Community*, 244.

13. Ibid. 61.

14. Ibid., 62.

Second, the operant method is a socializing vehicle to facilitate students to participate actively in the context of their socialization with desired behaviors. In order to increase desired behaviors, Berns introduces three pedagogical strategies belonging to the operant method: positive reinforcement (such as encouragement, physical contact, and praise), negative reinforcement (such as time-out and punishment), and shaping (such as feedback and learning by doing).[15]

Third, the observational method, also called modeling, is a socializing vehicle to help students learn appropriate social behavior and attitudes vicariously by observing and imitating another person's behaviors and their consequences in their socialization process.[16] As students observe and imitate other people's behaviors, they summarize what they observe, keep it in their memory, make rules about behaviors, get back appropriate information, and act it out at the appropriate time.[17]

Fourth, the cognitive method focuses on a way to help students process information effectively and to abstract meaning from experiences of their socialization process. Berns introduces instruction and reasoning as the examples of pedagogical strategies belonging to the cognitive method.[18] For effective teaching, Berns states that instruction needs to be specific enough to understand and remember and that reasoning needs to be rational enough for students to act and respond with appropriate rationale.

Fifth, the sociocultural method is a socializing vehicle that influences and ensures that students conform to their sociocultural groups such as family, peers, school, and religious community. By interacting with sociocultural groups through group pressure, tradition, rituals, routines, and symbols, students acquire knowledge of their societal customs, stories, beliefs, norms, and symbols, as well as ways of solving certain problems. For example, when students participate in indigenous traditional seasonal

---

15. Ibid., 6--65. According to Berns, through the dynamic, bidirectional feedback between the teacher and students, students have a chance to take in another person's perspectives, to know the knowledge of results, to have a increased learning motivation, and to have information on measuring up to standards of behavior or performance. The pedagogical strategy of learning by doing provides students with a chance not only to participate in a certain learning activity but also to interact with others through physical, intellectual, and social skills and to construct and transform their experiences.

16. Berns, *Topical Child Development*, 220.

17. Ibid.

18. Berns, *Child, Family, School, Community*, 70.

rituals, they learn sociocultural values, attitudes, gender roles, and morals in their society.

Last, the apprenticeship method is a socializing vehicle that guides students as novices to achieve the ability to master tasks through guided participation. Based on Rogoff's study of human development that identifed apprenticeship as an effective educational method,[19] Berns asserts that apprenticeship demands three steps: (1) appropriate structuring activities in which students participate according to ability, (2) joint collaborative activities between students and the guide, and (3) transfer of responsibility for activity management to students.

With the deep understanding of students' ecological sociocultural contexts and their various socialization methods, Berns asserts that the teacher needs not only to build effective teaching strategies and curriculum with serious attention to the awareness of students' needs and abilities but also to guide them pedagogically with appropriate actions. In her book *Community-Based Intervention*, Berns suggests a six-step model for the building of critical conversations and actions within a community by helping people explore, critically reflect on, and cope with their life issues and take positive actions. The six-step model consists of: (1) defining the problem, (2) ensuring safety, (3) providing support, (4) examining alternatives, (5) making plans, and (6) obtaining commitment to positive action.[20] Since Berns' six-step model is suggested for the effective individual socialization within a community as one of the socialization agents, she does not limit contexts where the six models could be applied to a certain socialization agent such as family only, school only, peer groups only.

In the context of education in this book, Berns' six-step model can be applied to the relationship between the teacher and students. The first three steps are listening activities and the remaining steps are acting strategies. The first step is to define students' life issues from their perspectives. The teacher's use of active listening skills such as open-ended questions, empathy, genuineness, and positive regard is demanded in this step. Through active listening to students' issues and situations, the teacher can help students open and share their feelings and think on their main issues from their sociocultural life experiences. The second step is to ensure students' safety. Berns defines the concept of safety as the situation of minimizing

---

19. Rogoff, *Cultural Nature of Human Development*.
20. Berns, *Community-Based Intervention*, 85–89.

danger to self and others physically and psychologically.[21] That is, the teacher needs to guarantee the safety of the students in their current physical and psychological situations. The third step is to provide support through open communication with students. In the process of communication, the teacher needs to demonstrate his or her support by providing students with emotional support such as caring, accepting, non-judgmental, and non-possessive involvement, and by providing adequate informational support regarding students' issues. The fourth step is to examine alternatives critically and systematically. According to Berns, this critical process of analysis demands collaborative work between the teacher and students by using three elements: (1) people who know and care about the students in the present or past, (2) actions, behaviors and environmental resources that students can use for coping with their issues, and (3) constructive conversations that help students interpret and act on their issues. The list of alternatives decided through this process needs to be realistic and available for students to apply to their situations. The fifth step is to help students to make doable short-term plans of action based on the list of alternatives from the previous step. The plan includes coping mechanisms and various socializing mediators such as additional persons, groups, and other referral resources in their sociocultural environments. The process of making plans of action needs to be done as collaborative work between the teacher and students with attention to students' initiative, active, and independent participation. The sixth step is to help students to commit to follow through in practical ways on plans of actions. The commitment can be obtained by brief, simple expressions by the students, such as a written promise or a handshake. This commitment should be voluntary.

In Berns' ecological socialization pedagogy, I find several distinct, significant reconceptualized pedagogical concepts that mark Berns' theory as reconceptualized curriculum theory: (1) the teacher is not an information giver but a socializing agent, (2) curriculum is not textbook-oriented but contexts-reflected, (3) critical conversation between the teacher and students is an essential pedagogical resource, and (4) learning environments are not limited to the classroom but include the ecological socializing agents outside the classroom that currently affect the students' lives. First, the teacher is not an information giver teaching contents and social rules for appropriate behaviors in a class but a socializing agent who encourages students to become involved in the critical conversation about standards

21. Ibid., 87.

of conduct and to respond them with actions. Second, since knowledge is a means to an end rather than an end in itself, the teacher builds curriculum that is not predetermined by a textbook but constructed by students through a process of critical reflection on their life experiences in their sociocultural contexts. Third, the critical conversation between the teacher and students about students' multilayered sociocultural contexts is one of the most important pedagogical resources for the building of educational goals, objectives, contents and methods. Thus, open communication and close relationships with students' possible socializing mediators such as parents, peers, school board members, city council boards, and social service committees are demanded for the building of effective teaching in the context of education. Fourth, in the light of ecological socialization pedagogy, learning environments cannot be defined by the limitations of the classroom. Learning time and space as well as learning materials and technologies cannot be restricted to the classroom but extend to students' daily lives including their micro-, meso-, exo-, and macrosystem.

Because Berns understands that effective teaching takes place on the ground of an integrative understanding of the process of students' socialization within their ecological multilayered socialization structures, she identifies the role of teacher as a significant socializing facilitator. The teacher helps students critically reflect on their life experiences based on an understanding of students' unique combinations rooted in their sociocultural contexts and respond to them with actions. With serious attention to students' life experiences, the teacher provides learning environments for students to participate actively and cooperatively in a class with relevant learning materials and attention to appropriate learning styles.

Critical Reflections on Berns' Ecological Socialization Pedagogy

With attention to the ecological process of students' socialization within multilayered socializing environments, Berns' theory provides support for a significant reconceptualization of several pedagogical concepts in terms of students' life-reflected pedagogy. It gives the Presbyterian Church of Korea important educational foundations such as an inductive, life-reflected, and collaborative pedagogy. However, Berns' ecological socialization pedagogy alone is not adequate for analyzing Korean Presbyterian contexts of eucharistic pedagogy. It is a Western theory that has a limited capacity to reflect Korean students' life experiences from their own specific contexts when learning about the Eucharist.

Educational Foundations for an Alternative Eucharistic Pedagogy

First, Berns' socialization pedagogy naturally cannot account for Korean Presbyterian students' particular contexts, such as Confucianism, which is a dominant socializing environment in Korean society. Whereas Confucianism might be understood as one element of a macrosystem from Berns' socialization pedagogy in terms of moral value and rule,[22] Confucianism in Korean society is more than a macrosystemic socialization agent. As I observed in chapter 2, Confucianism is the most powerful and crucial socialization agent that influences Korean students' entire socialization process: micro-, meso-, exo-, and macrosystem.[23] Since the sixteenth century, it has been the ruling socioculture in the Korean people's daily lives in terms of family, school, business, politics, economics, ethics, and religion.[24] Furthermore, Berns' theory regards the family as one microsystemic socialization agent. In Korean society the family is more than a microsystem; it is the core of all socializing agents.[25] Confucianism, which directed the history, culture, politics, and education of Korea for over five hundred years,[26] understands the family as the essential hub of the individual socialization process.[27]

Second, a postcolonial perspective of the ritual practices of a religious community is not considered seriously in Berns' socialization pedagogy. While Berns pays attention to the influence of a community's ritual practices on the formation of students' self-identity, worldview, and lifestyle, as a Western scholar she does not show a serious interest in culturally biased ritual practiced in a local community from a postcolonial perspective. As I historically, theologically, and liturgically examined the serious weaknesses

---

22. Berns, *Child, Family, School, Community*, 530.

23. H. Y. Kim, *Wang Yang-Min and Karl Barth*, 3–4; Ching and Kung, *Christianity and Chinese Religions*, 85.

24. Adams, *Christ and Culture in Asia*, 65.

25. Oh, *Study on the Social Welfare Ideology of Confucianism*, 5. According to *PalJo-Mok* (Eight articles; 八條目) of *Tehak* (a book of four big Confucian scriptures: 大學), the whole steps of an ideal socialization process start from *SuShin* (building myself ; 修身) to *JeGa* (managing a family; 齊家), *ChiKuk* (ruling a nation; 治國), and *PyungChunHa* (making a universe peaceful and harmonized; 平天下). In the next chapter, I will suggest the reformation of Berns' microsystem, not rooted in Western society but in Korean society, in order to build a new eucharistic pedagogy for the Presbyterian Church of Korea on the ground of the distinctive characteristics and influences of the family's socializing functions in Korean society, which is a strong Confucian-based society.

26. Adams, *Christ and Culture in Asia*, 65.

27. I will depict the family as the essential hub of Korean students' socializing process in chapter 5.

of the current Korean Presbyterian eucharistic practices with attention to Western-centered eucharistic practices in detail in chapters 2 and 3, the postcolonial perspective of eucharistic practices in the Presbyterian Church of Korea demands that the Presbyterian Church of Korea build a new eucharistic pedagogy with attention to students' particular local contexts.

Nevertheless, Berns' theory is useful for this project because her use of the broader interdisciplinary study of human development based on biology, sociology, anthropology, psychology, economics, politics, ecology, and education, which provide the broader context for her pedagogical theory. As Berns understands that students' learning processes occur not only in a classroom but also in their entire life contexts ecologically, her theory with attention to the reciprocal dynamics between individuals' learning and their multilayered social contexts emphasizes the teacher's ecological understanding of the life experiences of students as an essential pedagogical process. This emphasis on in-depth and critical understanding of students' life contexts enables Berns' theory not to be limited to Western applications but to be broadly applicable to a variety of contexts, including Korean contexts.

In this project, which seeks to build an alternative eucharistic pedagogy for the Presbyterian Church of Korea with attention to students' local contextuality, Berns' theory may provide a strong theoretical foundation for Korean teachers and students to take into account their local contexts, such as the influence of Confucianism, the role of family, and the postcolonial context of school, church, and community. Furthermore, Berns' reconceptualized pedagogical concepts, such as teacher as a socializing agent, students as collaborative participants, critical conversations as a significant pedagogical strategy, and teaching contents which are context-reflected, may offer the Presbyterian Church of Korea some important educational implications with which to build a new eucharistic pedagogy.

With an ecological understanding of students' life contexts based on the broader study of human development, Berns' theory is more than just a Western theory; it is valuable and useful for this project in terms of an alternative pedagogical strategy. Berns' theory can provide the Presbyterian Church of Korea with a significant pedagogical frame to build a new contextualized pedagogy that is inductive, life-reflected, and collaborative.

Critical Examination of Korean Presbyterians' Eucharistic Experiences in View of Ecological Socialization Pedagogy with Attention to Korean Students' Particular Local Contexts

In 1972, the Presbyterian Church of Korea published *The Bible and Living* as the first curriculum series in a three-year cycle focusing on Christian life rooted in the Bible, Christ, and church.[28] In 1980, the Presbyterian Church of Korea published *The Word and Life* as the second curriculum series in a two- or three-year cycle focusing on church growth and Christian life based on the Bible.[29] In 2001, the Presbyterian Church of Korea published *God's Kingdom: Call and Responding* as the third curriculum series in a two- or three-year cycle based on students' age with attention to God's kingdom in the view of Bible, church, and the world.[30] In 2008, *God's Kingdom* was revised with minor additions to the supplementary teaching materials. This latest curriculum series from the Presbyterian Church of Korea classifies congregation members in ten groups according to their age throughout the whole lifespan: nursery, pre-kindergarten, kindergarten, first and second grades, third and fourth grades, fifth and sixth grades, middle school, high school, young adult, and older adult. *God's Kingdom* (2008) provides each group with its own curriculum and its companion books for teachers and ministers. In this chapter, I will examine the cultural, contextual, and pedagogical assumptions that lie behind the printed materials that are used for the Eucharist in the Presbyterian Church of Korea by analyzing current curriculum materials from *God's Kingdom* and current eucharistic texts from the BCW [PCK] in view of Berns' ecological socialization pedagogy.

In light of Berns' ecological socialization pedagogy, it becomes clear that Korean students' learning experiences of the Eucharist in a class and at the table of the Eucharist do not provide students space or reasons to name and critically reflect on what they have experienced from postcolonial and political perspectives in their daily lives. Moreover, the curriculum materials of the Presbyterian Church of Korea prescribe the role of teacher as an authoritarian and information provider through teacher-centered and content-centered teaching practices in classes on the Eucharist. These critical observations point to several educational tendencies of Korean

28. Curriculum Committee, *The Bible and Living*.
29. Curriculum Committee, *The Word and Life*.
30. Curriculum Committee, *God's Kingdom*.

Presbyterians' teaching/learning practices in the context of education on the Eucharist: (1) null curriculum—that is, avoidance of rather than attention to—eucharistic experiences, (2) a strong tendency toward separation between Christian education and the Eucharist, and (3) lack of reflection on students' ecological sociocultural life experiences.

Null Curriculum of Eucharistic Experiences in Terms of Western Culture-Centered, Hierarchical, Patriarchal, and Twofold Anthropocentric Eucharistic Practices

Berns' ecological socialization pedagogy presupposes that the processes of socialization in the context of education occur in the reciprocal dynamics between students' sociocultural life experiences through their multilayered social contexts and teachers' teaching context-inclusive contents and appropriate teaching methods.[31] From an ecological socialization perspective, effective teaching contents and methods need to incorporate students' real issues not only from their sociocultural experiences but also from their learning experiences in the context of education. The teaching of the Eucharist needs to build teaching contents and methods critically and creatively with attention to students' contexts not only by examining students' relationships with multilayered socialization agents but also by reflecting their life experiences including eucharistic experiences at the table of the Eucharist in a class on the Eucharist.

From the perspective of ecological socialization theory, the *God's Kingdom* curriculum does not deal with students' real issues from their life experiences as educational contents. Through the exclusion of students' real issues in the context of the Eucharist from *God's Kingdom*, Korean Presbyterian students may receive an implicit message that those elements are not important enough to study along with participation in the Eucharist. I call this reality of the current Korean Presbyterian curriculum the "null curriculum" of eucharistic experiences. In his book *The Educational Imagination: On the Design and Evaluation of School Programs*, Eliot W. Eisner asserts that the null curriculum exists in the context of school alongside the explicit curriculum and the implicit curriculum.[32] For Eisner, the null

---

31. Berns, *Child, Family, School, Community*, 43.

32. Eisner, *Educational Imagination*, 74. Eisner understands that students experience learning processes through three curriculums in school in terms of explicit, implicit, and null curriculum. According to Eisner, while the explicit curriculum is about what is

curriculum refers to that which is not taught or that which is excluded intentionally, but nevertheless influences students' learning.[33] He argues that what is not taught may be as important as what is taught in school because the absence of educational contents is not a neutral void.[34] Through the null curriculum, students may receive the message that what is intentionally excluded from educational contents is not important in their learning or in their society.

For example, when I examine a middle school lesson on the Eucharist from *God's Kingdom* in light of the null curriculum, I find that it does not give students any room or reasons to reflect on their own sociocultural contexts and interpret their eucharistic experiences from postcolonial and political perspectives. In the first part of the lesson, a teacher shows and explains a picture of *The Last Supper* by Leonardo da Vinci as the standard picture for teaching the Eucharist. The following questions from the teacher's explanations based on da Vinci's picture focus on Jesus' passion and death for the forgiveness of human sin.[35] In the second part of the lesson, the teacher asks students two questions, as follows. "In the light of the event of Jesus' suffering and death, what are students' responsibilities in their daily lives as Jesus' disciples?" "In the light of the event of Jesus' suffering and death, what are the changes in the students' thinking of themselves as Jesus' disciples?"[36] That is, even though Korean Presbyterian students participate in Western culture–centered, hierarchical, patriarchal, and twofold anthropocentric eucharistic practices in the Eucharist according to eucharistic texts from the BCW [PCK], the class of the Eucharist does not have any space for students to critically reflect on their life experiences from their sociocultural contexts, including eucharistic experiences from postcolonial and political perspectives.

---

consciously and intentionally presented and taught by the teachers, the implicit curriculum (or hidden curriculum) includes the norms and values of educational environments where learning takes place.

33. Ibid., 83.

34. Ibid.

35. Curriculum Committee, *God's Kingdom* (*Middle School Group*), 81. In order for the reader to have access to the entire set of lessons regarding the Eucharist from *God's Kingdom* under examination, I reproduce it in the appendix of this book by translating it into an English version.

36. Ibid., 82. See the appendix for my translation of curriculum texts on the Eucharist from *God's Kingdom*.

A historically accurate depiction of Jesus' Last Supper would depict the meal culture of the Mediterranean society of Jesus' time, but *The Last Supper* instead depicts the Western meal culture of da Vinci's time. The use of this painting in the *God's Kingdom* curriculum sends the message to students that Western culture is normative for eucharistic practices in terms of eucharistic foods, posture, and environment. For example, da Vinci's painting portrays that the disciples do not recline on couches but sit in chairs.[37] There are small loaves of bread and glasses of wine on the table, which is not round but long and rectangular. Moreover, the null curriculum of sociocultural study of the Mediterranean society of Jesus' period deprives Korean students of the chance to learn historical, cultural, and biblical roots of the Eucharist. Also, it reinforces an understanding of the Western meal culture as the most appropriate culture for the Eucharist.

From a political perspective, da Vinci's painting depicts hierarchy rather than equality among Jesus' disciples at the eucharistic table. At the long rectangular table, some disciples have a seat near Jesus and others do not. For Korean students who have lived under a strong hierarchical society, the different distance from the host is correlated to the hierarchical rank of the people at the table. In general, at a Korean traditional meal table, the host has a seat at the center and guests sit next to the host according to their sociopolitical ranks hierarchically and patriarchally. In the absence of any sociocultural investigations of the picture, Korean students may misunderstand the eucharistic table as the table of inequality and injustice among participants. According to Smith, this issue of equality and justice at a meal table was a concern in the Gospels as well as at Greco-Roman banquet meals. In his book *From Symposium to Eucharist*, Smith points out that meals in ancient Mediterranean society, including the Christian Eucharist, came from a common banquet tradition[38] and that the ancient banquets echoed "social codes" in the Greco-Roman world, such as social bonding, social obligation, social stratification, and social equality.[39] Smith

---

37. Smith, *From Symposium to Eucharist*, 46.

38. Ibid., 3. Smith suggests a new model for the understanding of "common banquet tradition" in consideration of the relation between meals in New Testament and their socio-cultural context. That is, he understands that meals in the ancient world—such as everyday meals, symposia, funerary banquets, sacrificial meals, mystery meals, everyday Jewish meals, Jewish festival meals, Christian Agape, and Christian Eucharist—do not come from separated different forms of meals but from the common banquet tradition from a socio-cultural, historical perspective.

39. Ibid., 5–6.

deals with the historical Jesus, focusing on Mark's understanding of the banquet ("the banquet of the king")[40] as compared to Luke's understanding ("the philosophical banquet").[41] He argues that Jesus created new communities at this table in terms of social equality, social openness, social obligation, and social bonding. Smith also maintains that Paul's banquet ideology was not separated from the Greco-Roman meal traditions but basically related to them because the community meal—in Antioch, Corinth, and Rome—was understood as the place of social equality, social bonding, social ethics, and social stratification.[42]

In terms of postcolonial and political issues, the null curriculum of a middle school lesson on the Eucharist does not provide students with any room or challenges to respond with appropriate actions to their specific local issues in the context of both the Eucharist and their daily lives with attention to the issues of liberation, justice, and equality. As I determined in chapter 3, the current eucharistic texts from the BCW [PCK] are Western culture–centered, hierarchical, patriarchal, and twofold anthropocentric. It is clear that the null curriculum also exists in these Eucharist materials. In this learning environment, Korean students are socialized to regard political and postcolonial issues as unimportant, even inappropriate for the contents of teaching the Eucharist.

In this sense, the null curriculum in *God's Kingdom* and eucharistic texts deprives Korean Presbyterian students of a chance to explore, reflect, and cope with their specific local issues in the context of education on the Eucharist. The use of these materials may cause Korean Presbyterian students to see their own sociocultural contexts and eucharistic experiences as unrelated, insignificant, or possibly inappropriate to their learning of the Eucharist.

Separation between Christian Education and the Eucharist

Berns' ecological socialization pedagogy regards ritual as one of the socializing vehicles in the process of individual socialization. Since a ritual in a religious community helps individuals learn, practice, and obtain the religious community's norms, customs, stories, and values, it is a multilayered socializing vehicle that is not limited to the religious community

40. Ibid., 240.
41. Ibid., 253.
42. Ibid., 174.

but connected to and interacting ecologically with other socializing agents belonging to microsystems, mesosystems, exosystems, and macrosystems. Within the multiple dynamics among ecological socialization structures, individuals' socializing experiences through the religious ritual cannot be separated or marginalized from a curriculum as a sociocultural text.

In this respect, the Eucharist, as one of the most important Christian rituals, should not be separated or marginalized from curriculum. However, *God's Kingdom* as the current curriculum series book of the Presbyterian Church of Korea clearly shows the strong tendency of separation between Christian education and the Eucharist. When I examine the contents of the curriculum, only two groups out of ten—the third- and fourth-grade group and the middle school group—deal with the Eucharist as a part of teaching contents. Furthermore, in both groups, only one out of fifty-two instructional weeks includes the Eucharist.[43] In accordance with *God's Kingdom*, if a person takes a Bible study class in Sunday school throughout his or her whole life, from nursery to older adult, in the Presbyterian Church of Korea, he or she will have a chance to learn the Eucharist for only two weeks: the first week during his or her third- and fourth-grade year and the second week of his or her middle school years. If the congregation member learns the Eucharist in extra classes such as a confirmation class for youth and/or an infant baptism preparation class for parents, he or she will have at most only one or two more opportunities to learn about the Eucharist through the extra classes.

For the relationship between Christian education and liturgy, many Christian educators such as John H. Westerhoff, Thomas Groome, Byron Anderson, Chang Bok Lim, and Sang Jin Park emphasize the formative characteristics of liturgical practices as significant educational practices. In his book *Will Our Children Have Faith?*, Westerhoff emphasizes Christian ritual as the heart of Christian education in that it not only transmits and sustains a faith community's customs, values, and beliefs but also gives a meaning and goal for individual life both in church and in the world.[44] Thus, he insists that educational ministry needs to help people to understand, prepare, and participate in rituals both in church and in the world, such as Sunday worship services and rites of passage. In his book *Sharing Faith: A Comprehensive Approach to Religious Education and Pastoral Ministry*, the

---

43. Curriculum Committee, *God's Kingdom* (*Third and Fourth Grade Group*), 5; *God's Kingdom* (*Middle School Group*), 5.

44. Westerhoff, *Will Our Children Have Faith?*, 58.

Way of Shared Praxis Groome argues that Christian liturgy is a source of forming and transforming congregation members' Christian life in church and their social contexts, to guide them to express their faith in a visible and tangible way, and to empower them to live their lives based on mission and justice.[45] In his book *Worship and Christian Identity: Practicing Ourselves*, Anderson notes that Christian worship teaches people in the process of liturgical practice. According to Anderson, a congregation member's identity is formed, shaped, and reformed socially through participation in liturgical practices, which are constitutive and normative, particularly those which come from their sociolinguistic religious culture.[46] In her book *Worship Education Program for the Successful Ministry*, Lim and K. J. Kim underline that God nurtures the faith of God's people and enhances it in the faith community through their participation in Christian liturgy.[47] The Eucharist, as one of the external means of God's grace, is where God leads people to have heavenly food and to form and transform their life style and values within the eucharistic community.[48] In his book *A Search for Christian Education Curriculum*, Sang Jin Park explains that Christian worship is one of the most important educational contexts because Christian education can help people know God better and participate in the presence of God within the sense of community through liturgical practices.[49] As Park describes the formative characteristic of Christian worship in terms of the formation of faith, he stresses that Christian worship must not be used to support educational goals, but instead Christian education needs to support Christian worship so that people may encounter and praise God more fully.

With this understanding of ritual as one of the most influential socializing vehicles in the process of an individual's Christian socialization, the strong tendency of separation between Christian education and the Eucharist may cause the curriculum of the Presbyterian Church of Korea to overlook one of the most significant educative contents and contexts. For this reason, both teachers and students in the Presbyterian Church of Korea may understand the Eucharist as a secondary or even optional content in

---

45. Groome, *Sharing Faith*, 347–48.
46. Anderson, *Worship and Christian Identity*, 123.
47. Kim and Lim, *Worship Education Program*, 10.
48. Ibid., 11.
49. S. J. Park, *Search for Christian Education Curriculum*, 263.

the curriculum of Christian education rather than as one of the essential educational contents linking to their multilayered socialization process.

Lack of Reflection on Students' Ecological Sociocultural Life Experiences

When I analyze *God's Kingdom* and the BCW [PCK] in light of Berns' ecological socialization pedagogy with attention to a postcolonial perspective, I find that in both there is a lack of reflection of students' life experiences based on their sociocultural contexts. The failure to incorporate reflections of students' life experiences is related to Korean history, or what Berns would call the "chronosystem" of the Presbyterian Church of Korea, such as early missionaries' propagation of the gospel, Japanese imperialism, the Korean War, military government, and the cramming system of education. Since the beginning of the Presbyterian Church of Korea, Christian education has been practiced and developed by foreign missionaries using the Nevius Methods, focusing on effectively conveying the information of Christian doctrines and Bible stories to non-Christians in Korean society.[50] For this reason, most Korean Presbyterians have understood the Bible as the only primary resource, learned through cognitive, information-centered, and deductive teaching methods.

Under Japanese imperialism (1910–1945) and the Korean War (1950–1953), harsh political oppression and severe economic conditions influenced the Presbyterian Church of Korea to focus on hope for eternal life after death in liturgies.[51] The Japanese government prohibited the Presbyterian Church of Korea from offering any political resistance against Japanese imperialism in the Sunday worship service and Bible study. Many Korean Presbyterians who resisted Japanese oppression by breaking the political restrictions were imprisoned or martyred. After the Korean War, severe poverty influenced Korean Presbyterians to find hope for the future not so much in their daily lives as in the promise of eternal life after death. In this situation, the reality of the lives of the congregants, such as political and economic injustice, was marginalized from Korean Presbyterian worship and Bible study. It reinforced a dichotomous understanding of the church and the world.

50. C. S. Park, *Influence of Confucianism*, 28; Clark, *Korean Church and the Nevius Methods*, 33–34.

51. E. K. Park, "Political Activism of Korean Churches," 199.

Educational Foundations for an Alternative Eucharistic Pedagogy

In the 1970s and 1980s, in an effort to suppress opposition to its policies, the military government of South Korea made laws prohibiting public schools and churches from mentioning and interpreting any sociopolitical issues.[52] In public education, this policy restricted the contents of teaching in public school only to public texts that had been already censored by the government. In churches, the military government restricted sermons, liturgical texts, and curriculum materials only to Christian doctrine and the Bible. Under these limitations, teaching in the church came to focus on conveying the information of Christian doctrine and the Bible deductively and cognitively. As the education system in both public schools and churches developed over several recent decades of Korean sociopolitical contexts, goal-oriented and instrumental teaching became a distinguishing characteristic of Korean public education.[53] In this respect, the lack of reflections of students' life experiences in *God's Kingdom* and the eucharistic texts from the BCW [PCK] echoes the limited understanding of students' eucharistic socialization agents in the Sunday school classroom and at the table of the Eucharist, focusing on the dynamics between the Bible, the teacher, and students. In the context of education, the result of these cultural tendencies is a marginalization, not only of Korean Presbyterian students' life experiences from sociocultural contexts, but also of teaching strategies, which are narrow, information conveyance–centered, deductive, and instrumental.

In this respect, first, *God's Kingdom* shows that there is no space for students' life experiences to be reflected on, shared, or discussed in a class regarding the Eucharist for both the third- and fourth-grade group and the middle school group in terms of learning objectives and methods. With regard to learning objectives, a lesson plan in *The Companion Book to God's Kingdom* for the third- and fourth-grade group outlines that the learning objectives of the Eucharist lessons are for the students to listen, to remember, and to retell the story of Jesus' last supper focusing on his passion and death for the forgiveness of our sins in the class.[54] These instructional materials do not make any reference to reflections on the learning of the Eucharist in the classroom or experiences at the eucharistic table. With regard to teaching method, lesson plans both in *The Companion Book to God's Kingdom* for the third- and fourth-grade group and for the middle

52. Ibid., 204.
53. Huh, "Problems and Prospects," 4.
54. Curriculum Committee, *Companion Book (Third and Fourth Grade Group)*, 55.

school group describe the role of a teacher as an information giver who leads students to find appropriate answers from the Bible verses to questions about the Eucharist, focusing in the classroom on Jesus' passion and death.[55] In the lesson on the Eucharist, there are no pedagogical practices to help the students reflect on or connect the information of the Eucharist in a class to their life experiences from their sociocultural contexts.

In both of these important curriculum documents, the lack of reflection on students' life experiences is closely related to the limited understanding of students' eucharistic socialization agents, only focusing on the mono-relationship[56] between the teacher and students in a class on the Eucharist and at the table of the Eucharist, in terms of that class-limited microsystem. In *God's Kingdom*, for the third- and fourth-grade group and the middle school group, the limited understanding of students' socialization agents is easily observed in the teachers' questions. Eleven out of thirteen questions are short-answer questions composed deductively from the teacher's explanation of Jesus' suffering and death, checking the students' cognitive remembering of Jesus' words and actions at the Last Supper.[57] In the limited understanding of the Sunday school class as the only socialization agent of students who learn the Eucharist, ignoring or marginalizing other socialization agents not only belonging to the microsystem but also interacting with the mesosystem, exosystem, and macrosystem, the Bible story of Jesus' Last Supper and death is understood as the only primary resource for the teaching of the Eucharist. With this limited focus on the relationship between the teacher and students with attention to the conveyance of the Bible story, the teaching of the Eucharist becomes teacher-centered rather than a collaborative effort between the teacher and students. In *God's Kingdom* and its companion books, whereas the teacher is described as an initiating, active leader who engages himself or herself in the process of presenting and exploring the biblical, theological, and pastoral meanings of the Eucharist as well as conveying them in the class, students are described as passive followers who depend on questions given by their teacher. For

---

55. Ibid., 55–57; Curriculum Committee, *Companion Book* (*Middle School Group*), 87–88.

56. The phrase "mono-relationship between the teacher and students" refers to the teacher's relationship with students depending on the teacher's single, authoritative, and hierarchical teaching and not reflecting students' local contexts in the contents of teaching, and without any communication with their socialization agents or environments.

57. Curriculum Committee, *God's Kingdom* (*Third and Fourth Grade Group*), 34–36; *God's Kingdom* (*Middle School Group*), 80–82.

Educational Foundations for an Alternative Eucharistic Pedagogy

example, the lesson plan for teaching the Eucharist for the middle school group in *God's Kingdom* depicts the importance of the teacher's role: to be fully aware of teaching contents such as the biblical stories of Jesus' last supper; to show the *The Last Supper* by Leonardo da Vinci as teaching supplementary material and ask questions; and to guide students to remember and restate what they heard through the teaching session.[58] *The Companion Book to God's Kingdom* for the third- and fourth-grade group for the teacher and ministers also emphasizes the teacher's preparation for teaching the Eucharist in terms of the ability to transmit and summarize the biblical information of Jesus' Last Supper, to control the students' attention, and to guide them to remember and restate what they learned from the session.[59] While presenting a description of the active role of the teacher, the curriculum materials make no account of the role of students in either book. Therefore, the class-limited understanding of the eucharistic socialization agent and the teacher-centered pedagogy focusing on conveying cognitive information of the Eucharist enforce the teaching of the Eucharist in the Presbyterian Church of Korea in a manner that overlooks and dismisses students' life experiences.

Second, the eucharistic texts from the BCW [PCK] also fail to link students' eucharistic practices to their life experiences from their ecological socialization environments. Only one out of eleven eucharistic prayers—prayer K—includes an opportunity for participants to reflect on their life experiences. Moreover, it involves just one brief, simple sentence, an opportunity to reflect on participants' microsystemic life experiences with attention to the sick and the weak in the end of the epiclesis: "May the Lord give (the Lord's) peace to the sick and the weak."[60] In the other ten eucharistic prayers there is no space for participants to reflect on their life experiences from their sociocultural contexts. In prayer B, there is one sentence that might be evaluated to indicate implicitly the reflection of Korean Presbyterians' macrosystemic life experiences, such as a political situation of armistice: "Let us be people [who] plant peace in this land."[61] However, since the sentence does not include any specific expressions regarding the real life experiences of Korean Presbyterians by words such as "unifica-

---

58. Curriculum Committee, *Companion Book* (*Middle School Group*), 87–88.

59. Curriculum Committee, *Companion Book* (*Third and Fourth Grade Group*), 55–56.

60. Reforming Committee, *Book of Common Worship* [PCK], 212.

61. Ibid., 68.

tion," it is not enough to conclude that prayer B includes an opportunity for participants to reflect on their life experiences from their sociocultural contexts. In this respect, the lack of reflections of students' life experiences in the eucharistic texts may cause the gap between eucharistic experiences in a sanctuary and their daily lives in the world to worsen into a separation; further, it may even exclude participants' socialization agents in their sociocultural contexts altogether.

Pedagogical Implications

Critical analysis of *God's Kingdom* and the eucharistic texts from BCW [PCK] in the view of Berns' ecological socialization pedagogy with attention to a postcolonial perspective demonstrates that the current curriculum of teaching of the Eucharist and students' eucharistic experiences in the Presbyterian Church of Korea have limited capacity to help students participate in the Eucharist actively with attention to the reality of their sociocultural contexts and reflect and live their daily lives as transformed eucharistic lives. The limited understanding of the boundaries of students' socialization agents in a class and their chronosystem within several decades may not facilitate their active participation in the educative contexts of the Eucharist, but may instead encourage them to be passive followers. The lack of critical reflection on students' multilayered socializing environments rooted in students' specific local contexts such as Confucianism and Western-oriented eucharistic practices may be fatal hindrances for Korean Presbyterian students to experience the Eucharist as an event that transforms their daily lives in the world. In this respect, critical analysis of *God's Kingdom* and the eucharistic texts from the BCW [PCK] through the critical conversations between Berns, Phan, and Lee offer the Presbyterian Church of Korea significant educational resources for the building of an alternative eucharistic pedagogy: (1) curriculum on the Eucharist as a process of ecological socialization, (2) critical reflections and actions on students' realities as essential teaching strategies, and (3) reforming the teaching on the Eucharist rooted in an Asian way of thinking.

First, the curriculum of the Eucharist needs to be reconceptualized as ecological socialization, in that students' learning experiences about the Eucharist are correlated to their ecological socialization environments. *God's Kingdom*, which is built on a non-contextual and information-centered curriculum, does not give students a chance to consider their sociocultural life issues from their ecological socialization environments as significant educational sources for a context curriculum. It mostly depends on receiving cognitive information about the Bible, with an emphasis on listening and memorizing the story of Jesus' suffering and death without any reflections of students' specific local contexts. This non-contextual learning experience may cause students to misunderstand the Eucharist as a past event to be memorized cognitively. However, the Eucharist is a transformative three-tense integrated event. It is not only to be remembered but also to be celebrated as a heavenly banquet with the anticipation of a new hope to overcome participants' life issues in the light of the triune God's grace. Therefore, teaching on the Eucharist needs to be contextual, incorporating students' realities from their sociocultural contexts. Students' eucharistic practices need to be reflected in their learning experiences in the process of multilayered examinations of their socialization environments. Contextual teaching on the Eucharist can help students understand the Eucharist as a life-transformative event empowering then to name and critically reflect on their life experiences as well as to cope with their life issues in the light of the triune God's gracious works around the table of the Eucharist in terms of creation, redemption, and liberation. Eucharistic experiences cannot be separated from the teaching about the Eucharist, and therefore liturgical contextualization will be essential to building the new eucharistic curriculum for the Korean Presbyterian Church. These changes may include the reformation of eucharistic texts, foods, music, clothes, gesture, movements, and space to more naturally reflect the local culture. Since liturgical contextualization regards Scripture as its essential source along with tradition, local culture, and social change,[62] an expanded list of scriptures with eucharistic themes needs to be included. In terms of the relevance of the texts to students' life experiences, scriptures with eucharistic themes may be discussed and chosen through critical conversations in the class about the Eucharist and used at the table of the Eucharist. This will help Korean Presbyterian students understand and participate in the Eucharist not as a past event to be recollected cognitively but as a formative event to reflect on, reinterpret, and reshape their life experiences creatively and critically in the light of the triune God's works at the table of the Eucharist.

Second, critical reflections and actions on students' realities from their sociocultural contexts are indispensable in the building of the curriculum

---

62. Schreiter, *Constructing Local Theologies*; Bevans, *Models of Contextual Theology*; Jo, "Asian Understanding of the Baptism."

of the Eucharist as essential teaching strategies because students' experiences of their sociocultural life contexts are continuously changing. In order for teachers to understand students' experiences of their specific life contexts, this collaborative work needs to happen through active and mutual communication between students and teachers in a class. The teacher will help students have critical conversations between their life stories and the meta-stories of the Bible, by using Phan's liturgical contextualization methods such as socioanalytic mediation, hermeneutical mediation, and practical mediation. With regard to Confucianism as a dominant macro-systemic socialization agent in Korean society, the teacher will help Korean Presbyterian students to recognize the influences of Confucian traditions and culture on their life experiences.[63] Through the conversation, these critical reflections deal not only with students' complicated situations of socialization agents such as their families, peers, schools, media, communities (microsystem) but also the social, economic, religious, political, and cultural changes from the direct and indirect interrelationships of socialization agents (mesosystem, exosystem, and macrosystem). The process of critical reflection may help students be ready to reinterpret what they experience in their local contexts and to discuss and share a new hope for the transformation of their real lives on the ground of the triune God's works at the table of the Eucharist. In this respect, the process of critical reflection and action as significant teaching strategies can be fulfilled in the collaborative relationship between teachers, students, and socializing mediators such as parents, school teachers, peers, and community members. Under the teacher-centered, hierarchical, deductive teaching atmosphere identified in the current Korean Presbyterian curriculum on the Eucharist, students do not have a safe space in the class to reflect and react to their real issues. Under the supportive, collaborative, and reciprocal relationship between the teacher and students as well as between the teacher and socialization mediators such as their parents, school teachers, peers, and community members, the critical reflection and action in students' life experiences can be practiced and fulfilled. Therefore, the critical reflection

---

63. Ching and Kung, *Christianity and Chinese Religions*, 85. Ching points to the Korean Christians' tendency to believe in God based on Confucian ways of thinking and living. "Whether they like it or not, Korean Christians . . . cannot but assert themselves as Christians of Confucian background and values. This implies . . . that Korean Christians, as long as they are Koreans as well as Christians, cannot avoid the religio-cultural legacy of Confucianism, which has been the sole cumulative tradition during the past five centuries in Korea."

and action through the collaborative works will provide a safe space for both the teacher and students to bring their life realities to the class about the Eucharist and at the table of the Eucharist and to reflect, reinterpret, and reform them creatively and critically.

Third, the context-based curriculum of the Eucharist allows Korean Presbyterian students to learn and experience the Eucharist not only through context-reflected contents but also through an Asian way of thinking. Because a Western culture oriented–liturgy is the current Korean Presbyterian liturgical norm, an ecological socialization understanding of students' learning experiences calls for this project to deal with students' eucharistic experiences from a postcolonial perspective and to reform the current Korean Presbyterian eucharistic pedagogy with attention to Korean students' epistemological approach to eucharistic experiences. Since an Asian way of thinking is one of the most fundamental elements for Korean Presbyterian students to interpret what they experience in their life contexts, a pedagogical imperative is the reformation of the curriculum on the Eucharist rooted in the Korean students' epistemology: an inclusive both/and way of thinking and a communal way of thinking. In the both/and way of thinking, all juxtapositions in the context of the teaching on the Eucharist need to be included in the process of reformation of a eucharistic pedagogy, not as supplementary elements but as complementary elements. For example, juxtapositions between God's stories and students' life stories, between eucharistic foods and daily meals, and between eucharistic experiences at the table of the Eucharist and Christian life in the world need to be considered and reflected inclusively in the curriculum of the Eucharist. From a communal epistemological perspective, the relationship of students' eucharistic learning experiences to their specific life realities needs to be understood to be reciprocal and inductive rather than hierarchical and deductive. These Asian epistemological approaches can be applied to the process of building an alternative eucharistic pedagogy for the Presbyterian Church of Korea, through a creative reformation of teaching objects, contents, methods, and environments. In this sense, the teaching on the Eucharist rooted in a Korean epistemology will help Korean students participate in the contexts of learning about the Eucharist actively by interpreting the Eucharist and practicing it from an indigenous epistemological perspective.

CHAPTER 5

Building a New Eucharistic Pedagogy for the Presbyterian Church of Korea

THIS BOOK SEEKS TO propose a new eucharistic pedagogy for the Presbyterian Church of Korea. In light of the extensive critique of current Korean Presbyterian eucharistic and curricular practices, this chapter seeks to build a reformed eucharistic pedagogy, including both classroom activities and the actual celebration of the Eucharist, in an effort to create life-reflected and life-transforming eucharistic pedagogy. Since the arrival of Christianity in Korea over one hundred years ago, the Eucharist has been celebrated by Korean congregation members in the Korean language in local churches. However, the Eucharist still seems foreign to many Korean Christians. With an overwhelming understanding of Western culture as the most appropriate culture for Christian liturgy and of Korean culture as an anti-Christian or idolatrous culture, Korean Presbyterians must set aside their Korean understandings of ritual in order to enter into Western culture–oriented eucharistic practices. After all, Western culture–oriented eucharistic practices have been recognized and practiced as sacrosanct traditional liturgical practices at the table of the Eucharist, reinforced through classes on the Eucharist in the Presbyterian Church of Korea. In this context, Korean congregation members' daily lives have been marginalized in class and at the table of the Eucharist whether consciously or unconsciously. In order to help Korean students participate in the Eucharist actively as a genuine formative liturgy for their faith and Christian life, the current Korean Presbyterian eucharistic pedagogy needs to be reformed critically and creatively with attention to the reciprocal relationship between students' eucharistic experiences and their specific local contexts.

Building a New Eucharistic Pedagogy for the Presbyterian Church of Korea

This chapter suggests a new eucharistic pedagogy with attention to Korean Presbyterian students' contextuality. As I mentioned chapters 1 and 4, with Berns' theory as a framework with attention to its pedagogical strategy, I propose a theoretical shift of eucharistic pedagogy: from deductive to inductive, from class-limited to life-reflecting, and from teacher-centered to student-collaborative teaching approaches. In light of Phan and Lee's liturgical contextualization work, the new eucharistic pedagogy deals with the reciprocal relationship between students' eucharistic experiences and their specific local contexts. The new eucharistic pedagogy envisions that Korean students not only recognize and proclaim God's continuous power and reign over their specific local contexts but also envision and respond to their lives together in the light of the gospel with new hope and actions at the table of the Eucharist. For the building of the new eucharistic pedagogy, first, I will formulate the definition of the new eucharistic pedagogy. Second, I will reconceptualize elements of the eucharistic pedagogy such as teaching contents, learning objectives, the role of the teacher, the role of students, and pedagogical strategies from a newly defined eucharistic pedagogy for the Presbyterian Church of Korea. Third, I will propose five steps for a new eucharistic pedagogy for the Presbyterian Church of Korea, including pedagogical guidelines for teachers and students. And finally, I will describe three generative educational principles for the Presbyterian Church of Korea based on a new eucharistic pedagogy.

Defining a Contextualized Eucharistic Pedagogy

On the basis of critical conversations between the current curriculum and eucharistic texts in the Presbyterian Church of Korea and an ecological socialization pedagogy with attention to the sociocultural contexts of students, I propose a contextualized eucharistic pedagogy as a new eucharistic pedagogy for the Presbyterian Church of Korea. I define a contextualized eucharistic pedagogy *as teaching strategies that help Korean Presbyterian students participate in the Eucharist actively as a formative liturgy with contextualized eucharistic practices by reflecting critically and responding creatively on their life experiences.*

In this definition, the word *formative* means giving a form or shape for students to experience God's grace in a tangible mode such as bread and wine, to express gratitude to God within a faith community, and to be empowered to live their lives as Christian lives in the world.

S. W. Kim understands that, at the table of the Eucharist, participants have an opportunity to be nurtured as Christians in terms of Christian faith and Christian life by participating in the four eucharistic gestures of taking, blessing, breaking, and giving.

Through these four eucharistic gestures, participants give their offering to God at the offertory (taking); recall God's works, express thanksgiving for God's grace, and invoke God's presence in eucharistic prayer (blessing); engage themselves in the passion of Jesus at the fraction (breaking); and participate in the resurrection of Jesus in hope and gratitude (giving). Paul Galbreath mentions that participants' Christian lives are shaped in the process of participating in the four eucharistic gestures: taking as "receiving," blessing as "invoking God's presence," breaking as both "dividing what we have" and "acknowledge[ing] the brokenness of our lives and our need to seek God's healing," and giving as "self-giving."

Four eucharistic gestures provide the significant criteria of receiving, invoking, acknowledging, and self-giving for participants to be nurtured as Christians both at the table of the Eucharist and in the world. As Korean Christians begin to participate more actively in the Eucharist, their faith and lives will be nurtured in accordance with liturgical practices. A new eucharistic pedagogy identifies that the Eucharist is a *formative* liturgy for students' faith and Christian life.

The phrase *contextualized eucharistic practices* refers to eucharistic practices reflecting students' specific local contexts in view of an Asian way of thinking. In order to reflect students' local contexts, eucharistic practices need to be developed critically and collaboratively through ongoing conversations among the teacher, students, the eucharistic presider, and their other socialization mediators such as family members, peer groups, school teachers, and community colleagues. Since students' microsystems intrinsically have a mutual, interactive relationship with meso-, exo-, and macrosystems under the chronosystem of their daily lives, the critical conversations need to deal ecologically with the structures of the students' socialization process in their multilayered sociocultural contexts. Life-embedded eucharistic practices need to reflect ways of thinking rooted in the local society and culture, because students' socialization occurs not in the vacuum of a certain epistemology but on the ground of their culture and society. Therefore, *contextualized eucharistic practices* for the Presbyterian Church of Korea need to echo Asian ways of thinking such as both/and thinking and relational thinking, both at the eucharistic table and in the class on the Eucharist.

The phrase *reflecting critically* refers to remembering and reinterpreting what students have experienced in their daily lives and at the table of the Eucharist with attention to the presence of the risen Jesus Christ in daily life. At the table of the Eucharist, the risen Jesus Christ empowers participants to recall, anticipate, and participate in God's reign in the world with justice and equality.

In this respect, critical reflecting on students' life experiences challenges the oppressive aspects of Confucian traditions and culture that are deeply rooted in their lives to be discovered, reinterpreted, and liberated. In deep consideration of the current Korean Presbyterian eucharistic contexts, which are Western culture–oriented, sacrosanct, hierarchical, and male liturgist–oriented, the Presbyterian Church of Korea needs a new approach, one that incorporates postcolonial, political, and feminist perspectives with students' multilayered life experiences both in the church and the world.

The phrase *responding creatively* refers to actions taken after critical reflections on students' experiences both at the table of the Eucharist and in their daily lives through the creative process of ritualizing eucharistic practices. Ronald L. Grimes understands ritual not as static, structural, and conservative but as flowing, processual, and subversive. In order to emphasize the "processual phase in the life history of a rite," he uses intentionally the term "ritualizing" (the gerund form) for indicating "emergent constructed ritual" intentionally.

In this book, the term "ritualizing" refers to an ongoing process, requiring creativity and connection to people's life contexts rooted in ways specific to a particular culture, rather than a given and pre-established process based on a universal way.

Therefore, the phrase *responding creatively* through the process of ritualizing eucharistic practices means the creative contextual process of reform and evolution of eucharistic practices through critical conversation between current eucharistic practices and participants' specific local contexts. It must include two processes: critical examination of current eucharistic practices and planning of renewed eucharistic practices in light of participants' specific local contexts. The process of ritualizing needs to make progress not through the hierarchical, deductive acts of a few members who have authority and power but through collaborative acts by all participants' critical reflecting, reinterpreting, sharing, revising, and practicing ritual practices.

In order to build the process of collaborative, non-hierarchical, and creative ritualizing eucharistic practices, the new pedagogy pays serious attention to the critical role of the presider as a full, complete participant and partner. In the case that the teacher is not an ordained minister who presides at the Eucharist, unless the eucharistic presider participates in the whole process of ritualizing eucharistic practices as a participatory partner, co-reflector, and co-designer, the whole pedagogical process may end in futility and lead to separation or conflict between the class on the Eucharist and the table of the Eucharist. Furthermore, the ritualizing effects of the Eucharist need to include the process of participants' making a plan for commitments and actions in their daily lives as eucharistic lives both personally and communally. That is because the Eucharist is not a ritual of limited influence, one that is performed only within a specific place (the sanctuary) and a specific time (Sunday morning), but a ritual of extended influence, one that is practiced in participants' daily lives so as to be transformed into "the norm for the Christian life."

This pedagogy includes both the table of the Eucharist and the class on the Eucharist as the educational context of the Eucharist because learning the Eucharist takes place at both reciprocally. At the table of the Eucharist, students learn the Eucharist by participating actively. In the classroom on the Eucharist, they learn the Eucharist by reflecting and ritualizing critically and creatively. Through the ongoing, cyclic, and critical conversations between learning at the table of the Eucharist and in the classroom on the Eucharist, students learn the Eucharist as a formative liturgy as it relates to their faith and lives.

Reconceptualization of Eucharistic Pedagogy

The contextualized eucharistic pedagogy of the Presbyterian Church of Korea is accompanied by the reconceptualization of significant elements of eucharistic pedagogy in both its settings, the classroom and the table of the Eucharist. In a contextualized eucharistic pedagogy, the objective of learning is not information but transformation; the content of teaching is not text-oriented but life-reflected; the role of the teacher is that of critical reflection guide and collaborative reformer; the role of the eucharistic presider is that of participatory partner and co-teacher; the role of student is that of critical reflector, active actor, and co-celebrant; and pedagogical strategies are not seen as instructive but as dialogical.

Learning Objectives Not for Information but for Transformation

The contextualized eucharistic pedagogy recognizes the formation and transformation of students' faith and their Christian lives as its primary teaching objective. Christian education is not so much about the information of Christianity, Christian faith, and Christian life as it is about the formation and transformation of students' faith and lives. Whereas conveying the biblical, theological, and liturgical information about the history of the Eucharist may help students to understand Christian faith and Christian life cognitively, it cannot form and transform their faith and Christian life.

That is why faith and Christian life are not given by others as cognitive information but as God's gifts. They are not static but experiential. In this account, the primary learning objectives of a new eucharistic pedagogy for the Presbyterian Church of Korea cannot be simply a matter of information on the Eucharist, that is, the Eucharist as a repetition of the Last Supper focusing on Jesus' death and suffering, which appears clearly in the current Korean Presbyterian curriculum materials. The primary learning objectives need to be about the formation and transformation of students' faith and their Christian life. As the contextualized eucharistic pedagogy regards the formation and transformation of students' faith and their Christian life as primary learning objectives, it helps them to actively participate in the Eucharist as a formative liturgy while reflecting, reinterpreting, and reshaping their life experiences rooted in a Confucianism with a eucharistic view.

The Content of Teaching Not as Text-Oriented but Life-Reflected

The contextualized eucharistic pedagogy demands that the teacher reform the content of teaching from text-oriented to life-reflected contents. Just as contextual theology understands not only traditional loci of Scripture and tradition but also local culture and social change as essential resources of the theological enterprise, the contextualized eucharistic pedagogy considers the students' contextuality. It recognizes students' daily life experiences rooted in their specific contextual situations as essential pedagogical resources in terms of stories (the Bible's stories and students' life stories) and rituals (Christian traditions and students' daily rituals). The content of teaching needs to reach out to the entire realm of students' life experiences in terms of the ecological, political, social, religious, racial, gender, and cultural dimensions, because these socializing environments influence students' learning experiences of the Eucharist directly or indirectly.

The content of teaching is not fully established before the class on the Eucharist but is instead formed in the process of recalling and reflecting students' experiences, both in their daily lives and in the sanctuary. Therefore, the content of teaching of the contextualized eucharistic pedagogy needs to be life-reflected and text-based. For the life-reflected pedagogy, Korean Presbyterian students' life experiences from their entire local contexts need not be marginalized but echoed in the teaching contents recognizing Korean society deeply rooted in Confucianism. For the text-based pedagogy, the texts of the Bible, doctrines, and traditions regarding the Eucharist need not be text-oriented, as the only resource of the content of teaching regarding the Eucharist, but text-based, as significant conversation partners for students to reflect on and use in order to reshape their life experiences. In this sense, the contextualized eucharistic pedagogy of which the content of teaching is life-reflected and text-based provides a space within eucharistic texts to include Korean Presbyterian students' life experiences.

Teacher as a Critical Reflection Guide and a Collaborative Reformer

In the contextualized eucharistic pedagogy, the teacher functions as a critical reflection guide and a collaborative socialization facilitator. For a critical reflection guide, the teacher needs to assist students to reflect on their experiences including eucharistic experiences in the sanctuary and daily experiences in the world with critical questions connecting to students' socialization agents from their local contexts. In order to make and offer appropriate critical questions, the teacher needs to understand students' current situations based on accurate and sufficient information of students' multilayered local contexts, which are interwoven with micro-, meso-, exo-, and macro-systemic dimensions. For this reason, the teacher needs to have close networks with socialization mediators such as eucharistic presiders, family members, peer groups, school teachers, and community colleagues.

Since the socializing mediators can provide the teacher with information about students' current situations and issues as well as engage themselves in the socialization process in the world and at the eucharistic table, they can influence students' learning about the Eucharist directly and indirectly in terms of the learning of social values, norms, behaviors, skills, knowledge, attitudes, orders, and lifestyle.

Throughout the whole process of ecological socialization, socialization mediators are indispensible pedagogical companions who support students' learning of the Eucharist. In this respect, the teacher needs to be an effective pedagogical intermediator between students and their other socialization mediators, including the eucharistic presider. For the building of a close and secure bond with students' socialization mediators, the teacher needs to show his/her support through explicit and implicit ways, such as welcoming socialization mediators as pedagogical partners, contacting them regularly with careful attention to students' situations, and by being non-judgmental and non-possessive with regard to students' sharing.

Furthermore, the understanding of students' current situations demands that the teacher cultivate a close, collaborative bond with students because the secure attachment rooted in an affectional tie between the teacher and students helps create a safe space to recall together, reflect together, and reshape together the students' experiences.

Such a secure attachment requires a non-hierarchical atmosphere for the teacher and students to communicate with one another in the class on the Eucharist. However, even while the teacher maintains a non-hierarchical stance in the classroom, the authority of the teacher should be established, so that the teacher may serve as a guarantor of the safe place in the face of resistance by some students. Depending on the diverse teaching contexts and students' specific local contexts, the teacher may use Berns' various socialization methods when designing pedagogical strategies for the Eucharist.

In the role of socialization facilitator, the teacher needs to help students participate actively in the Eucharist by reflecting on their experiences critically and by reforming current eucharistic practices collaboratively with students in the light of critical reflections on students' experiences in their multilayered social contexts. In the process of reforming eucharistic practices, contextual theology's four essential resources are Scripture, tradition, local culture, and social change.

On this account, the teacher needs to be equipped to provide students with not only biblical information on the Eucharist but also historical, theological, and liturgical understanding of the Eucharist.

The reformation of the Eucharist as a collaboration between the teacher, students, and their socialization mediators does not marginalize the process of cognitive learning about the Eucharist. It is based, but not centered, on cognitive learning about the Eucharist. Thus, reformation of the Eucharist requires critical and creative conversations between cognitive learning about the Eucharist and empirical and collaborative reflections on students' experiences.

Eucharistic Presider as a Participatory Partner and Co-Teacher

In the new eucharistic pedagogy, both in the class on the Eucharist and at the table of the Eucharist, the role of the eucharistic presider is very important. That is because, on the occasion that the teacher is not an ordained pastor and the eucharistic presider is not sympathetic to liturgical contextualization, the Eucharist will be conducted in the old way, beyond the work of liturgical contextualization. This may set up deep cognitive dissonance for students who are in the class where the Eucharist is understood differently, with attention to their specific local contexts. In this respect, the eucharistic presider's positive stance on eucharistic contextualization is a precondition for the new eucharistic pedagogy. However, this presupposition regarding a eucharistic presider's positive stance on eucharistic contextualization cannot be guaranteed in the Korean church, because most Korean Presbyterians have become accustomed to participating in the Eucharist with the understanding of the Eucharist as sacrosanct, hierarchical, male liturgist–oriented, solemnized, marginalized, and Western culture centered. Therefore, in order to build supportive relationships with eucharistic presiders and to have a common understanding of liturgical contextualization, the teacher needs to develop a pedagogical partnership with the eucharistic presider theologically, liturgically, pedagogically, and pastorally.

From the beginning of planning the curriculum on the Eucharist, the teacher needs to have a common understanding of theological and liturgical contextualization through ongoing mutual conversations about the relationship between faith and culture, between worship and education, between liturgical experiences and Christian life, and between faith and culture. For these ongoing mutual conversations, the teacher may have regular meetings with the eucharistic presider regarding the inclusion of open, complicated conversations at the intersection of multilayered fields that the new eucharistic pedagogy covers, such as contextual theology, critical pedagogy, liturgical contextualization, Korean culture, Asian religions, ecological socialization theory, and pastoral issues. For these regular meetings, the teacher may employ the weekly worship feedback meetings, monthly worship committee meetings, or conference meetings regarding educational ministry. In this process, the teacher's sharing of students' current specific local contexts from their multilayered socializing environments may help the eucharistic presider have a common understanding and sympathy for the reality of the educational context regarding the Eucharist.

After establishing this close collaborative relationship with the eucharistic presider, the teacher needs to help the eucharistic presider to participate in both the class on the Eucharist and at the table of the Eucharist as a partner and co-teacher. As a participatory partner, the eucharistic presider engages himself or herself in the entire process of the new eucharistic pedagogy. In the class on the Eucharist, the eucharistic presider participates in the class activities by listening to students' particular local contexts and issues together, recalling eucharistic experiences together, examining them together, reforming together, and envisioning together.

As a co-teacher, the eucharistic presider collaborates with the teacher to guide students to reflect their life experiences, including eucharistic experiences, critically by helping the teacher ask students critical questions in the class on the Eucharist. Also, the eucharistic presider helps the teacher and students reform eucharistic texts and practices collaboratively, critically, and practically based on sound theological, liturgical, and pastoral foundations.

In the process of ritualization of the Eucharist, the eucharistic presider may provide students with not only biblical, theological information about the Eucharist but also pastoral information on the local church's specific sociocultural situations. During this process, the eucharistic presider becomes a co-designer with students and the teacher of the ritualization of the Eucharist. Moreover, it is the eucharistic presider who conducts the Eucharist with the newly ritualized eucharistic texts and practices at the table of the Eucharist. In this sense, the eucharistic presider is invited as a participatory partner and co-teacher both in a class on the Eucharist and at the table of the Eucharist throughout the whole process of generating the new eucharistic pedagogy.

Students as Critical Reflectors, Active Actors, and Co-Celebrants

In the contextualized eucharistic pedagogy, students are understood as critical reflectors, active actors, and co-celebrants who engage themselves both in the class and at the table of the Eucharist. As critical reflectors, students are called to participate in a class on the Eucharist by reflecting critically on their life experiences rooted in a Confucian-undercurrent lifestyle rather than to attend the class passively without making any connections to their daily lives. Moreover, this critical view toward students' experiences from their local contexts, such as Western-centered eucharistic practices and Confucianism, helps them participate in the Eucharist as a formative liturgy that challenges and transforms their daily lives. As active actors, students make critical reflections on their life experiences, and they respond with appropriate actions for the transformation of their issues from their specific local contexts. Since socializing environments are changing constantly, these actions are formed and practiced creatively both at the table of the Eucharist and in their daily lives. As eucharistic co-celebrants, the students are called to participate in the class and at the table of the Eucharist through collaborative work on the contextualization of their eucharistic practices. In class, students as co-celebrants have a chance to reflect on their eucharistic experiences along with the teacher and to reform eucharistic texts and practices with attention to their specific local contexts. At the eucharistic table, students as co-celebrants have a chance to participate actively with a eucharistic presider through contextualized eucharistic texts and practices. As students and a eucharistic presider give thanks together, eat together, and pray together with contextualized eucharistic texts and practices, they have an opportunity to remember students' life experiences together, reflect on them together, and envision them together in light of the gospel. In this way, students can be engaged as co-celebrants rather than "passive audiences" or followers.

Pedagogical Strategies Not as Instructive but as Dialogical

The contextualized eucharistic pedagogy rejects an instructive teaching and takes a dialogical teaching as a basic pedagogical strategy. As I criticized in chapters 2–4, Korean students' current eucharistic practices and learning experiences are Western culture oriented, sacrosanct, hierarchical, and patriarchal. These characteristics have been formed and reinforced with the teacher's instructive teaching methods, using a one-way, top-to-bottom, deductive approach to eucharistic teaching. In this educational context of the Eucharist, students do not have a safe space to bring their life experiences or issues in their learning process, reflect on them critically, and respond to them with critical thinking and actions. However, as the term "contextualized eucharistic pedagogy" indicates, the strategy of this eucharistic pedagogy can be basically understood as contextual. In order to make eucharistic pedagogy authentically contextual, it demands that both the teacher and the students have inductive, critical, and collaborative dialogues regarding students' specific local contexts. Since this dialogical approach to eucharistic teaching is correlated to a both/and way of thinking, student's active participation in these dialogues may change the teaching/learning atmosphere from exclusive to inclusive, from hierarchical to hospitable, and from teacher centered to collaborative.

In the process of active participation in these open dialogues including recalling and reflecting students' life experiences, students realize that they are called to be equal conversation partners with the teacher in a new eucharistic pedagogy. Their life experiences are welcomed to be recalled and linked to their learning of the Eucharist as essential pedagogical resources. Moreover, this dialogical approach to eucharistic teaching is correlated to a complementary relational way of thinking. Just as yin cannot exist by itself but it exists only in correlation to yang in yin-yang symbolic thinking, the process of dialogue presupposes that the relationship between learning about the Eucharist (in a classroom and at the Eucharist) and eucharistic life (in the world) needs to be understood not as conflicting dualism but as complementary dualism. Through this dialogical approach, focusing on the harmony between eucharistic learning and eucharistic living, the student's learning boundary may be extended from a classroom to their entire life contexts. In this way, the new contextualized eucharistic pedagogy reconceptualizes the pedagogical strategy of the Eucharist *from* an instructive method, that is, one-way, top-to-bottom, and deductive teaching approaches, *to* dialogical methods, that is, inductive, critical, and collaborative teaching approaches.

Reformation of Eucharistic Pedagogy

This new contextualized eucharistic pedagogy is built on the ground of the on-going, critical, and collaborative works between the teacher, students, and students' socialization mediators including the eucharistic presider, with attention to the real life experiences and specific local contexts of the students. This reformed, redefined, and reconceptualized pedagogy may be implemented in the classroom and at the table of the Eucharist in the Presbyterian Church of Korea, using these five concrete steps.

Building a Eucharistic Pedagogy for the Presbyterian Church of Korea

Five Steps of the Contextualized Eucharistic Pedagogy

This new contextualized eucharistic pedagogy draws upon Berns' life-reflecting pedagogy as a pedagogical strategy, but reconceives and modifies her Western pedagogy to be more effective in the specific local contexts of Korean Presbyterian students. I suggest reforming Berns' six-step model in light of Phan's inculturation methods and Lee's Asian epistemology from postcolonial, political, and feminist perspectives. Through the critical conversation between their life stories and the meta-stories of the Bible, this pedagogy helps students reflect on their specific local contexts in light of the gospel in the context of learning about the Eucharist.

My reformed Korean Presbyterian eucharistic pedagogy is composed of a five-step cycle: (1) ecological scanning of students' specific local contexts, (2) critical reflection on students' issues in light of eucharistic themes in scriptures, (3) contextual ritualization of eucharistic practices, (4) participation in the contextualized Eucharist, and (5) reaffirmation of commitment with plans for concrete actions.

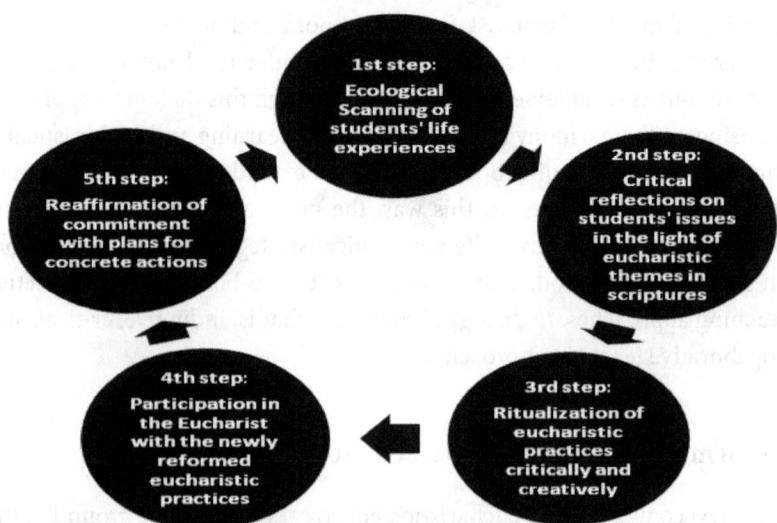

Figure 2: The Five-Step Cycle of the Contextualized Eucharistic Pedagogy

As students follow these pedagogical steps, they are guided to critical contextual conversations between their eucharistic experiences at the table of the Eucharist and their learning experiences in a class on the Eucharist with attention to their multilayered specific local contexts.

Building a New Eucharistic Pedagogy for the Presbyterian Church of Korea

First Step: Ecological Scanning of Students' Life Experiences

The first step is to scan the multilayered local contexts of the students from an ecological socialization perspective. This ecological scanning is a starting place on the way to a contextualized eucharistic pedagogy. Because a sound liturgical contextualization work requires both a liturgist and congregational members to be aware of their own local culture and contexts in depth, the first step is to try to help students, the teacher, and the eucharistic presider to recognize students' life experiences and issues together. In a class on the Eucharist, the teacher encourages students to share their life experiences in their specific local contexts with attention to their multilayered socialization environments. If the teacher is not an ordained pastor who presides over the Eucharist, the teacher invites the eucharistic presider to participate in this step as an active participant in sharing his or her own life experiences in the classroom. In the view of Asian epistemologies, which are not so much either/or as both/and and not so much analytic as dialogic, this step chooses students' autobiographical sharing as a pedagogical strategy rather than theoretical analysis. With an ecological socialization understanding of the relationship between individuals and society based on interdynamic processes as ongoing, reciprocal, communal, and creative works, the scanning of students' specific contexts through autobiographical sharing includes not only the complicated situations of socialization agents such as their families, peers, schools, media, communities (microsystem) but also the social, economic, religious, political, and cultural changes from the direct and indirect interrelationships of socialization agents (meso-, exo-, macro-, and chronosystem).

Because Confucianism is the most influential macrosystemic socialization agent in the local context of Korean Presbyterian students, the scanning process of their socialization environments pays special attention to Confucian influences. Special emphasis is placed on the family, since Confucianism has been formed around the two basic socio-moral and political ideologies of *Chung* (忠; loyalty) and *Hyo* (孝; filial piety) in Korean society. The family in Confucian society is the primary center of individuals' socialization in their daily lives.

In a strong Confucian Korean society, most individuals' socialization processes in their daily lives are dominated and controlled hierarchically and patriarchally by their family, whether explicitly or implicitly, in matters such as making friends, deciding on jobs, and even having a religious faith.

Thus, in the process of scanning students' life contexts, the family cannot be considered as just one of many microsystematic socialization agents such as peer groups, school, community, and media. The Confucian understanding of the family as the primary center of individual socialization needs to be applied not only to microsystemic socializing environments but also to meso-, exo-, and macrosystemic socialization environments. In terms of the family as the central locus of Confucian society, the reformed and reconceived teaching content needs to take serious account of students' experiences in their families. In this respect, for the new eucharistic pedagogy to be contextual with serious attention to Confucian influences on the dynamics among Korean Presbyterian students' socialization agents, the diagram of ecological socialization as suggested by Berns needs to be modified. The new structure of ecological socialization is what I call a "family-centered ecological socialization."

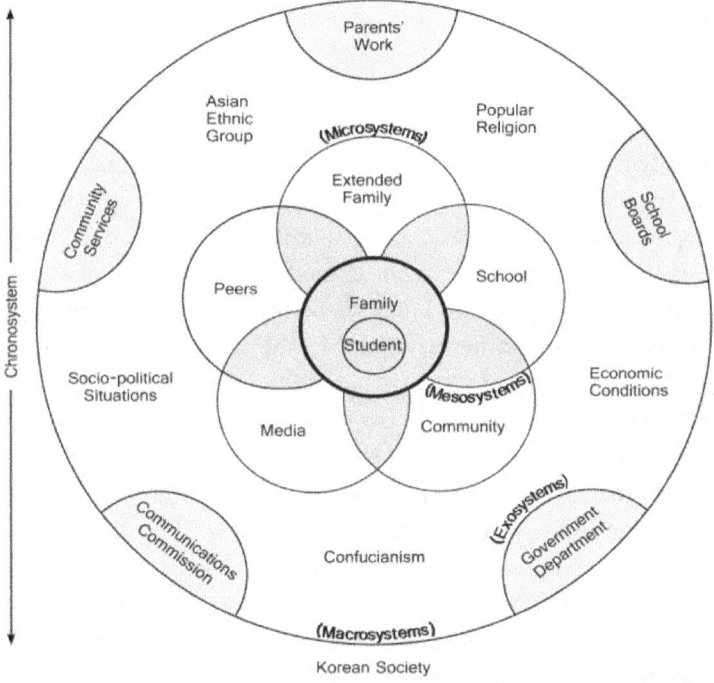

Figure 3: Contextualized Diagram of Korean Students' Ecological Socialization

In this diagram, the family is located at the center of the socializing process. This does not mean that the contextualized structure of ecological socialization supports the centrality of the biological family, nor that the scanning of students' life experiences based on the contextualized structure focuses on their family lives alone. The diagram identifies the position and role of the family as the hub of students' socialization process in a strong Confucian Korean society. It also shows that Korean students' family experiences are deeply correlated to their socialization process within other ecological socialization agents.

In this respect, the scanning of students' life experiences in light of a newly contextualized diagram encourages students to recall and share their ecological life experiences, including their eucharistic experiences, with attention to the family-centered ecological socialization process. The teacher needs to ask students questions about their life experiences, bringing serious attention to the correlations and influences of family lives on other socializing environments in terms of inequality and injustice. In the first step of a eucharistic pedagogy, the scanning needs to include the recalling of experiences and practices of the Eucharist. In the second and the third steps, later critical questions related to other socializing issues and themes such as hierarchicalism, ageism, patriarchalism, and classism can be related to the Eucharist. For effective dialogue with students in the classroom, the teacher needs to use active listening skills such as open-ended questions, verbally/nonverbally communicating empathic understanding, reflection of feelings, keeping silence, and positive regard.

This process offers students a safe place not only to examine critically their family lives, which previously have been easily accepted and socialized without any critical view, but also to realize that their family lives are mostly influencing their socialization process in Korean society. Through this process, the teacher demonstrates his/her support by providing students not only with emotional support such as caring, acceptance, a non-judgmental attitude, and non-possessive involvement, but also with adequate informational support regarding students' issues.

In situations in which the teacher is not a eucharistic presider, this process helps the eucharistic presider to understand students' specific local contexts more deeply and to have a common sympathetic ground of eucharistic pedagogy with the teacher and students. Depending on the students' particular issues, their socialization mediators who are involved in their issues directly or indirectly in their specific contexts, such as family members, peer groups, school teachers, and community colleagues, may be invited to be pedagogical supporters who know the students and who may share with the teacher information about students' daily lives. In the process of ecological scanning in a class on the Eucharist, the role of the teacher is not so much to analyze students' life experiences as to guide students to share and observe their own specific contexts critically and ecologically. In this step, the critical ecological scanning of students' life experiences based on the collaboration between the teacher, students, and students' other socialization mediators may enable the teacher, students, and the eucharistic presider to observe and face students' issues in light of their specific local contexts.

Second Step: Critical Reflections on Students' Life Experiences in Light of Eucharistic Themes in Scripture

The second step is to reflect on students' issues critically in light of eucharistic themes in Scripture in a class on the Eucharist. This process starts by choosing eucharistic themes in Scripture through open conversations between students and the teacher. The eucharistic themes in Scripture include not only the passages about the story of Jesus' Last Supper (Matt 26:26–30, Mark 14:22–26, Luke 22:14–20, and 1 Cor 11: 23–26) but also the stories of Jesus' ministries that are related to meals with Jesus. The stories of Jesus' meals with sinners, the story of five loaves and two fish, the story of two disciples on the road of Emmaus, the story of breakfast with Jesus at the sea of Tiberias, and the story of early church members' communal meals in their homes all exemplify eucharistic themes in Scripture. If the teacher is not an ordained pastor who presides at the table of the Eucharist, the teacher needs to invites the eucharistic presider to participate in these open conversations as a collaborative participant by observing students' dialogues and by helping the teacher provide biblical information about the eucharistic scriptures in the class on the Eucharist. In this process, the students must have a safe space to choose the eucharistic scriptures through open conversations focusing on the relevance of the texts to students' life experiences. The teacher also needs to provide a safe space to view the eucharistic themes in Scripture with suspicion with attention to students' oppressed situations from political, postcolonial, and feminist perspectives. Through the suspicion of the eucharistic themes in Scripture, students may have a chance not only to overcome conventional interpretations of eucharistic scriptures but also to link the Eucharist to their life issues in terms of justice and equality.

Building a New Eucharistic Pedagogy for the Presbyterian Church of Korea

Through this critical conversation between students' stories and eucharistic themes in Scripture and, a new perspective on students' life experiences may begin to be formed. It helps students have a chance to have a critical view on their life experiences, which are deeply rooted in a Confucian undercurrent lifestyle, in light of eucharistic themes in Scripture. For most Korean students, Confucianism has been considered as an absolute, sacrosanct lifestyle without any critical reflection.

For this reason, Korean people, whether Christian or non-Christian, rarely have an opportunity to examine their Confucian way of life—hierarchical, patriarchal, children marginalizing, text oriented, and tradition respecting as it is—from a critical perspective.

However, this step provides Korean students with a safe space to examine critically their life experiences rooted in Confucianism by reflecting on them in light of eucharistic themes in Scripture. With regard to the role of the teacher, the eucharistic themes in Scripture can be recalled and reflected through the process of collaborative conversations between the teacher and students. The teacher needs to help students reflect on their experiences in light of eucharistic themes in Scripture by asking critical questions. If the teacher is not an ordained pastor who presides at the table of the Eucharist, the teacher needs to encourage the eucharistic presider to participate in these conversations as a collaborative co-teacher who may ask critical questions to students in the class on the Eucharist. The following exemplify critical questions: "What are common grounds and differences between your daily meal tables with neighbors and Jesus' common meal tables with people?" "In the light of eucharistic themes in scriptures including the biblical story of the Good Samaritan, how often did your daily meal table express love and hospitality with your neighbors in terms of outcasts who are in need?"

Third Step: Ritualization of Eucharistic Practices Critically and Creatively

The third step is to ritualize eucharistic practices critically and creatively in a class on the Eucharist. In this step, the term ritualization means that Korean Presbyterian students and teachers examine current eucharistic practices and plan the renewed eucharistic practices by reinterpreting and reforming current eucharistic practices creatively with attention to their specific local contexts through a critical examination of eucharistic practices. For this process, I use the Nairobi Statement's four models about the relationship between culture and liturgy in order to examine and renew Korean eucharistic practices critically and creatively. The Nairobi Statement provides ecumenical guidance on culture and liturgy from a liturgical contextualization perspective by suggesting four models to approach the relationship between culture and liturgy: a trans-cultural model, a contextual model, a counter-cultural model, and a cross-cultural model.

If the teacher is not an ordained pastor who presides at the table of the Eucharist, the eucharistic presider must have a significant role as a participatory partner in the process of ritualization of eucharistic practices by reflecting together, examining together, and reforming together in the class on the Eucharist.

First, in view of a trans-cultural model, there are invariable elements in eucharistic practices beyond diverse local cultures. According to the Nairobi Statement, trans-cultural elements in Christian worship are defined as gathering together in God's name; Scripture reading; narratives of Christ's birth, ministries, death, resurrection, and ascension; shared eucharistic meals as God's gifts; and going out into the world for God's mission. In order to help students understand and discover the trans-cultural elements of eucharistic practices, the teacher not only reminds them of the sound biblical, theological, and liturgical information about the Eucharist that they learned in the second step, but also asks critical questions on their eucharistic experiences with attention to their trans-cultural elements, such as: "On the basis of the Bible and theological and liturgical traditions, what would be invariable elements of the Eucharist?" "In your eucharistic experiences in the past, what were core narratives and practices? Why?" If the teacher is not an ordained pastor who presides at the table of the Eucharist, the teacher needs to encourage the eucharistic presider to be a participatory partner who supports the teacher, supplements the teacher's classroom knowledge of eucharistic texts and practices, and asks critical questions. This model helps Korean students reflect on and learn the transcultural elements of the Eucharist in a class on the Eucharist and at the table of the Eucharist as it is experienced universally with other churches.

Second, from a contextual point of view, liturgical contextualization is regarded as an indispensible work in order for the gospel to be deeply rooted in Korean Presbyterian students' specific local cultures. A contextual model understands Jesus' incarnation as the theological and liturgical mandate of liturgical contextualization.

This approach emphasizes that the values and patterns of the specific culture of the students can be used for Christian liturgy as far as they correspond to the gospel's values and meanings. In this respect, the Nairobi Statement suggests dynamic equivalence and creative assimilation as useful methods of contextualization. The former is about contextual re-expressing of liturgical elements through the local community's thoughts, languages, and rituals. It avoids mere literal translation of text, word for word, without considering participants' specific local contexts. The latter is about socioreligious borrowing, from theological and liturgical perspectives, of relevant rites and terms from local culture. In both methods, a significant criterion is that local cultural elements need to considered and used with critical reflection in terms of theology, liturgy, and ministry. For this process, the teacher needs to guide students to discuss their eucharistic experiences by linking them to their own local cultures. "When you partook of eucharistic foods at the table of the Eucharist, did you recall meals in your daily life?" "As you participated in the Eucharist, did eucharistic texts, clothes, and music help you reflect on your life-experiences?" "During your last Eucharist, were there any eucharistic practices or elements that you felt were foreign?" "If some practices did not reflect your local culture in the Eucharist, how can we re-express them to link them to your local contexts?" This discussion guides students to present their own issues in the context of current eucharistic texts and practices and to provide a place to reform them by using methods of dynamic equivalence and creative assimilation. If the teacher is not an ordained pastor who presides at the table of the Eucharist, the teacher needs to invite the eucharistic presider into the classroom to collaborate in doing dynamic equivalence and creative assimilation together. Through the method of dynamic equivalence in the class, the teacher and the eucharistic presider may facilitate a conversation with students to reform eucharistic texts and practices critically by examining and comparing them with the relevant rites and terms of local culture. Furthermore, the teacher and the eucharistic presider may help students reform current eucharistic texts and practices creatively and collaboratively in light of theological, liturgical, and pastoral examination and comparison of local culture and Christian liturgy. In this context, the dialogues between students, the teacher, and the eucharistic presider in the classroom may enrich and supplement the reformed eucharistic prayer and practices at the table of the Eucharist in the future.

Third, in view of a counter-cultural model, whereas each culture has sinful components that are contrary to the values of the gospel implicitly or explicitly, Christian worship challenges and changes prevailing cultural patterns and values. Christian worship supports the transformation of selfish and dominant groups and powers from oppression to liberation in light of the message of gospel.

In this respect, Korean Presbyterian students may experience their active participation in the Eucharist as counter-cultural because it is different from the current prevailing Korean cultural patterns and values. In the course of this eucharistic experience, some prevailing cultural characteristics of Korean Presbyterian students' daily lives rooted in Confucianism may be recognized, challenged, and transformed in terms of hierarchalism, patriarchalism, ageism, and conventionalism. From this point of view, the teacher may ask critical questions. "As you participated in the Eucharist, did you see equality and hospitality among the eucharistic community?" "Which parts of the eucharistic practices were hindrances for you to participate in the Eucharist as a place of equality and hospitality? And how can we change that practically?" These questions encourage students to take a critical view of the current eucharistic texts and practices with attention to eucharistic values such as justice, equality, hospitality, and liberation. If the teacher is not an ordained pastor who presides at the table of the Eucharist, the teacher needs to encourage the eucharistic presider to participate in this critical conversation as a partner and active listener in the class on the Eucharist. The eucharistic presider may help the teacher ask critical questions on the eucharistic practices and listen to students' sharing by using active listening skills.

Through this dialogue, the teacher, the eucharistic presider, and students may identify those parts of eucharistic texts and practices that may run counter to core eucharistic values such as justice, equality, hospitality, and liberation. Further, this dialogue may provide an opening for them to reform eucharistic texts and practices critically and collaboratively, with attention to core eucharistic values in the classroom on the Eucharist.

Fourth, a crosscultural model focuses on the ecumenical characteristics of liturgical practices across cultural barriers. The sharing of eucharistic elements such as symbols, hymns, instruments, clothes, posture, and movement across culturally diverse settings may enrich eucharistic practices both globally and locally. This model enables Korean Presbyterian students to experience the cultural diversity of liturgical practices across different

Building a New Eucharistic Pedagogy for the Presbyterian Church of Korea

cultures and also to enhance the mutual respect between Christianity and local cultures at the Korean eucharistic table as a multicultural liturgical context.

A crosscultural understanding of the Eucharist may help students remember that, in the eucharistic elements and practices, there are contextual diversities rather than one authoritative single tradition and culture. The dialogue and sharing of crosscultural elements of the Eucharist may provide the teacher and students liturgical resources to reform eucharistic objects and practices that echo Korean students' multicultural liturgical context. In this process, the teacher needs to assist students to reflect and discover crosscultural elements of the Eucharist critically by asking the following question: "If congregation members from different cultures participated in the Eucharist with us last Sunday, which eucharistic elements would be easy for them to understand, and which would be difficult?"

In the process of reflecting on eucharistic practices through these four models of the Nairobi Statement, it is important to note that Asian epistemologies, such as the both/and way of thinking and communal way of thinking, are already reflected through each model's critical questions. They are not deductive (text oriented) and hierarchical (teacher centered) but inductive (life reflected) and reciprocal (collaborative between teacher, eucharistic presider, and students). In terms of the both/and way of thinking, juxtapositions at the table of the Eucharist such as between God's stories and students' life stories, between eucharistic foods and daily meals, and between eucharistic experiences at the table of the Eucharist and Christian life in the world are included in the critical questions. In the process of ritualizing eucharistic practices, students' specific sociocultural contexts in all their socializing environments will be considered critically as essential resources of liturgical contextualization reflected in order to reform eucharistic practices creatively. Korean folk songs, traditional literature, Korean foods, Korean arts, Asian architecture, Korean economic conditions, political situations, and social issues can be the very examples of them. Through the multilayered four critical lenses of the Nairobi Statement's four models, the students' local cultures and contexts are reflected on and incorporated into eucharistic texts, eucharistic objects, eucharistic action, music, space, and eucharistic atmosphere, critically and creatively. For example, eucharistic texts such as the eucharistic invitation, eucharistic prayer, the Words of Institution, and prayer after Communion will be reformed, focusing on the contextuality of eucharistic texts that link, reflect, and express Korean Presbyterian students' life issues to the eucharistic scriptures.

Eucharistic objects such as eucharistic foods, the eucharistic chalice and plate, table cover, clothes, and music need to be contextualized with attention to their cultural appropriateness to reflect Korean Presbyterian students' local cultures and daily lives. Eucharistic actions and space such as a presider's and congregation members' gestures, movements, and posture at the table of the Eucharist will remain or be reformed with serious consideration of whether or not they help participants experience eucharistic values such as thanksgiving, hospitality, equality, and justice. In terms of communal ways of thinking, these contextualized works of eucharistic practices are attained by the collaborative works between the teacher and students. If the teacher is not an ordained minister, the teacher needs to invite the eucharistic presider into these pedagogical activities in the classroom as a participatory partner and co-designer for the next celebration of the Eucharist. The eucharistic presider may engage himself or herself in this step by recalling earlier eucharistic experiences together with the students, discerning and categorizing them together, reforming them together, and designing the next Eucharist together in light of the eucharistic reflection on students' life experiences. This step of ritualization of eucharistic texts and practices includes a concrete, detailed plan for the next celebration of the Eucharist, such as making rice cakes, decorating the sanctuary and the table, and proposing new servers, words, actions, and gestures. In this process of ritualizing the Eucharist, the teacher and the eucharistic presider encourage students to participate actively in the work of contextualization by designing the next eucharistic celebration together with students' arts, photos, clothes, or things that reflect their specific local contexts from their home and classroom, bringing them to the table of the Eucharist, and using them as parts of the eucharistic ritual. If the plan for the preparation of the Eucharist is not available within the eucharistic community, the eucharistic presider needs to help the teacher and students make a new plan, providing pastoral situations within the eucharistic community as well as theological and liturgical concerns.

Fourth Step: Participation in the Contextualized Eucharist

The fourth step is to participate in the Eucharist that has been newly envisioned and ritualized through the previous three steps. The eucharistic presider leads the Eucharist with contextualized eucharistic texts and practices. At this eucharistic table, students' experiences from their specific local contexts are understood not as secondary, peripheral resources but as essential, primary resources at the table of the Eucharist.

As students participate in contextualized eucharistic texts and practices reflecting their specific local contexts, such practices will help Korean Presbyterian students participate actively in the Eucharist as a formative liturgy by reflecting on, reinterpreting, and reshaping their life experiences critically and creatively through life-reflected eucharistic practices and Asian epistemology. In the course of participating in the contextualized Eucharist, students will have a safe environment to recall and reflect ecologically on their life issues that are deeply rooted in a hierarchal, patriarchal, and conventional Confucian way of life. Through critical reflections on their own life issues with newly contextualized eucharistic texts and practices, students may have a new hope for God's reign in their daily life contexts and join a eucharistic prayer including a new dedication to future actions in their daily lives. With regard to Asian epistemological approaches to the Eucharist, the eucharistic practices dealing with eucharistic juxtapositions based on the both/and way of thinking may help Korean Presbyterian students understand the relationship between liturgical experiences and liturgical lives not as separate but as reciprocal. The eucharistic practices celebrated by all participants collaboratively in the view of communal ways of thinking may help students participate in the Eucharist as active co-celebrants.

Fifth Step: Reaffirmation of Commitment with Plans for Concrete Actions

The last step is to reaffirm students' commitments and make plans for concrete actions. After students have participated in the Eucharist, they are invited to have a critical review time in a class on the Eucharist. Since the Eucharist itself is a form of commitment, in this class, the teacher may help students reaffirm their commitments by encouraging them to reflect on what they experienced at the table of the Eucharist both personally and communally. In this process, the teacher needs to use appropriate communication skills such as open-ended questions, non-judgmental questions, non-possessive involvement, and positive reinforcement.

Based on this critical review of students' new hope and new visions through their eucharistic experiences, students are called on to make practical plans for their actions for transformative Christian lives. These plans will identify concrete actions for students to cope with their own issues in their specific local contexts, both at the church and in the world. The students' commitments and actions regarding the transformation of their daily lives as eucharistic lives can be supported and anticipated in various ways, such as writing a journal, making a verbal resolution to cope with their issues, praying a group prayer created with fellow students, singing songs with new lines reflecting students' plans, collaboratively drawing pictures reflecting their new visions, and making practical lists to do in their multilayered socializing environments. Moreover, Korean indigenous cultural elements such as art, hymns, musical instruments, gestures, and postures can be used in various ways to express students' commitments and actions.

These commitments and actions are disruptive to a hierarchical, patriarchal, Confucian-dominated culture. However, students will return to that culture in their daily lives. In order to support students' resistance of that culture, the teacher needs to help students to make commitments and take actions collaboratively with one another in the classroom and with socializing mediators in their entire socialization environments in terms of micro-, meso-, exo-, and macrosystems. In this step, parents, siblings, other family relatives, school colleagues, school teachers, church friends, church session members, school board members, and local politicians can be the examples of their socializing mediators. As the students engage in these collaborative commitments and actions, socializing mediators may play important pedagogical roles as companions, partners, supporters, and fellows.

Since this pedagogy is cyclical, the fifth step returns to the first step via students' new eucharistic lives reflecting on their commitments and actions in their daily lives. When the pedagogical cycle begins again from the first step in a classroom, the newly ritualized eucharistic practices become the typical eucharistic practices to be recalled, reflected, and reformed again in the five steps of eucharistic pedagogy. Through these cyclical steps, this eucharistic pedagogy may guide students to learn about the Eucharist as an ongoing critical, creative, and contextualized process between eucharistic learning (in a classroom and at the sanctuary) and eucharistic life (in the world).

Building a New Eucharistic Pedagogy for the Presbyterian Church of Korea

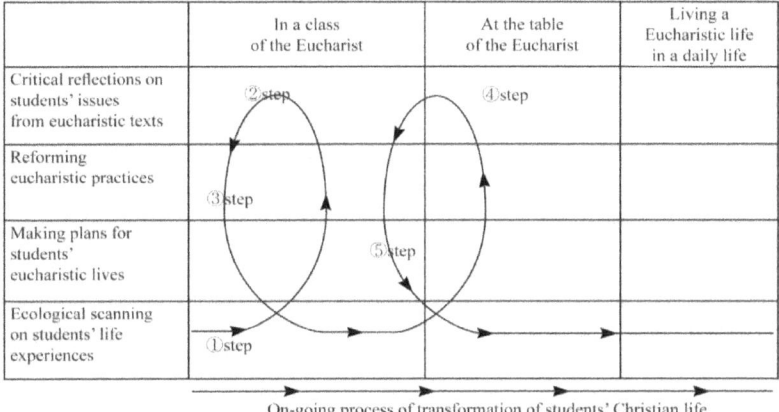

Figure 4: The Five-Step Cycle of Eucharistic Learning

Three Generative Educational Principles from the New Eucharistic Pedagogy

This book suggests a contextualized eucharistic pedagogy through the reformation of eucharistic practices rooted in ways specific to Korean Presbyterian students' local culture from a critical view. Throughout the process of designing this new eucharistic pedagogy focusing on contextuality, I find three generative educational principles: (1) to be inclusive rather than exclusive, (2) to be dialogical rather than instructive, and (3) to form rather than transmit.

Principle One: To Be Inclusive Rather than Exclusive

This newly contextualized eucharistic pedagogy built on the ground of the both/and way of thinking guides students to approach their learning experiences on the Eucharist from an inclusive perspective. Whereas students' specific local contexts are marginalized in typical Christian education settings, including classes focused on the Eucharist and at the table of the Eucharist in the Presbyterian Church of Korea, they are valued as primary resources in the contextualized eucharistic pedagogy. As the new eucharistic pedagogy understands students' life experiences as essential resources for the eucharistic pedagogy with attention to contextuality, it helps students rediscover the multiple juxtapositions of their life experiences throughout the five steps of the contextualized eucharistic pedagogy built based on the both/and way of thinking.

From an inclusive perspective, students have an opportunity to observe and view their life issues through multiple lenses. In the first step of the ecological scanning of students' local contexts, students may recognize that all their life experiences in each socializing agent are interrelated. Furthermore, this inclusive perspective helps students extend their understanding of the boundaries of eucharistic pedagogy from class-limited learning to life-reflecting learning. Through an ecological understanding of their own local contexts, Korean Presbyterian students may realize that their life experiences in Confucian society, especially family experiences, are not independent from learning about the Eucharist but interrelated and connected, directly or indirectly.

In the second step of critical reflections on students' issues in the light of a eucharistic view, multiple juxtapositions that exist in the Eucharist may be discovered: biblical stories and students' life stories, eucharistic foods and daily meals, a eucharistic community in a church and secular communities in the world, eucharistic practices at the table and ritual practices in society, and so on.[1] Through the process of critical reflection based on an inclusive perspective that unites liturgical experiences and liturgical life, juxtaposed elements can be understood to be complementary to each other in the Eucharist, in terms of the inseparable relationship between Christian life and Christian liturgy. For example, an inclusive approach to dealing with the juxtaposition of the biblical stories and students' life stories will help students understand the biblical stories as meta-stories, which do not make students' life stories silent but guide students to experience the presence of God at the table of the Eucharist. For the juxtapositions between eucharistic foods and daily meals, the inclusive approach assists students in finding sacred moments from their daily meal tables such as a soup kitchen, a dinner with neighbors, a lunch with newcomers in a church, and a cultural community banquet.[2]

---

1. Lathrop, *Holy Ground*, 66–67.

2. D. Smith, *From Symposium to Eucharist*, 216; Galbreath, *Leading from the Table*, 27. Smith understands that there are correlations between eucharistic meals in the New Testament and daily meals in the Greco-Roman society as their sociocultural context. That is, eucharistic meals were formed and developed in the process of interdynamic influences between Christianity and Greco-Roman socioculture. For example, Smith asserts that Paul's banquet ideology was not separated from the Greco-Roman meal

In the third step, ritualization of the Eucharist, an inclusive approach enables existing eucharistic practices in the Presbyterian Church of Korea as Christian traditions to be authentically contextualized. Under the basic understanding of the reciprocal relationship between eucharistic practices at the table and ritual practices in a society, the existing Korean eucharistic practices may continue to be ritualized through critical conversations with students' specific local contexts in the class on the Eucharist. Through dynamic interactions with students' life experiences, the existing traditional eucharistic practices can be creatively reformed by students' active participation in the Eucharist, rather than formally repeated with no echoes of their own contexts at the table of the Eucharist.

The inclusive approach also is applied to the fourth and fifth steps of the contextualized eucharistic pedagogy. In the course of participating in the Eucharist with renewed eucharistic practices dealing with eucharistic juxtapositions inclusively, those daily life experiences that are connected to prevailing sinful, dehumanizing cultural patterns and values may be reflected critically in the light of a eucharistic view. Through their eucharistic experiences, students may be challenged and empowered to cope with their own issues from their specific local contexts with new hope, just as they are guided to make plans for concrete commitments and actions for transformative Christian lives.

As I pointed out in previous chapters, Korean Presbyterian students' life experiences have been marginalized in a context of eucharistic pedagogy both in classes on the Eucharist and at the table of the Eucharist. Furthermore, there is a strong tendency to separate learning about the Eucharist from participating in the Eucharist. However, the new eucharistic pedagogy based on an inclusive both/and way of thinking pays attention to juxtapositions in the educational context of the Eucharist, such as between faith and culture, between eucharistic experiences and ecological life experiences, and between liturgical practices and liturgical life. In this eucharistic pedagogy, students learn the Eucharist both in the classroom and at the table of the Eucharist reciprocally. In this basic understanding, the new eucharistic pedagogy enables students to have safe places to reflect on their life experiences critically through contextualized eucharistic practices in terms of

---

traditions but related to them in terms of the context of social bonding, social ethics, and social equality. On the basic understanding of the inseparable relationship between eucharistic practices and eucharistic life, Galbreath mentions the possibility of considering congregation members' serving and participation in a soup kitchen as the Communion table in their daily lives.

eucharistic texts, foods, objects, actions, and space. In this respect, Korean Presbyterian students' specific local contexts rooted in Confucianism are welcomed into open conversations equally with Christian traditions and the Bible, not as supplementary or hostile resources but as complementary and reciprocal resources. In terms of the rediscovery and critical reflections of students' eucharistic juxtapositions as an essential pedagogical process, the new eucharistic pedagogy understands that students' socializing mediators from their ecological socializing environments need to be connected and invited to be pedagogical supporters, companions, and sometimes active participants. If the teacher is not an ordained pastor who presides at the table of the Eucharist, then the role of the eucharistic presider is critical. Throughout the whole five steps of this new eucharistic pedagogy, the eucharistic presider is invited to be a participatory partner, active listener, co-designer, and co-teacher in the class on and the table of the Eucharist.

Principle Two: To Be Dialogical Rather than Instructive

The contextualized eucharistic pedagogy with attention to the critical reflections on students' specific local contexts facilitates students' learning experiences to be dialogical rather than instructive. Since the contextualized eucharistic pedagogy takes collaborative and critical reflections between the teacher, students, and students' socialization mediators as primary pedagogical strategies, it requires a non-hierarchical atmosphere for them to communicate with one another in the class on the Eucharist.

In the first step of the contextualized eucharistic pedagogy, as students share their life experiences in the class on the Eucharist, the teacher's role is to assist them in identifying their specific local contexts and finding their current issues for the building of teaching contents inductively, rather than to instruct deductively from already established teaching content. The dialogical sharing of students' life experiences, including eucharistic experiences between the teacher, students, and their socialization mediators, enables the eucharistic pedagogy to be inductive and further enables their life issues, such as political, gender, cultural, class, racial, religious, and social issues, to be considered as significant pedagogical resources.

In the second step of the critical reflections on students' life experiences, a dialogical approach is applied to the interdisciplinary conversations between the traditions of the Eucharist and Korean local cultures. It is through non-hierarchical, interdisciplinary dialogues that the Korean

Presbyterian traditions of the Eucharist, which have been formed and developed under strong postcolonial influences, can be decentralized from the cultural superiorism of Western culture and destigmatized from the misunderstanding of Korean local culture as anti-Christian.

In the third step of ritualization of eucharistic practices, students examine current eucharistic practices and plan renewed eucharistic practices according to the Nairobi Statement's four lenses (liturgical practices as trans-cultural, contextual, counter-cultural, and cross-cultural). From a contextual perspective, students are encouraged to have equal conversations with their own culture in classes on the Eucharist. Through this process, contextual dialogues take place with indigenous cultures such as Korean folk literature, music, art, rituals, and architecture.

In the fourth step of the participation in the Eucharist, students as co-celebrants can experience the presence of God through the dialogical approach to God's gracious works. When students as co-celebrants participate in the Eucharist with newly contextualized eucharistic practices, they may engage in critical dialogue between what God has done through Jesus Christ and what students experience in their daily lives by remembering, reflecting, reinterpreting, and envisioning.

In the fifth step of making plans, a dialogical approach helps students to make real commitments and actions in their daily lives, because the transformation of students' Christian lives is possible only through their voluntary commitments and actions, not through external hierarchical oppression.[3]

For this reason the dialogical approach, rather than the instructive approach, is an essential pedagogical strategy that makes it possible for not only the teacher and students but also their socialization mediators to be collaborative partners in classes on the Eucharist and at the table of the Eucharist. Particularly if the teacher is not an ordained pastor who presides at the table of the Eucharist, the eucharistic presider who is invited in the class on the Eucharist becomes an indispensible dialogue partner in the entire process of this new eucharistic pedagogy.

Principle Three: To Form Rather than Transmit

The new eucharistic pedagogy with attention to students' contexts and their corresponding actions guides students' learning experiences and

---

3. Berns, *Community-Based Intervention*, 89.

focuses on forming students' Christian lives rather than on transmitting information about the Eucharist. As I examined in chapter 3, eucharistic pedagogy in the Presbyterian Church of Korea has a strong tendency to be understood and practiced focusing on teaching students to *know about* the Eucharist by studying history, biblical texts, denominational doctrines, theological meanings, and liturgical orders of the Eucharist. However, the contextualized eucharistic pedagogy proposed here as an alternative eucharistic pedagogy for the Presbyterian Church of Korea is built on teaching students to *know* the Eucharist by participating in the Eucharist, reflecting on their life experiences, and envisioning the transformation of their lives both in classes on and at the table of the Eucharist.

In this respect, a contextualized eucharistic pedagogy based on students' specific local contexts requires its pedagogical contents and methods to deal with not only *what* students *need to know* about the Eucharist by using the Bible and Christian traditions but also *who* they *are* and *will be* through educational experiences on the Eucharist in the class, at the table of the Eucharist, and in the world. In this pedagogy, Confucianism and Korean Presbyterian students' local cultures are not rejected or discarded but welcomed as a starting place in order to build a foundation of contextual pedagogy for the Presbyterian Church of Korea. Through critical reflections and conversations between eucharistic texts and students' specific local contexts, Korean Presbyterian students may find specific life issues that are deeply rooted in Confucian culture to be challenged and changed. In an open-ended encounter between eucharistic practices and various students' specific contexts, there can be ongoing, creative, and critical learning experiences of the Eucharist. The contextualized eucharistic pedagogy focusing on the formation of students' Christian lives may allow students to liberate their eucharistic learning experiences from text-limited learning to life-reflective learning.

The new contextualized eucharistic pedagogy for students in the Korean Presbyterian Church focuses on formative learning and teaching and encourages Korean Presbyterian students to participate in the Eucharist actively as a formative liturgy by participating in context-embedded eucharistic practices, by reflecting and reforming them critically and creatively, and by envisioning their Christian lives transformed.

Conclusion

Summary

This book explores a new pedagogy of the Eucharist for the Presbyterian Church of Korea. It starts with a critical and historical analysis of eucharistic practices in the Presbyterian Church of Korea. The analysis identifies that Korean Presbyterian eucharistic practices have been formed and developed to be sacrosanct, hierarchical, male liturgist oriented, solemnized, and Western culture centered. It identifies several cultural, theological, and liturgical formative roots, such as Confucianism, frontier worship style, Nevius Methods, and the liturgy of the American Presbyterian church. In this eucharistic context, most Korean Presbyterians have experienced and understood the Eucharist as a predetermined, gloomy liturgy that is unequal in terms of gender, age, and position. As a result, in the Korean Presbyterian context separations exist not only between the Eucharist and participants' daily lives, but also between liturgists and participants.

However, the Eucharist is a formative liturgy which forms and transforms participants' faith and their lives through their participation in the presence of God, by praising God's works together, eating a common meal together, and envisioning God's reign in the world together. It is a liturgy that is contextual rather than predetermined. It is a liturgy where all people are invited by Jesus Christ to eat a common meal in hospitality and justice rather than inequality or separation based on gender, age, and functional differences.

In this respect, in order to help students participate in the Eucharist as a formative liturgy in the Presbyterian Church of Korea, this book suggests building a new eucharistic pedagogy with attention to students' contextuality both at the table of the Eucharist and in classes on the Eucharist. For the study of the relationship between students' contextuality and eucharistic practices, this book draws on the work of Peter Phan and Jung Young Lee as conversation partners. Phan understands liturgical contextualization in Asian churches as multiple dialogues between the gospel, cultures, the poor, and religions. He emphasizes that congregants' life experiences need to be an effective source for the eucharistic liturgy.[4] Lee's liturgical contextualization work focuses on the reinterpretation and reformation of liturgical practices rooted in Asian epistemologies. When I examined current eucharistic practices in the Presbyterian Church of Korea in light of Phan

4. Phan, *Being Religious Interreligiously*, 272.

and Lee's liturgical contextualization works, I found significant liturgical implications for building an alternative eucharistic pedagogy: (1) valuing congregants' life experiences as important resources for eucharistic texts, (2) reforming eucharistic objects to better reflect Korean culture, (3) reinterpreting congregants as active co-celebrants in equality and justice, and (4) revitalizing the value of eucharistic foods as essential signs.

For an educational framework for my pedagogical theory, this book uses Roberta Berns' ecological socialization pedagogy as its pedagogical strategy with attention to the dynamics between students' learning experiences and life experiences from their socializing environments. Berns asserts that students learn through the ecological interdynamics between four basic structures: microsystem, mesosystem, exosystem, and macrosystem. In her ecological understanding of learning experiences, Berns emphasizes that effective teaching takes place on a foundation of an integrative understanding of the process of students' socialization within their ecological multilayered socialization structures. As a significant socializing facilitator, a teacher needs to build close networks and communication channels with socialization mediators in the context of education in order to understand the socialization process of students from their multi-layered socializing environments. As occasion demands, the teacher may invite these mediators, such as students' parents, peer groups, community colleague, and neighbors, as indispensible pedagogical companions in the context of education. In this respect, Berns' theory provides significant educational implications for an inductive, life-reflected, and collaborative pedagogy. However, because of Berns' theory's limited capacity to reflect Korean students' particular local contexts, such as Confucianism and Western culture–oriented eucharistic practices, this book invites Phan and Lee to critique the historic and current eucharistic and curricular practices of the Presbyterian Church of Korea. In light of the critique based on Phan and Lee, this book has used Berns' theory as a pedagogical strategy to construct and propose an alternative pedagogy that includes a process for revised Eucharistic practices and classroom practices. When I critically examined current curriculum and texts of the Eucharist in the view of Berns' theory with attention to Korean students' local contexts, I found that there are three educational tendencies in Korean Presbyterians' teaching/learning practices of the Eucharist: (1) null curriculum of eucharistic experiences, (2) separation between Christian education and the Eucharist, and (3) lack of reflection of students' ecological sociocultural life experiences.

Building a New Eucharistic Pedagogy for the Presbyterian Church of Korea

Based on my critical analysis of the current curriculum and eucharistic texts in the Presbyterian Church of Korea in the light of an ecological socialization pedagogy focused on the sociocultural contexts of students, this book suggests a new eucharistic pedagogy for the Presbyterian Church of Korea. I call it a "contextualized eucharistic pedagogy" and define it as *teaching strategies that may help Korean Presbyterian students participate in the Eucharist as a formative liturgy with contextualized eucharistic practices by reflecting critically and responding creatively on their life experiences.* This new eucharistic pedagogy demands significant reconceptualization of elements of eucharistic pedagogy. The primary learning objectives are not information about the Eucharist but about formation and transformation of faith and life. Teaching contents need to be changed from text oriented to life reflected. The role of the teacher is to act as a critical reflection guide and a socialization facilitator. Students are expected to be critical reflectors, active actors, and co-celebrants in the classroom and at the eucharistic table.

This book suggests a five-step cycle of contextualized eucharistic pedagogy for the Presbyterian Church of Korea: (1) ecological scanning of students' specific local contexts, (2) critical reflection on students' issues in light of eucharistic themes in scriptures, (3) contextual ritualization of eucharistic practices, (4) participation in a contextualized Eucharist, (5) reaffirmation of commitment with plans for students' concrete actions. The first step starts from students' autobiographical sharing of their life experiences, including eucharistic experiences, from their multilayered socialization environments. The second step helps students have a safe environment to critically examine their life experiences rooted in a Confucian-based society by reflecting on them in light of eucharistic themes in Scripture. The third step is to ritualize eucharistic practices critically and creatively based on the four models of the Nairobi Statement: a trans-cultural model, a contextual model, a counter-cultural model, and a cross-cultural model. The fourth step is to participate in the Eucharist that has been newly envisioned through the previous three steps, and the last step is to include as classroom practices activities reaffirming commitment with plans for students' concrete actions.

Finally, this book identifies that this new eucharistic pedagogy is built on the foundation of three educational principles specific to Korean Presbyterian students' contexts: inclusive, dialogical, and formative. First, based on the both/and way of thinking, this new eucharistic pedagogy guides students to approach to their learning experiences of the Eucharist from an inclusive perspective: the contents of teaching (not only biblical, theological, and liturgical information about the Eucharist but also ecological life experiences of students), the places of learning (not only in the classroom but also at the table of the Eucharist), pedagogical participants (not only the teacher and students but also their socialization mediators including the eucharistic presider). Second, since the collaborative and critical reflections are primary pedagogical strategies, the new eucharistic pedagogy requires a non-hierarchical atmosphere for both students and the teacher to communicate with one another in classroom activities about the Eucharist. Third, the new eucharistic pedagogy focuses on forming students' Christian lives rather than focusing on transmitting information regarding the Eucharist. It demands its pedagogical contents and methods to be concerned *both* about what students need to know about the Eucharist *and* who they are and will be through educational experiences of the Eucharist in a Korean context. Thus, in the new eucharistic pedagogy, students' life experiences rooted in their specific local cultures are welcomed and reflected rather than rejected or excluded as essential pedagogical resources for the content of teaching.

Suggestions for Further Research

This book suggests a new model for eucharistic pedagogy for the Presbyterian Church of Korea through critical conversations about students' learning experiences of the Eucharist emphasizing their specific local contexts. This study has envisioned how Korean culture—such as Korean literature, music, dance, foods, architecture, and rituals—can be accepted and used in the process of reforming Korean Presbyterian eucharistic practices both in classroom activities and actual celebration of the Eucharist. Since Christian education covers the entire church life and daily life in the world, the contextual work of Christian education requires the entire church ministry to be inter-related, inter-influenced, and inter-acted. Since Christian education covers the entire church ministry, the contextual work of Christian education in Korea will never be completed by building and practicing a contextualized eucharistic pedagogy that is suggested in this book. It will require ongoing interdisciplinary studies that are connected to entire areas of ministry in Korean local churches, such as worship, liturgy, mission, social service, counseling, church education, and so on, thereby extending the research of this book.

Building a New Eucharistic Pedagogy for the Presbyterian Church of Korea

Even though this study investigates a contextual pedagogy limited to the context of the Eucharist in Korea, this task needs attention and study in a larger context beyond the context of the Presbyterian Church of Korea. Because the gospel is the worldwide truth that cannot be limited to a certain culture but is to be incarnated into each local culture over the world,[5] this kind of contextual investigation as the conversation between the gospel and culture will not be optional but imperative to all churches.[6] In the last several decades, the needs and efforts of contextualization have already come out, not only in the context of Asian churches but also in churches all over the world through international conferences, church declarations, papal documents, and denominational statements.[7] Even though there is no universal answer or agreement about the relationship between gospel and culture in these discussions, a consensus has emerged that the gospel needs to be enfleshed into local cultures in order for people to live Christian lives to reflect a specific time and a particular place for the glory of God.

This book is an academic response to the generative contextual needs of the Presbyterian Church of Korea. Considering that the contextualization work of Christian practices is inevitable in the process of local church evangelization, it becomes clear that this work is urgent and essential for churches all over the world. We live in an age of globalization in which people are increasingly interconnected, politically, economically, and socioculturally.[8] All local congregations will benefit from the contextual dialogue between congregation members' eucharistic experiences and their continuously changing local contexts. In developing an authentic Christian

---

5. Chupungco, "Lima Text," 106. Chupungco asserts that the church spread over the world is to be incarnated "in the genius and traditions of various people" through the proclamation and celebration of the gospel "in a pluriformity of cultural expressions."

6. Wedig, "Evangelism, Inculturation." According to Wedig, since evangelization is not only a conveyance of the gospel but a creative encounter between the gospel and culture, Christian worship which is of no cultural relevance to local people becomes "an ineffective means of evangelization."

7. For inculturation discussions on Africa, see Browne, *African Synod*; For inculturation discussions on Asia, see Phan, *Asian Synod*; "Ecclesia in Asia". For a collection of the final statements of Federation of Asian Bishops' Conferences, see Federation, *For All Peoples of Asia*; for the texts of "The World Council of Churches' Jerusalem Statement on Intercultural Hermeneutics" (1995), "The Lutheran World Federation's Nairobi Statement on Worship and Culture," and "The World Council of Churches Commission on World Mission and Evangelism (WCC-WCME) Ecumenical Conference in Salvador, de Bahia, Brazil" (1996), see Scherer and Bevans, *New Directions*; see also Gallagher, *Clashing Symbols*.

8. Jang, *Constructing a Public Practical Theology*, 192.

education that transforms congregation members' faith and Christian life, each local church needs to help its members hear the gospel in their own native tongue and through their own local cultural contexts.

I hope that this study will offer a pedagogical approach that can be applied by local churches around the world so that their congregation members participate in the Eucharist actively with attention to their own specific local contextuality. In addition, I believe that local churches all over the world are called to participate in this contextual investigation for the sake of building an authentic Christian education to transform students' faith and Christian lives.

Appendix A

Translation of Eucharistic Texts of the Presbyterian Church of Korea

Eucharistic Prayer A[1]

Eucharistic prayer A is for an ordinary Sunday worship service including the Eucharist.

Invitation—Presiding minister

Brother and sisters in Jesus Christ, this is a rite in which we remember Jesus' death and resurrection until he will come again. This rite enables us to overcome our sins, to strengthen us in the midst of suffering, to be equal to the task with responsibility, to live a faithful life in this world, and to have a mind of peace and hope for eternal life. Now, let us go to Christ through a table that he prepared.

Words of Institution—1 Corinthians 11:23–29—Presiding minister

Epiclesis—Presiding minister

Gracious God, thank you for sending your son Jesus Christ as a human being to this world and saving us through Jesus' sacrificial death. The Lord Jesus died as a perfect and holy sacrifice for the forgiveness of our sins. You commanded us to do this remembrance of Jesus until Jesus' second

---

1. Reforming Committee, *Book of Common Worship* [PCK], 58–59. Eucharistic prayer A is for an ordinary Sunday worship service including the Eucharist

Appendix A

coming. Merciful God, we ask you to bless and make this rice cake and cup holy through the Holy Spirit. By receiving the rice cake of eternal life and cup of salvation, we want to remember Jesus' suffering, his death by shedding his blood, his resurrection with authority, and his glorious ascension once again. We ask the Holy Spirit to help us to receive life and grace in this table where Jesus provides. In the name of Jesus, we all pray. Amen.

Apostles' Creed—All together

Communion of the People—Presiding minister and eucharistic servers

Rice cake

The Lord Jesus, on the night he was betrayed, took a rice cake, gave thanks, broke it and gave it to his disciples. I also give you this rice cake in the name of Jesus. You may partake of this rice cake in remembrance of Jesus' broken body. Let us pray.

Jesus said, "This is my body, which is for you; do this in remembrance of me." At this table that our Lord established, we will take this rice cake as a sacramental food. Lord, help us recognize your broken body and make this rice cake we partake of the rice cake of eternal life. In the name of Jesus Christ. Amen.

The minister and those assisting receive Communion, and then serve the rice cake to the congregation.

Cup

After supper he took the cup and blessed it and he said, "This cup is the new covenant in my blood; do this, whenever you drink it, in remembrance of me." As we drink this cup, we experience our hearts renewed in the blessing of covenant. Let us pray.

Appendix A

God of holiness, we are about to take this cup. May your blood lead us to reach eternal life. Help us love each other through your love and make our cup overflow. In the name of Jesus Christ. Amen.

The minister and those assisting receive Communion, and then serve the cup to the congregation.

Eucharistic Prayer B[2]

Eucharistic prayer B is for an ordinary Sunday worship service including both Baptism and the Eucharist.

Apostles' Creed—All together
Hymn—All together
Words of Institution—1 Corinthians 11:23–29—Presiding minister

The presiding minister may choose Words of Institution either from 1 Corinthians 11:23–29 or the Synoptic Gospels [Matthew 26:26–28, Mark 14:22–24, Luke 22:14–20]. After reading the Words of Institution, the presiding minister may give a brief guidance.

The Eucharist is not only for remembrance. It is a place for us to recall, reenact, and meditate on the Lord's broken body and shed blood for us. For the Lord's body and blood to be my body and blood, we need to rededicate a new life. And, through this Eucharist, we need to be one in Jesus Christ who is a peacemaker. This is the will of our Lord who invites us to participate in this Eucharist.

Epiclesis—Presiding minister

This prayer is very important because it is about invoking the Holy Spirit to be present with the rice cake and the cup and, through the works of the Holy Spirit, to lead those who receive them to encounter the Lord.

---

2. Ibid., 67–70. Eucharistic prayer B is for an ordinary Sunday worship service including both the Baptism and the Eucharist.

Appendix A

Our Lord who broke your own flesh and shed your own blood, we come to this place with unclean hearts and bodies. Now we are standing in front of the Eucharist reenacting the Lord's flesh and blood.

Come to this place and lead us to experience deeply your flesh and blood within our mouths and bodies. May you guide us to encounter you in this place. In the presence of the Holy Spirit, we may participate in the holy Eucharist. In the name of Jesus Christ who broke his own body and shed his own blood for us, Amen.

Breaking the Rice Cake—Presiding minister

According to Words of Institution, a presiding minister reenacts Lord's actions to take, bless, and break the rice cake.

The Lord Jesus, on the night he was betrayed, ate the Passover with his loving disciples. At that time, he took rice cake, gave thanks, broke it, and gave it to his disciples. Jesus said, "This is my body, which is for you; do this in remembrance of me." You may take this rice cake as Lord ordered.

Proclamation of Participation—Presiding minister

Now you may reflect on the Lord's flesh, broken for us. And then, you may eat it with your thankful heart.

Partaking the Rice Cake—All together
Taking the Cup—Presiding minister

According to Words of Institution, a presiding minister reenacts Lord's actions to take the cup, bless it, and give it to his disciples.

After supper the Lord took the cup and blessed it, he said, "This cup is the new covenant in my blood for you; take it and drink it." You may drink the cup as the Lord said.

Appendix A

Proclamation of Participation—Presiding minister

Now, you may take the cup and reflect on the Lord's shed blood for the forgiveness of our sin. And then, you may drink it with your sincere and thankful heart.

Drinking the Cup—All together
Prayer after Communion—All together

Loving God, thank you for allowing us to participate in the Eucharist by your merciful grace. Thank you for your renewing the grace of forgiveness and salvation. Thank you for helping us reaffirm that we are the Lord's bodies. Thank you for guiding us to love each other and to be one.

May your flesh and blood reign over our bodies. Let us be people who follow the Gospel. Let us be people [who] plant peace in this land. Let us be the light of the nation that witnesses Christ's death and resurrection. Let us be children who give glory to the only God. In the name of Jesus, Amen.

Hymn of Thanksgiving—"Now, I Have a New Life" (#436)—All together

Eucharistic Prayer C[3]

Eucharistic prayer C is for an ordinary Sunday worship service including both Baptism and the Eucharist.

Invitation—Presiding minister

This is the joyful feast of the people of God. They will come from east and west, and from north and south, and sit at the table in the kingdom of God.

---

3. Ibid., 78–81. Eucharistic prayer C is for an ordinary Sunday worship service including both the Baptism and the Eucharist.

Appendix A

This is the Lord's Table. Our Lord invites those who trust him to share the feast that he prepared. Let us participate in a heavenly banquet that the Lord prepared for us.

Great Thanksgiving—Presiding minister

The Lord be with you.

And also with you.

Lift up your hearts.

We lift them to the Lord.

Let us give thanks to the Lord our God.

It is right to give our thanks and praise.

Holy God, Father almighty, Creator of heaven and earth, you commanded light to shine out of darkness, divided the sea and dry land, created the vast universe and called it good. You made us in your image to live with one another in love. You gave us the breath of life and freedom to choose your way. You promised yourself in covenant, told us your purpose in commandments through Moses, and called for justice and love in the cry of prophets.

Lord God almighty! Great and wonderful are your works. Therefore all nations praise you who are justice and truth forever. Only God is holy.

We praise you, most holy God, for sending your only Son to live among us, sharing our joy and sorrow. He told your story, healed the sick, and was a friend of sinners. Obeying you, he took up his cross and died that we might live. We praise you that he overcame death and is risen to rule the world. He is still the friend of sinners.

Now, we take the rice cake and drink the cup in remembrance of him and will tell all nations of the Lord Jesus who died and was resurrected to save us from our sinfulness.

Appendix A

Gracious God, pour out your Holy Spirit upon these your gifts of rice cake and cup. Make them be for us the body and blood of Christ that we may be for the world the body of Christ, redeemed by his blood.

Now, as the Lord has taught us, we are to pray: Our Father in heaven, hallowed be thy name, your kingdom come, your will be done, on earth as in heaven. Give us today our daily bread. Forgive us our debts, as we forgive our debtors, but deliver us from evil. For thine is the kingdom, the power, and the glory, forever. Amen.

Words of Institution—1 Corinthians 11:23-29—Presiding minister

The Lord Jesus, on the night of his arrest, took the rice cake (the presiding minister takes the rice cake), and after giving thanks to God, he broke it (the presiding minister breaks the rice cake), and gave it to his disciples, saying: Take it and eat. This is my body, given for you. Take it (the presiding minister stretches out own left hand) and eat it (the presiding minister stretches out own right hand). Do this in remembrance of me.

In the same way he took the cup (the presiding minister takes the cup), saying: This cup is the new covenant sealed in my blood, shed for you for the forgiveness of sins. Receive it and drink it (the presiding minister stretches out own hand).

The Lamb of God—All together

All congregation members sing a song rather than read it.

The Lamb of God who takes away the sin of the world, have mercy upon us.

The Lamb of God who takes away the sin of the world, give us peace.

Proclamation of Participation—All together

All congregation members or choir members sing songs of Psalms.

Appendix A

> Now, you may take the Lord's rice cake and the cup. As we reflect on the Lord's broken flesh for us, we may receive the gifts of grace. Participate in the Eucharist with holy hearts.

The minister and those assisting receive Communion, and then serve the rice cake to the congregation.

The presiding minister/communion servers: (*giving the rice cake*) The body of Christ.

Congregation members: *Amen.*

The presiding minister/communion servers: (*giving the cup*) The blood of Christ.

Congregation members: *Amen.*

If congregation members take the rice cake and the cup at the eucharistic table, they may have the rice cake by dipping it into the cup or before drinking the cup separately.

Prayer after Communion—Presiding minister

Lord, we thank you that you have fed us with the rice cake and the cup. We thank you that you give us your love and grace in this Sacrament. God, thank you for this grace given to us who do not deserve to receive it. May you guide us as people who have received your rice cake and the cup to live life. May you lead us to witness the glory of life through us who have received the foods of life. In the name of Jesus Christ. Amen.

When Jesus had sung a hymn, he went out to the Mount of Olives.

Hymn of Thanksgiving—All together

Eucharistic Prayer D[4]

Eucharistic prayer D is for Sunday worship services in Advent.

---

4. Ibid., 121–23.

Appendix A

Invitation—Presiding minister

Loving brothers and sisters, this is the joyful feast of the people of God. They will come from east and west, and from north and south, and sit at table in the kingdom of God.

This is the Lord's table. Our Lord invites those who trust him to the feast that he prepared. Listen, this is the witness from Mark who is the Lord's disciple.

"While they were eating, Jesus took bread, gave thanks and broke it, and gave it to his disciples. He said, take it; this is my body. Then he took the cup, gave thanks and offered it to them, and they all drank from it. He said to them, this is my blood of the covenant, which is poured out for many." (Mark 14:22–24)

Great Thanksgiving—Presiding minister

The Lord be with you.

And also with you.

Lift up your hearts.

We lift them to the Lord.

Let us give thanks to the Lord our God

It is right to give our thanks and praise.

Holy God, Father almighty, Creator of heaven and earth, You commanded light to shine out of darkness, divided the sea and dry land, created the vast universe and called it good. You made us in your image to live with one another in love. Thank you for giving us life and breath. Thank you for giving us the privilege to live by following your way. Through the ancients of faith, you told your will and proclaimed your justice. Bearing no relation to the change of nature, you have been faithful to the children of the Lord in equality and kindness. Almighty God, how wonderful your works are! We give our hearts to the holy Lord.

Appendix A

Congregation members: Holy, holy, holy Lord, God of power and might, heaven and earth are full of your glory. Hosanna in the highest. Blessed is he who comes in the name of the Lord. Hosanna in the highest.

You are holy, O God of majesty, and blessed is Jesus Christ, your Son, our Lord. You sent Jesus to us. He lived as one of us, knowing joy and sorrow. He healed the sick, fed the hungry, and became a friend of sinners. Obeying you, he took up his cross and died that we might live. We praise you that he overcame death and is risen to rule the world. He is still the friend of sinners. We trust him to overcome every power that can hurt or divide us, and believe that when he comes in glory, we will celebrate victory with him. Now, we take the rice cake and drink the cup in remembrance of him and will tell all nations of the Lord Jesus who died for us, taking away the sin of the world, and was resurrected. Gracious God, pour out your Holy Spirit upon these your gifts of rice cake and cup. Make them be for us the body and blood of Christ. By taking this rice cake, may you make us receive a new life and live as your children until we participate in a *feast with the Lord in your glory.*

Congregation members: God who called us from death to life, we give you all our things. In our Lord Jesus Christ, we thank you for your love and salvation with all generations and churches.

Lord's Prayer—All together
Communion of the People—Presiding minister and eucharistic servers

(The rice cake and the cup)

Eucharistic Prayer E[5]

Eucharistic prayer E is for a Christmas Sunday worship service.

5. Ibid., 127–29.

Appendix A

Invitation—Presiding minister and congregation members

In the time of the glory of heaven and the peace of the earth, those who listen to the joyful news of Christ's birth and praise him are invited to this holy table.

As God comes to us with the hope of salvation, we come before you with thanksgiving and joy.

The Lord be with you.

And also with you.

Lift up your hearts.

We lift them to the Lord.

Let us give thanks to the Lord our God for God's salvation

It is right to give our thanks and praise.

Great Thanksgiving—Presiding minister

Holy God, Father almighty, Creator and Ruler of heaven and earth, we praise the Lord and give glory to the name of the Lord. We gather in this place within the remembrance of Jesus Christ you gave us as a gift. For when the time came, God sent him to us and made him be good news. Dwelling in us, Christ revealed the mystery of the Word of God. Now we praise God with joy with choirs of angels and with all the faithful of the earth.

Sanctus—"Holy Holy Holy! Lord God Almighty!" (#8)—All together

Words of Institution—1 Corinthians 11:23-29—Presiding minister

The Lord Jesus, on the night of his arrest, took the rice cake, and after giving thanks to God, he broke it, and gave it to his disciples, saying: "This is my body, given for you. Do this in remembrance of me."

Appendix A

In the same way he took the cup, saying: "This cup is the new covenant sealed in my blood. Whenever you drink it, do this in remembrance of me."

God of dignity, we are filled with joy for the birth of Christ. As we proclaim Christ's death and resurrection, we are waiting for Christ's coming again.

Lord's Prayer—All together

Communion of the People—Presiding minister and eucharistic servers

(The rice cake and the cup)

Prayer after Communion—Presiding minister

Almighty God, we praise you for giving us Jesus Christ who came to us and saved us from our sinfulness. We thank you for Jesus Christ who was born in Bethlehem according to the Word of God. In Jesus, the Lord became flesh, dwelt among us, and lived in sorrow and joy with us. We give you glory for your abundant grace and love. Eternal God, we give you glory. In the name of Jesus Christ who is the Lord of Lords and the king of kings, forever and ever. Amen.

Eucharistic Prayer F[6]

Eucharistic prayer F is for an Epiphany Sunday worship service.

Great Thanksgiving—Presiding minister
Lord's Prayer—All together
Words of Institution—Presiding minister
Communion of the People—Presiding minister and eucharistic servers

(The rice cake and the cup; hymn or Psalm may be played)

6. Ibid., 132–33.

Appendix A

Prayer after Communion—Presiding minister

The Lord be with you.

And also with you.

Lord, Pour the spirit of love of God upon us. And, make us who have one heavenly food one. In the name of Jesus, Amen.

Or

Lord, you gave us yourself.

Now, we give other people ourselves.

The love of the Lord made us new people.

As people of love, we will serve the Lord with joy.

May you fill us with the glory of the Lord.

Help us give glory to you through all things.

Eucharistic Prayer G[7]

Eucharistic prayer G is for the Palm Sunday worship service.

Great Thanksgiving—Presiding minister

The Lord be with you.

And also with you.

Lift up your hearts.

We lift them to the Lord.

Let us give thanks to the Lord our God for God's salvation.

It is right to give our thanks and praise.

---

7. Ibid., 143–45.

Appendix A

Holy God, almighty, forever and ever, it is right to give our thanks and praise to you, creator of heaven and earth. In eternal love, God created us for God's glory. When we were sinful and even chained by sins and death, your love was faithful. The Lord commanded people to cleanse their hearts and prepare the Passover with joy. The Lord told them to pray with whole hearts, to work by grace, and to be renewed through the Word of God and sacraments.

Lord, come to us in the abundance of grace that you prepared for your loving people. Therefore, we praise your name with eternal songs with all your people on earth and with choirs of angels.

Congregation members: Holy, holy, holy Lord, God of power and might, heaven and earth are full of your glory. Hosanna in the highest. Blessed is he who comes in the name of the Lord. Hosanna in the highest.

You are holy, Lord, and blessed is Jesus Christ, your Son, our Lord. He made himself nothing and became flesh. Jesus humbled himself and became obedient to death, even death on a cross. Bearing the burden of our sins and death, he gave himself.

Through his passion, death, and resurrection, the Lord gave the church a new life. The Lord set us free from the slavery of sin and death. The Lord gave us a new covenant through water and the spirit.

The Lord Jesus, on the night of his arrest, took the rice cake, and after giving thanks to God, he broke it, and gave it to his disciples, saying: "This is my body, given for you. Do this in remembrance of me." In the same way he took the cup, saying: "This cup is the new covenant sealed in my blood. Whenever you drink it, do this in remembrance of me."

Therefore, we proclaim the mystery of our faith in remembrance of Jesus Christ's wonderful works. As we participate in the sacrifice of the Lord, we give ourselves as a holy and living sacrifice.

Christ has died,

Christ is risen,

Christ will come again.

Appendix A

Gracious God, pour out your Holy Spirit upon us and upon these your gifts of rice cake and cup, that the rice cake we break and the cup we bless may be the communion of the body and blood of Christ. By your Spirit make us one with Christ, that we may be one with all who share this feast, united in ministry in every place. As this rice cake is Christ's body for us, send us out to be the body of Christ in the world. In union with your church in heaven and on earth, we pray, O God, that you will fulfill your eternal purpose in us and in all the world. Keep us faithful in your service until Christ comes in final victory, and we shall feast with all your saints in the joy of your eternal realm. All glory and honor are yours, almighty Father, now and forever. Amen.

Words of Institution—1 Corinthians 11:23–26—Presiding minister
Communion of the People—Presiding minister and eucharistic servers

(The rice cake and the cup)

Prayer after Communion—Presiding minister

Lord, thank you for filling our hearts with sacraments given in the name of the Father, the Son, and the Spirit. Save us by Jesus' resurrection. In the name of Jesus, Amen.

Eucharistic Prayer H[8]

Eucharistic prayer H is for an Easter vigil service.

Invitation—Presiding minister

This is a gracious place that the risen Lord prepared. Jesus who is the rice cake of life gave us rice cake and cup. He told us, "Do this in remembrance of me." The place of grace to provide people the foods of life has existed since Jesus was resurrected. Through his churches, it has existed since he ascended.

8. Ibid., 163–65.

Appendix A

Words of Institution—1 Corinthians 11:23-29—Presiding minister
Epiclesis—Presiding minister

Lord who died for us and was resurrected, thank you for providing the foods of life to us who have betrayed you in our daily lives. Today, we want to participate in a feast of life that the risen Lord gives us. Open our eyes to see the risen Lord. Make this sacrament holy in the presence of the Holy Spirit. In the name of Jesus Christ, we all pray. Amen.

Communion of the People—Presiding minister
and eucharistic servers

The Lord Jesus, on the night of his arrest, took the rice cake, and after giving thanks to God, he broke it and gave it to his disciples, saying: "This is my body, given for you. Do this in remembrance of me." In the same way he took the cup, saying: "This cup is the new covenant sealed in my blood. Whenever you drink it, do this in remembrance of me." And, Jesus carried the cross and died for us according to the prophet of the Bible. And, he was raised in three days.

The risen Lord met his disciples at a table. Jesus ate food with disciples who were going to a village called Emmaus. He also had food with his disciples including Peter at the sea of Tiberias. As the disciples ate food with Jesus, they realized that Jesus was resurrected.

Now we are before a holy table that risen Jesus prepared for us. Today, the Lord gives us the Lord's rice cake and cup. We may take the Lord's rice cake and cup according to the Lord's will.

Receiving the Rice Cake and the Cup—Presiding minister and
eucharistic servers

The minister and those assisting receive Communion, and then serve the rice cake and the cup to the congregation. Those who are baptized today receive the rice cake and the cup first, and then serve to other congregation members.

Appendix A

Prayer after Communion—Presiding minister

Eucharistic Prayer I[9].

Eucharistic prayer I is for a Pentecost Sunday worship service.

Invitation—Presiding minister

This is a rite of remembrance of Christ. We are purchased by the holy blood of the Lord. In this rite, we remember Christ until he will come again. This rite enables us to overcome our sins, to strengthen us in the midst of suffering, and to have a mind of peace and hope for eternal life. Now, you may participate in it with holy hearts.

Words of Institution—1 Corinthians 11:23-24—Presiding minister

Communion of the People—Presiding minister
and eucharistic servers

1. Breaking the Rice Cake—Presiding minister

The Lord Jesus, on the night he was betrayed, took a rice cake, gave thanks, broke it and gave it to his disciples. Jesus said, "This is my body, which is for you; do this in remembrance of me." Loving Lord, we are about to take the rice cake as you ordered. Holy Spirit, come to this place and make this rice cake holy as the rice cake of life. In the name of Jesus, Amen.

(The minister and those assisting receive Communion, and then serve the rice cake to the congregation.)

---

9. Ibid., 169–70.

Appendix A

2. *Taking the Cup—Presiding minister*

After supper the Lord took the cup and blessed it, and he said, "This cup is the new covenant in my blood for you. Whenever you drink it, do this in remembrance of me." Now, we are about to drink the cup as the Lord said. Clean people's sins only by your blood to save us. As we receive this cup, help us to become people who love one another, forgive one another, and help one another by following your love. In the name of Jesus, Amen.

(The minister and those assisting receive Communion, and then serve the cup to the congregation.)

Prayer after Communion—All together

Eucharistic Prayer J[10]

Eucharistic prayer J is for an intergenerational corporate Sunday worship service.

Invitation—Presiding minister

While inviting people to the Sacraments, the presiding minister may give a brief guidance.

Today's sacraments that God provides us are the bread and wine for us to live eternally. You may participate in it with thankful hearts.

Words of Institution—Presiding minister

While reading 1 Corinthians 11:23-29, the presiding minister breaks the rice cake and pours wine, facing the congregation members.

---

10. Ibid., 205–6.

Appendix A

Eucharistic Prayer and Lord's Prayer—Presiding minister

Communion of the People—All together

(Only baptized congregation members stand in a line before a eucharistic table and receive the rice cake and cup. The minister and those assisting receive Communion, and then serve the rice cake and the cup to the congregation. If congregation members take the rice cake and the cup at the eucharistic table, they may have the rice cake with the cup or by dipping it into the cup. Children who are with their parents observe their parents' participation in the Eucharist. Parents may prepare some food for their babies who cannot understand what the Eucharist is.)

Prayer after Communion—Presiding minister

Eucharistic Prayer K[11]

Eucharistic prayer K is for a Sunday worship service including a time for prayers of healing and wholeness.

Invitation—Presiding minister

Our Lord is the rice cake of life. Our Lord is a heavenly food for the hunger of the spirit. Our Lord is also spring water welling up for the thirsty in spirit. Our Lord is the resting place for the weary of spirit. This table is a feast that Jesus who is the rice cake of life and spring water provides us. This table is a gracious place to heal and renew our spirit which is hungry and thirsty and tired.

Epiclesis—Presiding minister

Gracious God, thank you for providing us a holy table of the Lord. Pour out your Holy Spirit upon us and upon these your gifts of rice cake and cup, that the rice cake we break and the cup we bless may be the communion of the body and blood of Christ. As we receive the Lord's body and blood,

11. Ibid., 211–13.

Appendix A

may you make our minds and bodies renewed and restore all things in us to health.

May the Lord give (the Lord's peace) to the sick and the weak. In the name of Jesus who died on the cross and was resurrected. Amen.

Words of Institution—John 6:47–57 or 1 Corinthians 11:23–26—Presiding minister

While reading Words of Institution, the presiding minister breaks the rice cake and pours wine.

The Lord Jesus, on the night he was betrayed, took the rice cake, gave thanks, broke it and gave it to his disciples. Jesus said, "This is my body, which is for you; do this in remembrance of me."

After supper the Lord took the cup and blessed it, and he said, "This cup is the new covenant in my blood for you. Whenever you drink it, do this in remembrance of me."

Communion of the People—All together

The minister and those assisting receive Communion, and then serve the rice cake and the cup to the congregation. Eucharistic servers stand with the rice cake and the cup before the eucharistic table. According to the situations of local churches, they may stand at multiple places.

Now a table that the Lord prepared is ready. By faith, come to the table and receive the body and blood of the Lord.

When congregation members receive the rice cake and the cup, eucharistic servers may say, "This is the body of the Lord," and "this is the blood of Christ." Congregation members receive them with a response of "Amen."

Appendix A

Prayer for healing—Presiding minister

> *Among the people who received the rice cake and the cup, the sick or the weak may come before the table and the minister may place hands on them for a healing prayer. The minister may use the following scriptures.*

"Have I not commanded you? Be strong and courageous! Do not tremble or be dismayed, for the LORD your God is with you wherever you go." (Joshua 1:9)

"Cease striving and know that I am God; I will be exalted among the nations, I will be exalted in the earth." (Psalm 46:10)

"Peace I leave with you; my peace I give to you; not as the world gives do I give to you. Do not let your heart be troubled, nor let it be fearful." (John 14:27)

Appendix B

Translation of Curriculum Texts about the Eucharist in the Presbyterian Church of Korea

Lesson 11. Jesus as the bread of life (for 3rd and 4th grade group)[1]

Scripture: John 6:54–59

I. Opening & Presenting and Exploring: Following Jesus' Life

1. Lord's Supper

This is my (_____). This is my (_____).

Whoever eats my (_____) and drinks my (_____ has (_____).

For my (_____) is real (_____) and my (_____) is real (_____).

After reading John 6:54–59, fill in the blanks.

2. Washing Disciples' Feet

In order to set disciples an example that they should do as Jesus has done for them, Jesus, the Lord and Teacher of disciples, has washed their feet. (John 13:1–15)

---

1. Curriculum Committee, *God's Kingdom (Third and Fourth Grade Group)*, 34–36.

Appendix B

3. Praying at Gethsemane

Jesus went to a place called Gethsemane, and he fell with his face to the ground and prayed, not for His will but God's will. (Matthew 26:36–46)

4. Standing before Pilate, the governor

5. The Soldiers Mock Jesus

Jesus was found guilty through unjustified trial by Pilate. Pilate washed his hands and said, "I am innocent of this man's blood."

6. The Crucifixion: Dying on the Cross

"But He was pierced for our transgressions, he was crushed for our iniquities; the punishment that brought us peace was upon him, and by his wounds we are healed." (Isaiah 53:5)

I tell you the truth, he who (_____) has (_____).

Fill in the blanks in a picture of dying on the cross.

After listening to Jesus' life through 6 steps, answer following questions.

1) Why did Jesus name Himself as the bread of life? After reading John 6:35–40, share your thoughts in your group.
2) Why did Jesus give us His life to us? (John 3:16–17)
3) How can we have eternal life? Share your thoughts in your group.

II. Responding: Thinking of Jesus

This week is Holy Week when we remember what Jesus has done for the forgiveness of our sins. Remembering Jesus, check the following sentences regarding daily life statements for Holy Week, and try to live a pious life in the light of them.

Appendix B

Daily Life Statement for Holy Week

With all my heart to participate in Jesus' passion, I swear to live a pious daily life by keeping my promises in this week.

___ I will read the Bible every day.
___ I will fast one meal every day (or only on Friday).
___ I will join an early morning prayer meeting every day.
___ I will have a family worship every day.
___ I will make an offering for the poor.
___ I will pray for my friends who will be invited to Easter worship service.
___ I will sing gospel songs rather than secular songs.
___ I will not watch TV (or DVD) or reduce my watching time.
___ I will not play video games.
___ I will spread the Gospel to my friends.
___ I will not read comic books.
_____ Month/Day Year
_____ Name

III. Closing: Remembering Jesus

As we read the Bible, let us remember Jesus' passion and death.

Monday	Tuesday	Wednesday	Thursday	Friday	Satruday
John 13:1–15	Luke 22:7–20	Matthew 26:31–46	Matthew 26:47–55	Isaiah 53	1 John 1

Lesson 25. Jesus as the bread of life (for youth group)[2]

Scripture: 1 Corinthian 11:23–29
Reference Scripture: John 6:35, 41–59

---

2. Curriculum Committee, *God's Kingdom* (middle school group), 80–82.

Appendix B

I. Opening: Opening Our Hearts

Let us share our knowledge of th picture of *The Last Supper* by Leonardo Da Vinci. What do you know about it?

II. Presenting and Exploring: Listening to the Word of God

1. When did Jesus have the last supper with his disciples?
2. Even though Jesus knew that he would be betrayed by his disciples, he still had the last supper with them. Why?
3. After you read 1 Corinthians 11:23–26, share your thoughts on the meaning of bread and wine.
4. What does this Bible verse mean? "If anyone eats of this bread, he will live forever." (John 6:51) In the light of another Bible verse "anyone who believes has everlasting life" (John 6:47), share your thoughts in your group.
5. What do you call this liturgy that remembers Jesus' last supper with his disciples? Let's learn its meaning and participants' appropriate attitude.

III. Responding and Closing: Reflecting Myself

1. "In the light of the event of Jesus' suffering and death, what are students' responsibilities in their daily lives as Jesus' disciples?"
2. "In the light of the event of Jesus' suffering and death, what are the changes in the students' thinking of themselves as Jesus' disciples?"

Appendix C

Examples of Contextualized Eucharistic Texts

A. Contextualized Eucharistic Texts for a Thanksgiving Sunday Service

I. Madang (마당, an open place for communal celebration)[1] of Offering

Following the presiding minister who wears Korean traditional clothes, all congregation members go out of the sanctuary and sit in a circle in the courtyard of the church. The table of the Eucharist is placed at the center of the circle. As the signal of the beginning of the Eucharist, one communion server comes to the table and strikes a gong, which is a Korean percussion instrument. According to the direction of the presiding minister, all people come and put their offerings on the table, which they bring from their houses or farms, and go back to their seats. Communion servers bring and put the rice cake and the cup at the center of the table. During this offering time, people may sing a song of Poong-Nyun-Ga (풍년가), which is a traditional Korean folk song of celebration for a good harvest accompanied by Korean folk instruments.[2] The lines of the song may be added variously based on specific local situations.

---

1. H. J. Park, *Study of Madang Play*, 12–13. The word *madang* refers to an open public place where community members gather for communal celebration rites such as a community thanksgiving, a traditional percussion performance, and seasonal folk games. For several decades, however, the word *madang* has been used not only as a spatial concept, referring a particular open place, but also for an occasional concept, referring to a specific event or situation. According to H. Park, in a hierarchal, authoritative, and conservative Korean society, *madang* has been an exceptional place where people participate in rituals in an atmosphere of equality, justice, and hospitality that transcends age, gender, class, or economics.

2. Y. J. Park, *Korean Classic Music*, 28. Korean folk instruments comprise a wide range

Appendix C

1. Because God gave us seeds, lands, rain, air, and nature on the earth
   Today we have a good harvest of fruits and grains for this year.
2. Because God blessed us abundantly in our fields and lives,
   Now we give thanks and praise God's grace and faithfulness.

Invitation

Standing at the table, the presiding minister invites the people to the Eucharist, using the following invitation to the table of the Eucharist.

Presider—Brothers and sisters in Jesus Christ, this is the joyful feast of the people of God. They will come from north and south, and from east and west, and sit at the table in the kingdom of God. (During invitation of the Eucharist, the whole view of the local town may be presented on a screen.)

(C[3]—Here may be added one or more of Jesus' meal stories[4] as well as Scripture about Jesus as the bread of life.[5])

Presider   This is the Lord's Table. Jesus our Lord invites those who trust him to share the feast that he prepared. With joy and thanksgiving, let us give our praise to God.

---

of string, wind, and percussion instruments such as Gayageum (가야금, a Korean harp with twelve strings), geomungo (거문고, a Korean harp with six strings), Taegeum (대금, a large transverse bamboo flute), piri (피리, a Korean flute), Yanggeum (양금, a hammered dulcimer with metal strings), Haegeum (해금, a Korean fiddle), Ajeng (아쟁, a harp with seven strings), ggoenggwari (꽹과리, a small gong), jing (징, a large gong), janggo (장고, an hourglass drum), and buk (북, a barrel drum).

3. This open-ended eucharistic text may vary depending on participants' specific local contexts. Line C is an improvised line that will be crafted in step 3 (contextual ritualization of eucharistic practices) of the contextualized eucharistic pedagogy with attention to congregation members' specific local contexts.

4. The story of Jesus' eating with the sinners, the story of five loaves and two fish, the story of two disciples on the road of Emmaus, the story of Jesus' Last Supper, the story of breakfast with Jesus at the sea of Tiberias; all can be examples of Jesus meal stories.

5. John 6:35, 48, 51.

Appendix C

I. Madang (마당, community celebration gathering) of Thanksgiving

The participants stand. If there are people who are not able to stand among congregation members, the presiding minister needs to guide them to their seats at the front in order to secure a clear view of the presiding minister when others stand.

Presider   The Lord be with you.

People   **And also with you.**

Presider   Lift up your hearts.

People   **We lift them to the Lord.**

Presider   Let us give thanks to the Lord our God.

People   **It is right to give our thanks and praise.**

Presider   We all praise you, holy God. You created the heaven, the earth, and us.

People   **With love and goodness, you created all things.**

(C   Here may be added more specific examples of farming products, grains, crops, fruits, foods, or locales.)

Presider   You made us in your image to live with one another in love.

People   **From generation to generation, you have guided and kept us to be your people in our daily lives with faithfulness and kindness.**

(C   Here may be added several significant local, socio-cultural, and historical events.)

The people may sing a song of Joo-Chan-Ga (주찬가) which is a contemporary Korean folk gospel song with the accompaniment of Korean folk instruments. The lines of the song may be added variously based on specific local farm products.

Appendix C

1. Holy, holy, holy Lord, God of creation.
   All things you created, heaven, earth, and us
   Hallelujah, hallelujah, Ulsiguna-jota, Jiwhaja-jonne

2. Holy, holy, holy Lord, God of creation.
   You blessed us through your creations.
   Thanks for rice, cabbage, radish and apple.
   Hallelujah, hallelujah, Ulsiguna-jota, Jiwhaja-jonne,[6]
   Praise God of creation.

3. Holy, holy, holy Lord, God of creation.
   Blessed is one who comes in the name of the Lord.
   Hosanna in the highest.
   Hallelujah, hallelujah, Ulsiguna-jota, Jiwhaja-jonne.
   Praise God of creation.

   The presiding minister continues:

Presider   We all praise you, for your Son, Jesus Christ as our Savior.

People   **You sent him to live among us with human nature, to share our joy and sorrow together, and to save us from death.**

(C   Here may be added several aspects of Jesus' ministry of salvation through his birth, baptism, life, death, resurrection, and ascension.)

Presider   We all remember your Son, Jesus Christ,

People   **By taking this rice cake and this cup, we celebrate his life, death and resurrection.**

The people may sing a song of Arirang (아리랑),[7] which is the most representative Korean traditional folk song with the accompaniment of Korean folk instruments.

Arirang arirang arariyo, arirang arirang arariyo

Christ has died, Christ is risen, Christ will come again

---

6. Tobagi Korean Language Compilation Committee, *Bori Korean Dictionary*, 1198. The words *ulsiguna-jota, Jiwhaja-jonne* are a Korean folk echoic phrase for joy and delight, accompanied by hand clapping.

7. Ibid., 862. The words *arirang, arirang, arariyo* are Korean folk echoic words for the mixed emotion of hope from despair, joy from sadness, and liberation from oppression.

Appendix C

The presiding minister continues:

Presider   We all pray that you pour your Holy Spirit upon us and upon these earthly gifts of rice cakes and wine.

People   **As we share these foods together, may they be the communion of the body and blood of Christ.**

Presider   Make us one with Christ and one with all who share this feast together.

People   **Inspire us and encourage us to live our daily lives as your faithful disciples.**

(C—Here may be added participants' specific local issues from the classroom on the Eucharist in terms of socio-political, economic, gender, ethnic, and ecological issues from their ecological socializing environments such as family, school, peer group, church, community, media, and society. At this moment, art objects, photos, or things from home or the classroom on the Eucharist can be presented to congregation members as liturgical supplementary resources around the table of the Eucharist. The presiding minister will offer participants enough time to see and meditate about their local issues and relative resources as well as pray for them.)

Presider   Renew our lives in this world,

People   **With your mercy, with your healing, your justice, your faithfulness, your peace, and your power.**

(C—Here may be added more signs of God's grace.)

Presider   We all praise you, Triune God, the Father, the Son, and the Holy Spirit.

People   **Through Christ, with Christ, in Christ, in the unity of the Holy Spirit, all glory and honor are yours, almighty God, now and forever.**

All   **Amen.**

Appendix C

Lord's Prayer

The minister leads all participants to sing or say the Lord's Prayer. If they sing, the tune and melody of the song may come from Sa-Joo-Ga (예수님이 좋은 걸), which is a contemporary Korean folk gospel song.

Our Father in heaven, hallowed be your name Your kingdom come

Your will be done, on earth as in heaven Give us today our daily bread

Forgive us our sins as we forgive Save us from the trial deliver us from evil

For the kingdom, the power, the glory are yours now and forever. Amen.

I. Madang (마당, community celebration gathering) of Eating Together

Breaking of the Rice Cake

The presiding minister breaks the rice cake, singing a pansori[8] with the text below. The presiding minister may choose the words of Institution either from 1 Corinthians 11:23–29 or the Synoptic Gospels (Matthew 26:26–28, Mark 14:22–24, Luke 22:14–20). When the minister takes and breaks the rice cake and fills the cup, he or she needs to do it in full view of the people.

Presider   The Lord Jesus, on the night before he died, took bread,

And after giving thanks to you,

he broke it, and gave it to his disciples, saying:

Take, eat. This is my body, given for you. Do this in remembrance of me.

In the same way he took the cup, saying:

This cup is the new covenant sealed in my blood,

---

8. S. H. Park, *Study on the Use of Culture*, 7. *Pansori* is a form of folk music developed in the southwestern part of Korea from the 16th century to the 20th century. One singer, accompanied by a single drummer, chants an epic story in a performance. In the *pansori* performance, there are three major elements: *chang*, which are the songs themselves; *ballim*, the gestures and body movements enhancing the descriptive power of the performance; and *aniri*, the recitativo parts, which set the scenes. In 2003, UNESCO listed *pansori* as one of the masterpieces of the Oral and Intangible of Humanity.

Appendix C

Shed for you for the forgiveness of sins.

Whenever you drink it,

Do this in remembrance of me.

Communion of the People

Then holding out both the rice cake and the cup to the people, the minister says:

Presider   Jesus said: I am the bread of life. Whoever comes to me will never be hungry, and whoever believes in me will never be thirsty. The gifts of God

People   **For the people of God.**

Following the presiding minister's leading, people come forward the table of the Eucharist and receive the elements. If there are participants who are unable to walk or come forward, servers should first take the eucharistic food to them. During Communion, Samulnori[9] may be played in the courtyard.

In giving the rice cake:

Communion server   The body of Christ, the rice cake of life.

People   **Amen.**

In giving the cup:

Communion server   The blood of Christ, the cup of salvation.

People   **Amen.**

---

9 Joo, *Study of Historical Development*, 11–12. *Samulnori* is music played with the four basic Korean percussion instruments: *ggoenggwari* (꽹과리, a small gong), *jing* (징, a large gong), *janggo* (장고, an hourglass drum), and *buk* (북, a barrel drum). Though derived from traditional Korean farmers' music, *samulnori* became popular and spread quickly as a new genre of music in Korea. Jae Yeon Joo explains that *samulnori* has been developed based on yin-yang symbolic thinking. That is, *janggo* and *buk*, which are made of wood, stand for yang, whereas *ggoenggwari* and *jing*, which are made of metal, stand for ying. Whereas *janggo* and *ggoenggwari*, which are big, stand for yang, *buk* and *jing*, which are small, stand for yin. These four instruments do not conflict with each other but have a harmony between the big and the small, the heavy and the light, the wood and the metal, each keeping its own sound.

Appendix C

I. Madang (마당, community celebration gathering) of New Hope

All people stand and hold hands in a circle. The presiding minister leads prayer after communion.

Prayer after Communion

Presider We all give our thanks to you for feeding and nourishing us with your gifts at this feast.

People **Empower us to participate in your ministry in this world as your disciples with courage and hope.**

(C Here may be added more specific events or places related to participants' local contexts)

All **Strengthen us in your service that our daily living may be part of the life of your kingdom, glorifying you, loving people, and serving the world. In the name of Jesus Christ who moves us from sorrow to joy, from oppression to liberation, and from death to life. Amen.**

After prayer, the presiding minister leads all people to dance ganggangsulae[10] by using the following texts together. The presiding minister leads a chant and the people follow with the chorus. During ganggangsulae, Samulnori may be played in the courtyard.

Presider Give thanks to our God

People **Ganggangsulae.**

Presider Who sends us into the world.

---

10. Hong, *Research into the Characteristic*, 9–10. *Ganggangsulae* is a five-thousand-year-old traditional Korean group circle dance. People dance together, singing and playing hand in hand. It is associated with the celebration of thanksgiving for a good harvest. The song of *ganggangsulae* includes the line of the hope and blessing of the whole community, and the individual members' well-being in their daily lives. The word *ganggangsulaeg* is a Korean folk echoic word for hope and blessing. In 2009, UNESCO listed *ganggangsulae* as one of the masterpieces of the Oral and Intangible Heritage of Humanity.

Appendix C

People	**Ganggangsulae.**
Presider	Empowers us to be faithful disciples.
People	**Ganggangsulae.**
Presider	Helps us cope with injustice and inequality.
People	**Ganggangsulae.**
Presider	Helps us serve your people in need.
People	**Ganggangsulae.**
Presider	With your love and mercy in our schools.
People	**Ganggangsulae.**
Presider	Helps us be peace makers.
People	**Ganggangsulae.**
Presider	In the conflict of our work places.
People	**Ganggangsulae.**
Presider	Helps us welcome your people.
People	**Ganggangsulae.**
Presider	With love and equality in our faith community.
People	**Ganggangsulae.**

(C Here may added various prayer-lists for participants' hope and desire connected to their specific local issues and situations.)

Appendix C

B. An Example of A Contextualized Eucharistic Text for a Korean Reunification Sunday Service

I. Madang (마당, an open place for communal celebration) of Offering

The table of the Eucharist is placed at the center of a big circle. Following the presiding minister who wears Korean traditional clothes, all congregation members come to the table and sit in the circle. The table of the Eucharist is placed at the center of the circle. As the signal of the beginning of the Eucharist, one communion server comes to the table and strikes a gong, which is a Korean percussion instrument. According to the direction of the presiding minister, communion servers bring and put the rice cake and the cup at the center of the table. Beside the table, they also bring and set up a big wooden cross bound up with two fabrics: blue standing for South Korea and red standing for North Korea. Through a worship bulletin, the presiding minister may inform people that the rice cake is made of rice flour from both North and South Korea, and that the wine is also from both North and South Korea. It also includes the information that the cross is made of two sticks: one from Baekdu mountain in North Korea and the other from Halla mountain in South Korea. If there are congregation members who have family connections to North Korea, communion servers are composed of both those who have family connections to North Korea and those who have not, young and old, and male and female. During this offering time, people may sing a song with the melody of So-Mang-Ga (소망가), which is a traditional Korean folk gospel song of peace, justice, and unity accompanied by Korean folk instruments.

Blessed are you, God of peace and justice

We give our offering to you

Blessed are you, God who calls us one

We give offerings of our life and the gifts of the earth

Appendix C

Invitation

Standing at the table, the presiding minister invites the people to the Eucharist, using the following invitation to the table of the Eucharist. During the invitation, a whole view of Korea may be presented on a screen.

Presider   Brothers and sisters in Jesus Christ, this is the joyful banquet of the people of God. They will come from north and south, and from east and west, and sit at the table in the kingdom of God. (If there are congregation members who have family connections to North Korea, a presiding minister may repeat "from north and south" two or three times slowly.)

(C   Here may be added a story of Jesus' meal with the sinners.[11])

Presider   This is the Lord's Table. Jesus our Lord invites those who believe in him to join the banquet that he prepared. With joy and thanksgiving, let us praise our God.

People   **Amen.**

I. Madang (마당, community celebration gathering) of Thanksgiving

The participants stand. If there are congregation members who are not able to stand, the presiding minister needs to guide them to their seats at the front in order to secure a clear view of the presiding minister when others stand.

Presider   We give thanks to you, creator God. With your mighty hands, you created the heaven, the earth, and us in peace and harmony.

(C   Here may be added more specific examples of God's creations in terms of peace and harmony.)

All   **Blessed be our God.**

---

11. Matthew 9:10–12.

Appendix C

Presider   Creator God, you called people to obedience for the life of love and justice.

People   **Even as they have been unfaithful to your commands, you have kept warning them against disobedience and guiding them to obedience for love and justice in their daily lives.**

(C   Here may be added several specific biblical stories of people's disobedience to God.)

All   **We praise your goodness with thanksgiving.**

The people may sing a song with the melody of Dong-Du-Koong[12] Praise God (덩덕쿵 찬양해), which is a contemporary Korean folk gospel song with the accompaniment of Korean folk instruments.

Dong du koong Dong du koong God of creation

God called us to live in love and justice

Dong du koong dong du koong God of creation

God leads us to live in peace and harmony

Presider   We all praise you for your Son Jesus Christ, our Savior.

People   **You gave him to us as a peace maker to make the two into one and to tear down the barrier, the dividing wall of hostility. He preached good news, released the oppressed, proclaiming the year of the Lord's favor, and saved us from death.**

(C   Here may be added several aspects of Jesus' peace ministry of salvation through his entire life.)

Presider   We all remember your Son Jesus Christ as a peace maker.

People   **We celebrate his death and resurrection by taking this rice cake and this cup.**

---

12. Tobagi Korean Language Compilation Committee, *Bori Korean Dictionary*, 276. The words *dong-du-koong* are a Korean folk echoic phrase for joy and delight, accompanied by hand clapping.

Appendix C

The people may sing a song with the melody of Miryang Arirang (밀양 아리랑),[13] *a Korean traditional folk song with the accompaniment of Korean folk instruments.*

> **Ari arang suri surirang arariga nanne**
>
> **Christ has died, Christ is risen**
>
> **Ari arang suri surirang arariga nanne**
>
> **Christ will come again**

Presider   We all pray that you pour out your Holy Spirit upon us and upon these gifts of rice cakes and wine.

People   **As we share these gifts together, make us one with Christ and one with each other.**

All   **Through our communion with Jesus who is and is to come, inspire us to open our eyes to this nation which has been divided into north and south over 60 years since 1950.**

(C   Here may be added participants' specific local issues related to Korean War from the classroom on the Eucharist. These issues may be unification issues, family separation issues, concerns about human rights and severe famine in North Korea, concerns about nuclear weapons, and issues of religious oppression. At this moment, art objects, photos, or things from home or the classroom on the Eucharist can be presented to congregation members as liturgical supplementary resources around the table of the Eucharist. The presiding minister will offer participants enough time to see and meditate about their local issues and relative resources as well as pray for them.)

---

13. Joh, *Study on the Original Arirang*, 7–12. According to Joh, the song *Arirang* has been formed, developed, and sung among Korean people as the soul song of Korea within the history of Korea, especially in hard times such as Japanese imperialism, the Korean War, and military government. Depending on specific local sociocultural contexts, over three thousand different versions of *Arirang* have been known and sung. *Miryang Arirang*, formed originally around the city of Mirayng in Kyungsang province, is one of them. In 1998, UNESCO established the prize *Arirang* in order to encourage to safeguard proclaimed masterpieces of the oral and intangible heritage of humanity. The words *ari-arirang, suri-surirang, arariga-nanne* are Korean folk echoic words for the inclusive emotion of joy and sadness, liberation and oppression, and suffering and hope.

Appendix C

Presider   May God be present with all your people who live in situations of division, suffering, injustice, and brokenness,

People   **With your justice, your love, your peace, and your power.**

(C   Here may be added more values and signs of God's reconciliation works.)

Presider   We all praise you, Triune God, the Father, the Son, and the Holy Spirit.

People   **Through Christ, with Christ, in Christ, in the unity of the Holy Spirit, all glory and honor are yours, almighty God, now and forever.**

All   **Amen.**

Lord's Prayer

The minister leads all participants to sing or say the Lord's Prayer. If they sing, the tune and melody of the song may come from Jungson Arirang (정선 아리랑),[14] *a Korean traditional folk song of hope and happiness with the accompaniment of Korean folk instruments.*

Our Father in heaven, hallowed be your name Your kingdom come

Your will be done, on earth as in heaven Give us today our daily bread

Forgive us our sins as we forgive Save us from the trial deliver us from evil

For the kingdom, the power, the glory are yours now and forever. Amen.

---

14. Ibid., 16. As a version of *Arirang*, *Jungson Arirang* was formed originally around the city of Jungson in Gangwon province.

Appendix C

I. Madang (마당, community celebration gathering) of Eating Together

Breaking of the Rice Cake

The presiding minister breaks the rice cake, singing a pansori which is Korean traditional narrative music with the text below accompanied by a single drummer. The presiding minister may choose the words of Institution either from 1 Cor 11:23-29 or the Synoptic Gospels (Matt 26:26-28, Mark 14:22-24, Luke 22:14-20). When the minister takes and breaks the rice cake and fills the cup, he or she needs to do it in full view of the people.

Presider   The Lord Jesus, on the night before he died, took bread,

And after giving thanks to God,

he broke it, and gave it to his disciples, saying:

Take, eat. This is my body, given for you.

Do this in remembrance of me.

In the same way he took the cup, saying:

This cup is the new covenant sealed in my blood,

Shed for you for the forgiveness of sins.

Whenever you drink it,

Do this in remembrance of me.

Communion of the People

Then the presider holds out both the rice cake and the cup to the people.

Presider   Jesus said: my flesh is real food and my blood is real drink. Whoever eats my flesh and drinks my blood abides in me, and I in him or in her.

The gifts of God.

People   **For the people of God.**

Appendix C

Following the presiding minister's leading, people come forward to the table of the Eucharist and receive the elements. If there are participants who are unable to walk or come forward, servers should first take the eucharistic food to them. During Communion, people may join the drum dance[15] together with the accompaniment of Samulnori.

In giving the rice cake:

Communion server   The body of Christ, the rice cake of life.

People   **Amen.**

In giving the cup:

Communion server   The blood of Christ, the cup of salvation.

People   **Amen.**

I. Madang (마당, community celebration gathering) of New Hope

All people stand and hold hands in a circle. The presiding minister leads the prayer after communion.

Prayer after Communion

Presider   At this table, we all give our thanks to you for feeding and nourishing us with your gifts.

People   **Grant us strength and courage to join in your ministry of love and justice in this world.**

Presider   In our daily lives in families, schools, work places, communities, and society,

---

15. Goh, *Study for the Historical Development*, 18–20. The "drum dance" is a Korean traditional group dance for a communal unity and harmony beyond the conflict and separation in a group or community. Since the third century, it has been performed and developed by people in Korean society. As a performer starts to play a drum, people perform a dance together in free style with improvisations.

Appendix C

People **Help us be peace makers, as we are called to build your kingdom by coping with injustice and inequality and by supporting our neighbors in need. Particularly, empower us to be peace makers to those who are suffering from the Korean War not only emotionally but also politically, economically, and ethically.**

(C Here may be added more specific upcoming events or people related to issues of the Korean War.)

All **In the name of Jesus Christ who moves us from separation to reunion, from oppression to liberation, and from death to life. Amen.**

After the prayer, following the presiding minister, all congregation members go out of the sanctuary and stand together in a circle in the courtyard of the church. A communion server brings a young plant of Mugungwha (an ornamental hibiscus shrub), the national flower of Korea, to the center of the circle. Around the planting place, there are two lumps of soil: one comes from South Korea and the other comes from North Korea. The presiding minister says:

Presider Here is a young plant of *Mugungwha*. As we plant it together today, we will see how it will grow well in this land under God's abundant grace and our continuous cooperation. Let us pray.

Gracious God, as we plant with one heart this young tree in this ground, may you plant and realize your Kingdom in both North and South Korea. Help us participate in your ministry of love and justice as peace makers in our daily lives within families, schools, work places, local communities, and society. In the name of Jesus Christ, our Savior,

All **Amen.**

According to the presiding minister's direction, all congregation members may plant the Mugungwha together by taking soil and putting it on the ground. During the planting, the people may sing a song together with the melody of Hope for Unification (우리의 소원은 통일) which is the most famous children's song for the hope of unification in both South and North Korea. The song may be accompanied by Korean folk instruments.

Appendix C

Today we see the kingdom of God in our land

By faith, we go out into the darkness Help us be the light

By faith, we go out into the silence Make us be the awakening sounds

By faith, we go out into the corruption Help us be the salt

(C   Here may be added various concrete prayer lists for participants' hopes and desires related to the issues of the Korean War according to their congregational situations.)

Bibliography

Adams, Daniel J. *Christ and Culture in Asia: Explorations from Korea.* Quezon City: New Day, 2002.
Anderson, E. Byron. *Worship and Christian Identity: Practicing Ourselves.* Collegeville, MN: Liturgical, 2003.
Baek, Young Sun. *Is Confucianism Unfair Thought?: The Equality of Confucianism.* Seoul: Ewha Women University Press, 2001.
Bal, Mieke. *Double Exposures: The Subject of Cultural Analysis.* New York: Routledge, 1996.
Berns, Roberta M. *Child, Family, School, Community: Socialization and Support.* 7th ed. Belmont, CA: Wadsworth, 2007.
———. *Community-Based Intervention.* Stanford, CT: Thomson Learning, 2008.
———. *Study Guide for Berns' Child, Family, School, Community: Socialization and Support.* 7th ed. Belmont, CA: Wadsworth, 2007.
———. *Topical Child Development.* Florence, KY: Wadsworth, 1994.
Bevans, Stephen B. *Models of Contextual Theology.* Maryknoll, NY: Orbis, 2002.
Bower, Peter C. *The Companion to the Book of Common Worship.* Louisville: Geneva, 2003.
Bradshaw, Paul F. *Eucharistic Origins.* New York: Oxford University Press, 2004.
———. *Reconstructing Early Christian Worship.* Collegeville, MN: Pueblo, 2010.
Bronfenbrenner, Urie. "Ecological Systems Theory." In *Six Theories of Child Development: Revised Formulations and Current Issues,* edited by R. Vasta, 187–250. London: Jessica Kingsley, 1992.
———. *The Ecology of Human Development: Experiments by Nature and Design.* Cambridge, MA: Harvard University Press, 1979.
———. "Interacting System in Human Development Researching Paradigms: Present and Future." In *Persons in Context: Developmental Processes,* edited by N. Bolger, A. Caspi, G. Downey, and M. Moorehouse, 39–44. New York: Cambridge University Press, 1988.
———. *Making Human Beings Human: Bioecological Perspectives on Human Development.* London: Sage, 2005.
Bronfenbrenner, Urie, et al. *Examining Lives in Context: Perspective on the Ecology of Human Development.* Washington, DC: American Psychological Association, 1995.
Browne, Maura. *African Synod: Documents, Reflections, Perspectives.* Maryknoll, NY: Orbis, 1996.
Browning, Robert L., and Roy A. Reed. *Sacraments in Religious Education and Liturgy.* Birmingham, AL: Religious Education Press, 1985.
Byars, Ronald P. *Lift Your Hearts on High.* Louisville: Westminster John Knox, 2005.
Calvin, John. "The Sacraments." In *Institutes of the Christian Religion,* translated by Tony Lane and Hilary Osborn, 1276–1302. Grand Rapids: Baker, 1987.

Bibliography

Carvalhaes, Cláudio. "Globalization and the Borders of Liturgical Practices: Redrawing the Lines of Eucharistic Hospitality." PhD diss., Union Theological Seminary, 2007.
Ching, Julia, and Hans Kung. *Christianity and Chinese Religions*. London: SCM, 1993.
Chupungco, Anscar J. "Lima Text as a Pointer to the Future: an Asian Perspective." *Studia Liturgica* 16/1–2 (1986).
———. *Liturgical Inculturation: Sacramentals, Religiosity, and Catechesis*. Collegeville, MN: Liturgical, 1992.
———. *Worship: Beyond Inculturation: Sacramentals, Religiosity, and Catechesis*. Washington, DC: Pastoral, 1994.
Clark, Charles Allen. *ChonChiMunDap JoYe (What Is the Presbyterian Law?)*. Seoul: Korean Religious Books and Tracts Society, 1917.
———. *Digest of the Presbyterian Church of Korea (Chosen)*. Seoul: Korean Religious Books and Tracts Society, 1918.
———. *The Korean Church and the Nevius Methods*. New York: Revell, 1930.
———. *Mokhoehak (The Ministry of the Pastors)*. Seoul: Christian Literature Society of Korea, 1955.
———. *MokSaJiBop (The Works of Pastors)*. Seoul: Korean Religious Books and Tracts Society, 1919.
Coe, Shoki. "Contextualization as the Way toward Reform." In *Asian Christian Theology: Emerging Themes*, edited by D. J. Elwood, 48–55. Philadelphia: Westminster, 1980.
Curriculum Committee of the Presbyterian Church of Korea. *The Bible and Living*. Seoul: Korean Presbyterian Publishing, 1972.
———. *The Companion to the Book of God's Kingdom for the Middle School Group*. Seoul: Korean Presbyterian Publishing, 2008.
———. *The Companion to the Book of God's Kingdom for the Minister*. Seoul: Korean Presbyterian Publishing, 2008.
———. *The Companion to the Book of God's Kingdom for the Teacher*. Seoul: Korean Presbyterian Publishing, 2008.
———. *The Companion to the Book of God's Kingdom for the Third and Fourth Grade Group*. Seoul: Korean Presbyterian Publishing, 2008.
———. *God's Kingdom: Call and Responding*. Seoul: Korean Presbyterian Publishing, 2008.
———. *God's Kingdom: Call and Responding for Third and Fourth Grade Group*.
———. *God's Kingdom: Call and Responding for Middle School Group*.
———. *The Word and Life*. Seoul: Korean Presbyterian Publishing, 1980.
Davies, Daniel Michael *The Missionary Thought and Activity of Henry Gerhard Appenzeller*. Madison, NJ: Drew University Press, 1985.
Decker, L. E., and V. A. Decker. *Engaging Families and Communities: Pathways to Educational Success*. Fairfax, VA: National Community Education Association, 2001.
Driver, Tom F. *Liberating Rites: Understanding the Transformative Power of Ritual*. Boulder, CO: Westview, 1998.
Education and Resource Ministry of the Presbyterian Church of Korea. *The Catechism of the Presbyterian Church of Korea*. Seoul: Korean Presbyterian Publishing, 2002.
Eliot W. Eisner, *The Educational Imagination: On the Design and Evaluation of School Programs* (Upper Saddle River, N.J.: Prentice Hall, 1985
Epstein, J. L. *School, Family, and Community Partnerships: Preparing Educators and Improving Schools*. Boulder, CO: Westview, 2001.
Federation of Asian Bishops' Conferences. *For All Peoples of Asia*. 3 vols. Vol. 1, *Documents from 1970 to 1991*, edited by Gaudencio Rosales and C. G. Arevalo. Maryknoll, NY:

Bibliography

Orbis, 1991. Vols. 2 and 3, *Documents from 1992 to 1996* and *Documents from 1997 to 2001*, edited by Franz Josef Eilers. Quezon City, Philippines: Claretian, 1997, 2002.

Flinders, David J., and Stephen J. Thornton. *The Curriculum Studies Reader*. New York: Routledge, 2004.

Foster, Charles. *Teaching in the Community of Faith*. Nashville: Abingdon, 1982.

Francis, Mark R. *Shape a Circle Ever Wider: Liturgical Inculturation in the United States*. Chicago: Liturgy Training Publications, 2007.

Fruseth, Inger, and Pal Repstad. *An Introduction to the Sociology of Religion: Classical and Contemporary Perspectives*. Burlington, VT: Ashgate, 2006.

Galbreath, Paul. *Leading from the Table*. Herndon, VA: Alban Institute, 2008.

Gallagher, Michael Paul. *Clashing Symbols: An Introduction to Faith and Culture*. New York: Paulist, 1988.

Gerrish, B. A. *Grace and Gratitude: The Eucharistic Theology of John Calvin*. Eugene, OR: Wipf and Stock, 2002.

Giroux, Henry. "Paulo Freire and the Politics of Postcolonialism." In *Paulo Freire: A Critical Encounter*, edited by P. McLaren and P. Leonard, 177–88. New York: Routledge, 1993.

Goh, En Mi. *A Study for the Historical Development of Drum and Drum Dance*. Seoul: Sookmyung Women University Press, 2003.

Gollnick, D. M., and P. C. Chinn. *Multicultural Education in a Pluralistic Society*. Upper Saddle River, NJ: Merrill/Prentice-Hall, 2005.

Grimes, Ronald L. *Reading, Writing, and Ritualizing: Ritual in Fictive, Liturgical, and Public Places*. Washington, DC: Pastoral, 1993.

Groome, Thomas. *Sharing Faith: A Comprehensive Approach to Religious Education and Pastoral Ministry, the Way of Shared Praxis*. Eugene, OR: Wipf and Stock, 1999.

Grusec, Joan E., and Paul Hastings. *Handbook of Socialization: Theory and Research*. New York: Guilford, 2008.

Gy, P. M. "The inculturation of the Christian Liturgy in the West." *Studia Liturgica* 20/1 (1990) 8–11.

Han, Jin Hwan. *A Historical and Theological Analysis of the Renewal of Worship of Korean Presbyterianism in the Context of the Directory for Worship of the Presbyterian Church of Korea*. Boston: Boston University Press, 1997.

Handel, Gerald, and Frederick Elkin. *The Child and Society: The Process of Socialization*. New York: Random House, 1989.

Haskins R., and C. Rouse. "Closing Achievement Gaps: School Readiness: Closing Racial and Ethnic Gaps." *The Future of Children* 15 (2005) 1–7.

Henderson, A. T., and N. Berla. *A New Generation of Evidence: The Family Is Critical to Student Achievement*. Washington, DC: National Committee for Citizens in Education, 1994.

Henderson, J. Frank, Stephen Larson, and Kathleen Quinn. *Liturgy, Justice, and the Reign of God: Integrating Vision and Practice*. New York: Paulist, 1989.

Hofius, Otfried. *Paulusstudien*. 2nd ed. WUNT 51. Tübingen: Mohr, 1989.

Hong, Sung Im. *A Research into the Characteristic of Ganggangsulae of Beguem-do*. Seoul: Dongduk Women University, 2010.

Huh, Hyung. "Problems and Prospects of Educational Evaluation Research in Korea." *A Colloquy of Korean Public Education Research* 19 (2004).

Irwin, Kevin W. *Models of the Eucharist*. New York: Paulist, 2005.

Bibliography

Jang, Shin G. *Constructing a Public Practical Theology a Trinitarian-Communicative Model of Practical Theology for the Korean Public Church*. New York: Princeton Theological Seminary Press, 2002.

Jo, Ki Yeon. "Asian Understanding of the Baptism." In *Theology of Korea and Culture*. Seoul: Christian Literature Society of Korea, 2002.

———. *Korean Protestant Church and Worship Revival*. Seoul: Korean Christian Institute, 2004.

———. *Theology and Practices of Worship Revival*. Seoul: Korean Christian Institute, 2002.

Joh, Yong Ho. *A Study on the Original Arirang*. Seoul: Soongsil University Press, 2011.

Joo, Jae Yeon. *A Study of Historical Development and Cultural Outcome*. Seoul: Korea University, 2010.

Jung, Jang Bok. "Examining the Lima Liturgy in the view of Korean Ritual Culture," *JangShin Theological Colloquy* 6 (1990) 346–58.

———. *Theology of Worship*. Seoul: Presbyterian College and Theological Seminary, 1999.

Kim, Byung Jin. "A Study of Korean Presbyterian Liturgy." PhD diss., Anyang Theological Seminary, 2004.

Kim, Cheol Ho. *A Study of Worship Renewal in Korean Church*. Jeon Ju: Hanil Jangshin Press, 2004.

Kim, De Hyun. *Ethical Researching about the Blessing of Korean Christianity*. Seoul: Presbyterian College and Theological Seminary, 2004.

Kim, Hyup Young. *Wang Yang-Min and Karl Barth: A Confucian-Christian Dialogue*. Lanham, MD: University Press of America, 1996.

Kim, Kyung Jin. "The Early Korean Presbyterian Worship through the History of the Formation." *Christian Thought* 513 (2001) 150–57.

———. *The Formation of Presbyterian Worship in Korea, 1879–1934*. Boston: Boston University Press, 1999.

Kim, Kyung Jin, and Chang Bok Lim. *Worship Education Program for the Successful Ministry*. Seoul: Korean Institute for Christian Ministry, 2009.

Kim, Myung Hyuk. *Ancestor Worship in the Korean Church*. Seoul: Evangelical Review of Theology, 1984.

Kim, Nam Soo. *Task for the Korean Hymnal of 21 Century*. Seoul: Korean Christian Theological Treatise, 1999.

Kim, Ne Ok. *A Study of Ancestor Worship: Focusing on Confucian Rite*. Seoul: Anyang University, 1997.

Kim, Se Kwang. *Worship and Contemporary Culture: Multimedia, CCM, Film, Language*. Seoul: Korean Christian Institute, 2005.

Kim, Soon Whan. "Cultural Application of the Eucharistic Elements for the Efficacy of the Korean Worship Services." In *Theology of Korea and Culture*, 143–55. Seoul: Christian Literature Society of Korea, 2002.

———. "The Future of the Korean Presbyterian Worship: Four Actions," *Korean Biblical Journal* 8 (2002) 265–89.

———. *A Study of the Liturgical Reconsideration and Direction for Korean Protestant Church*. Seoul: Korean Bible University, 2001.

———. *Symbol of the Eucharist and Korean Cultural Relevance*. Seoul: Handle, 1999.

———. *Worship in the Twenty-First Century: Seeking for the Encountering between Modern and Tradition*. Seoul: Korean Christian Institute, 2006.

Koh, Yong Soo. *Contemporary Christian Education Thought*. Seoul: Presbyterian College and Theological Seminary, 2003.

Bibliography

Korean National Commission for UNESCO. *Korean Anthropology: Contemporary Korean Culture in Flux.* Seoul: Hollym International Corporation, 2003.

Kyohoe, Yongdong. *Yongdong Kyohoe Paengyonsa, 1894-1994. (Centennial History of Yongdong Presbyterian Church).* Seoul: Yongdong Presbyterian Church, 1995.

Lathrop, Gordon W. *Holy Ground: A Liturgical Cosmology.* Minneapolis: Fortress, 2009.

Lee, Dong. *Confucian Asceticism and Christian Spirituality: Chinese Confucian Thought and Spiritual Exercises of St. Ignatius Loyola.* Seoul: Catholic University Press, 2002.

Lee, Jung Young. *Korean Preaching: An Interpretation.* Nashville: Abingdon, 1996.

———. *Marginality: The Key to Multicultural Theology.* Minneapolis: Fortress, 1995.

———. *The Trinity in Asian Perspective.* Nashville: Abingdon, 1996.

Lee, Jung Young, and Peter C. Phan. *Journeys at the Margin: Toward an Autobiographical Theology in American-Asian Perspective.* Collegeville, MN: Liturgical, 1999.

Levitt, Peggy. "Review of Chinese Christians in America." *Social Forces* 79 (2001) 1552.

Lutheran World Federation. "The Lutheran World Federation's Nairobi Statement on Worship and Culture." In *New Directions in Mission and Evangelization*, edited by James A. Scherer and Stephen B. Bevans, 23–28. Maryknoll, NY: Orbis, 1999.

———. "Nairobi Statement on Worship and Culture: Contemporary Challenges and Opportunities." In *Christian Worship: Unity in Cultural Diversity*, edited by S. Anita Stauffer, 23–28. LWF Studies 1/1996. Geneva: Lutheran World Federation, 1996.

Martin, Robert K. "Education and the Liturgical Life of the Church." *Religious Education* 93 (2003) 43–64.

Ministry of Culture and Sports. *Religious Culture in Korea.* Seoul: Religious Affairs Office, 1996.

Moffett, S. A. *The Wi Wonip Koin Kyujo (Manual for Catechumens).* Seoul: Korean Religious Tract Society, 1913.

Muller, Ulrich. *Social Life and Social Knowledge: Toward a Process Account of Development.* New York: Erlbaum Associates, 2008.

Murphy, Debra Dean. *Teaching that Transforms: Worship as the Heart of Christian Education.* Eugene, OR: Wipf and Stock, 2007.

Nelson, C. Ellis *How Faith Matures.* Louisville: Westminster John Knox, 1989.

Neville, Gwen Kennedy, and John Westerhoff III. *Learning through Liturgy.* New York: Seabury, 1978.

Nevin, John Williamson. *The Mystical Presence: A Vindication of the Reformed or Calvinistic Doctrine of the Holy Eucharist.* Philadelphia: S. R. Fisher, 1846.

Nevius, H. S. C. *Kurisudo Mundap (Christian Catechism).* N.p., 1893.

Ng, Greer Anne. "Asian Sociocultural Values: Oppressive and Liberating Aspects from a Woman's Perspective." In *People on the Way: Asian North Americans Discovering Christ, Culture, and Community*, edited by David Ng, 63–104. Valley Forge, PA: Judson, 1996.

Oh, Seong Hae. *A Study on the Social Welfare Ideology of Confucianism.* Seoul: Han Sung University Press, 2002.

Ostdiek, Gilbert. *Catechesis for Liturgy: A Program for Parish Involvement.* Washington, DC: Pastoral, 1986.

Paik, George L. *The History of Protestant Missions in Korea, 1832-1910.* Pyeongyang: Union Christian College Press, 1929.

Park, Chul Soo. *The Influence of Confucianism in the Early Stage of Christian Missionary Work in Korea.* Seoul: Jeon-Ju University Press, 2003.

Bibliography

Park, Eng Kyu. "The Political Activism of Korean Churches Revisited: With Particular Attention to the Church and State Issue." *Presbyterian Church and Theology* 5 (2008) 149–82.

Park, Hee Jung. *A Study of Madang Play*. Seoul: Dankuk University Press, 2003.

Park, Sang Jin. *A Search for Christian Education Curriculum: Faith, Epistemology, and Christian Curriculum*. Seoul: Presbyterian College and Theological Seminary Press, 2004.

Pan, Shin W. "Christian Education on Conflict Resolution in Korean Protestantism: Based on Analysis of Korean Culture." *Journal of Christian Education & Information Technology* 7 (2005) 325–45.

Park, Si Hyun. *A Study on the Use of Culture and Art Education in the Preservation, the Intangible Cultural Heritage Pansori*. Kwang Ju: Jeonnam University, 2010.

Park, Young Jin. *Korean Classic Music Singing Educational Methods through Using Korean Folk Instruments*. Yongin: Yongin University, 2002.

Phan, Peter C., editor. *Asian Synod: Texts and Commentaries* (Maryknoll, NY: Orbis Books, 2002)

———. *Being Religious Interreligiously: Asian Perspectives on Interfaith Dialogue*. Maryknoll, NY: Orbis, 2004.

———. *Christianity with an Asian Face: Asian American Theology in the Making*. Maryknoll, NY: Orbis, 2003.

———. "Culture and Liturgy: Ancestor Veneration as a Test Case." *Worship* 76 (2002) 403–30.

———. "Ecclesia in Asia: Challenges for Asian Christianity," *East Asian Pastoral Review* 37/3 (2000), 215-32

———. *In Our Own Tongues: Perspectives from Asia on Mission and Inculturation*. Maryknoll, NY: Orbis, 2003.

Pieris, Aloysius. "An Asian Paradigm: Inter-Religious Dialogue and Theology of Religions." *The Month* 254 (1993) 131–32.

Pinar, William, et al. *Understanding Curriculum: An Introduction to the Study of Historical and Contemporary Curriculum Discourses*. New York: Peter Lang, 2002.

Presbyterian Church of Korea (Chosen). *Constitution of the Presbyterian Church of Chosen, 1919*. Seoul: Korean Religious Books and Tracts Society, 1919.

———. *Yesugyo Changnohoe Honsang Yesikso (Forms of Marriage and Burial of the Presbyterian Church of Korea): A Supplement on the Administration of Baptism and the Lord's Supper and on the Ordination of Pastors and Elders*. Seoul: Chang Mun Sa, 1925.

Presbyterian Church in the United States. *The Constitution of the Presbyterian Church in the United States of America*. Philadelphia: Presbyterian Board of Publication and Sabbath-School Work, 1910.

———. *The Directory for the Worship of God in the Presbyterian Church in the United States*. Richmond, VA: Presbyterian Committee of Publication, 1910.

Presbyterian Church (USA). *Book of Common Worship*. Louisville: Westminster John Knox, 1993.

Reforming Committee of Korean Presbyterian Common Worship. *Book of Common Worship of the Presbyterian Church of Korea*. Seoul: Korean Presbyterian Publishing, 2008.

Research Committee of Korean Church History. *Christian Thoughts of Korean Church*. Seoul: Yonsei University Press, 1998.

Bibliography

Rogoff, B. *The Cultural Nature of Human Development.* New York: Oxford University Press, 2003.

Scherer, James A., and Stephen B. Bevans, editors. *New Directions in Mission and Evangelization.* 3 vols. Maryknoll, NY: Orbis, 1992–1999.

Schreiter, Robert J. *Constructing Local Theologies.* Maryknoll, NY: Orbis, 1985.

Shorter, Aylward. *Toward a Theology of Inculturation.* London: Wipf and Stock, 1988.

Smith, Dennis E. *From Symposium to Eucharist: The Banquet in the Early Christian World.* Minneapolis: Fortress, 2003.

Smith, Dennis E., and Hal E. Taussig. *Many Tables: The Eucharist in the New Testament and Liturgy Today.* Eugene, OR: Wipf and Stock, 2001.

Smith, James. K. A. *Desiring the Kingdom: Worship, Worldview, and Cultural Formation.* Grand Rapids: Baker Academic, 2009.

Soltau, T. S. *Yebae ChopKyoung.* Seoul: Korean Religious Books and Tracts Society, 1934.

Son, Sung. "Historical Relationship between Buddhism and Confucianism in Korea." *Buddhism Review* 6 (1999) 67–78.

Son, Won Young. "Sunday School Culture and the Education of Christian Culture." In *Is There a Christian Culture in Korea?*, 131–54. Seoul: Handle, 2005.

Stookey, Laurence Hull. *Eucharist: Christ's Feast with the Church.* Nashville: Abingdon, 1993.

Takenaka, Masao. *God Is Rice: Asian Culture and Christian Faith.* Eugene, OR: Wipf and Stock, 2009.

TEF Staff. *Ministry in Context: The Third Mandate Programme of the Theological Education.* London: Theological Education Fund, 1973.

Thompson, Laurence G. *Chinese Religion: An Introduction.* 4th ed. Belmont, CA: Wadsworth, 1989.

Ting, K. H. "Eucharistic Homily." *Chinese Theological Review* 19 (2005) 128–29.

Tobagi Korean Language Compilation Committee. *Bori Korean Dictionary.* Seoul: Bori Press, 2011.

Underwood, H. G. *Chanyangga (Hymns of Praise).* Yokohama, Japan: Yokohama Seishi Bunsha, 1894.

———. *Songgyong Mundap (Bible Catechism).* N.p., 1895.

Warren, Ronald L., and Larry Lyon. *New Perspectives on the American Community.* Homewood, IL: Dorsey, 1983.

Webb-Mitchell, Brett P. *Christly Gestures: Learning to Be Members of the Body of Christ.* Grand Rapids: Eerdmans, 2003.

———. *School of the Pilgrim: An Alternative Path to Christian Growth.* Louisville: Westminster John Knox, 2007.

Wedig, Mark E. "Evangelism, Inculturation and the RCIA." *Worship* 76 (2002) 505–6

Welker, Michael. *What Happens in Holy Communion?* Grand Rapids: Eerdmans, 2000.

Westerhoff, John H., III. *J Will Our Children Have Faith?* Rev. ed. Harrisburg, PA: Morehouse, 2000.

White, James F. *Introduction to Christian Worship.* Nashville: Abingdon, 1990.

———. *Protestant Worship: Traditions in Transition.* Louisville: Westminster John Knox, 1989.

Wilhelm, Richard, and Cary Baynes. *The I Ching: or, Book of Changes.* 3rd ed. Princeton, NJ: Princeton University Press, 1967.

Yu, Yeol. *Understanding of Family and Community in Korean Society.* Pusan: Pusan Foreign Language University, 2009.

www.ingramcontent.com/pod-product-compliance
Lightning Source LLC
Chambersburg PA
CBHW071515150426
43191CB00009B/1532